NEW ESSAYS ON MUSICAL UNDERSTANDING

New Essays on Musical Understanding

PETER KIVY

CLARENDON PRESS · OXFORD
2001

OXFORD

UNIVERSITY PRESS

Great Clarendon Street, Oxford OX2 6DP

Oxford University Press is a department of the University of Oxford.
It furthers the University's objective of excellence in research, scholarship,
and education by publishing worldwide in

Oxford New York

Athens Auckland Bangkok Bogotá Buenos Aires Cape Town
Chennai Dar es Salaam Delhi Florence Hong Kong Istanbul Karachi
Kolkata Kuala Lumpur Madrid Melbourne Mexico City Mumbai
Nairobi Paris São Paulo Shanghai Singapore Taipei Tokyo Toronto Warsaw

and associated companies in Berlin Ibadan

Oxford is a registered trade mark of Oxford University Press
in the UK and in certain other countries

Published in the United States
by Oxford University Press Inc., New York

British Library Cataloguing in Publication Data

Data available

Library of Congress Cataloging in Publication Data

Data available

ISBN 0–19–825083–5
ISBN 0–19–924661–0 (pbk.)

1 3 5 7 9 10 8 6 4 2

Typeset by Hope Services (Abingdon) Ltd.
Printed and Bound in Great Britain by
Biddles Ltd, Guildford & King's Lynn
www.Biddles.co.uk

For Harold Aks,
Abram Klotzman, and Lois Wann

PREFACE

THE essays and lectures contained in this volume are *new*—and they are new in two different ways.

The volume constitutes a new collection of my pieces on the philosophy of music, most of which have been written since the publication of the first collection by Cambridge University Press in 1993. But most of these essays are new, as well, in that they have never been published before. Their history is as follows.

Chapter 1, Note-for-Note: Work, Performance and Early Notation, is an essay originally written as a talk in honour of Leo Treitler. The occasion was a conference devoted to his work, on 21 March 1998, at the Graduate Center of the City University of New York, on the occasion of his retirement. Professor Treitler, much to the joy of his students and colleagues, then decided not to retire after all.

The essay received a second airing at the annual meeting of the American Philosophical Association, Eastern Division, Washington DC, 24 December 1998, on an invited symposium. It is published now for the first time.

Chapter 2, Music, Will, and Representation: I was asked a few years ago to contribute an essay on music for a volume devoted to the philosophy of Arthur Schopenhauer, and this is the result. When the essay was finished the editor of the volume and I both agreed that it was not appropriate, so I put it away for future use. It is published now for the first time.

Chapter 3, On Hanslick's Inconsistency, is part of a longer paper that was read at a joint meeting of the Canadian Society for Aesthetics and the Canadian Philosophical Association in Montreal, 3 June 1995. It is published now for the first time.

Chapter 4, Making the Codes and Breaking the Codes: Two Revolutions in Twentieth-Century Music: early in 1998 I was invited by Christoph Metzger to give a lecture, under the auspices of the Berliner Gesellschaft für Neue Musik, on minimalism in music at a meeting devoted to the subject of minimalism in contemporary art. In the event I produced a lecture far too long for public presentation and had to cut it down to half its size for the occasion, in Berlin, 14 November 1998. The shortened version was published in German in the proceedings of the meeting: 'Die Einführung von Codes und der Bruch mit ihnen', in Christoph Metzger and Nina Möntmann (eds.), *Minimalisms* (Berlin: Reihe Cantz, 1998), 62–74. I am grateful to Christoph Metzger for permission to publish, in English, those portions of the lecture that appeared in the proceedings; it appears here in its complete form for the first time.

Chapter 5, Auditor's Emotions: Contention, Consensus, Compromise, was originally published in the *Journal of Aesthetics and Art Criticism*, 51 (1993), 1–12. I am grateful to the editor of the *Journal*, Philip Alperson, for permission to reprint it here.

Chapter 6, Experiencing the Musical Emotions: I was invited, in the summer of 1997, to deliver a lecture on music and the emotions for Geneva Emotion Week, an annual event sponsored by the Emotion Research Group of the University of Geneva. The lecture was given on 14 May 1999 to an audience made up mostly of psychologists. In its written form it had a substantial historical introduction that made the lecture too long for public presentation. I cut the historical part and some other segments, here and there, for the lecture, and then published this abridged version in the *British Journal of Aesthetics*, 39 (1999), 1–13, under the title, 'Feeling the Musical Emotions.' I am grateful to the editor of the *Journal*, Peter Lamarque, for permission to reprint those portions published therein. It is published here, in its original, uncut version for the first time.

Chapter 7, The Arousal Theory of Musical Expression: Rethinking the Unthinkable, was written especially for the present volume.

Chapter 8, Absolute Music and the New Musicology, was written on invitation, for the Sixteenth International Congress of Musicology, London, Royal College of Music, 14–20 August 1997. Illness prevented me from attending the Congress, and my paper was read *in absentia*. However I had an opportunity to present it in person a year later, at the Tenth International Conference on Nineteenth-Century Music, at the University of Bristol, 17 July 1998. The paper was published in the proceedings of the International Congress: *Musicology and Sister Disciplines; Past, Present and Future*, ed. David Greer (Oxford: Oxford University Press, 1999). It is reprinted here with permission of the editor.

Chapter 9, Movements and 'Movements': a rather unusual conference on Music and Social Movements was held at the Interdisciplinary Conference Center of the University of California, Santa Barbara, in the winter of 1997. I was invited to give a lecture at that conference, on 22 February 1997, and this chapter is the result. It was presented again at the Open University Conference on the Philosophy of Music in London, 22 April 1998, and is published here for the first time.

Chapter 10, Music in Memory and *Music in the Moment* was written especially for the present volume.

Chapter 11, How to Forge a Musical Work: the death of the great Nelson Goodman in the autumn of 1998 was a cause for universal distress in the philosophical community. The *Journal of Aesthetics and Art Criticism*, in recognition of Professor Goodman's monumental contribution to aesthetics and the philosophy of art, published a group of essays as a tribute to his memory, of which the present essay was one. It appeared in the *Journal of Aesthetics and Art Criticism*, 58 (2000), 233–5. It is reprinted here with the permission of the editor, Philip Alperson.

Many of these essays were written as lectures or talks for specific occasions, and were, therefore, tailored for the audiences that were to hear them. In publishing them now I have removed all specific references to those occasions and any other topical references that might be obscure to readers of this volume. But there is a certain chatty quality to the lectures and talks, as opposed to the pieces not specifically written for public presentation, that I have not attempted to remove. I have never thought formal prose was necessary or even particularly desirable for philosophical discourse, and neither, as is apparent from the dialogues, did Plato or Socrates. So, while not presuming to compare myself with these two illustrious founders of the Western philosophical tradition, I happily follow their example, as best I can.

Besides the informality of the essays and lectures published here, there is another sense in which this collection is 'informal.' For with the exception of the three pieces on music and the emotions that make up the second part, they cover a wide and disparate range of subjects, and what will be of interest to one musical reader may not be of interest to another (although all the topics were, obviously, of interest to *this* musical reader). So this is very much a collection to be browsed. Each essay is self-contained, and need not be read in connection with any other.

As diverse as these essays and lectures are, however, they *do* constitute, or at least are a part of, a consistent philosophy of music. Inconsistencies I know there are; for even philosophers, stubborn though they may be, learn something new from time to time, and have been known to change their minds. I am not proud of my inconsistencies, in the way Walt Whitman was of his, but I have let them stand rather than rewrite the earlier pieces to bring them into conformity with the later ones. So if you find an inconsistency, you are welcome to it, and you can decide for yourself which of the alternatives is the right one, if either. Probably I couldn't make up my own mind, which perhaps is the *real* reason I have not tried to get the inconsistencies out.

It now remains but for me to thank Peter Momtchiloff, of Oxford University Press, for his encouragement and help. He has not *made* me change anything. So whatever is wrong with this volume you can lay entirely at my door.

P.K.

Cape Cod
Summer 2000

CONTENTS

. . . as if correct judgment were not the crucial factor, just as it is in musical questions.

Aristotle, *Nicomachean Ethics*, trans. J. A. K. Thomson

PART I

Some History (and its Aftermath)

Part I

Sartre's Theory and its Alternatives

I

Note-for-Note:
Work, Performance, and Early Notation

One of the most extraordinary and valuable aspects to me of Leo Treitler's work as a Medievalist—and I am thinking, here, particularly about the work on the origins and early history of Western musical notation—is its implications for the philosophy of music. Nor is Treitler, I hasten to add, unaware of these implications, for he combines the skills and learning of a historian with a love and instinct for the big, speculative questions—a rare combination indeed, much to be admired.

It seems to me that no work of Treitler's exemplifies more fully this connection between the philosophy of music and the history of notation, in its earliest period, than the article he published in 1992, in *The Journal of Musicology*, called 'The "Unwritten" and "Written Transmission" of Medieval Chant and the Start-up of Musical Notation.' Its rather dry, prosaic title gives no hint of the deep conceptual issues it raises for the aesthetician. It is no exaggeration to assert that the whole repertory of questions concerning the ontology of the musical work, the relation of work to performance, the nature of performance, and the relation of both to notation itself is implied either directly or indirectly by Treitler's research, as laid out in this article. The variety of notations and notational functions that he reveals cannot help but shake anyone's conceptual scheme, if he or she is complacent enough to think that it can all be worked out on the basis merely of Beethoven's Fifth Symphony.

Indeed, so deep and various are the philosophical issues that this article raises that it would require a book, not a chapter, to do them justice. What I propose, therefore, is to tease out and pursue one or two trains of thought that the first reading of Treitler's article initiated in me, and that have, from time to time, exercised me since. To do anything more would be quite impossible.

I begin, where Treitler begins, with some of his sage advice, to be taken to heart by upstarts and interlopers, among whom I am certainly to be numbered, who try to say something about work, performance, and notation from, let us broadly say, a philosophical or, at least, extra-musicological vantage-point. He says: 'We—who are accustomed to musical scores as signs in which composers encode their works, as the instructions that guide performers, and as the objects of analysis and comparison for scholars and students—must strain to understand how a distant and complex musical culture that we view as the progenitor of our own thrived without the use of scores.'[1]

Treitler continues this thought:

Subordinating medieval material to these conceptions and expectations has meant evaluating early medieval notational material according to the measure in which it meets the standard of precision in a prescriptive denotation; envisioning performance in a scriptless musical world in terms of two satellite conceptions of the Romantic work concept: either as the reproduction of an autonomous 'text' that has been deposited in all its completeness in 'memory,' as a written text would be deposited in a book; or as an improvisation produced through the free exercise of the musical fantasy . . .[2]

He concludes: 'The effort to avoid such templates as constraints on medieval materials, though far from easy, will yield a more objective portrayal, and it will at the same time serve as a reminder of the narrow historicality of the work concept and its satellites.'[3]

The *Diabolus in musica*, here, is obviously the so-called Romantic work/performance ontology Treitler describes as embodying 'closure, unity and not least autonomy . . .'[4] I shall have some more to say about this in a moment; but for now I just want to register at least a mild warning about becoming paranoid in this regard. If the three characteristics Treitler mentions are the minimal requirements for the work/performance ontology, then it is surely not solely a Romantic concept; and if one understands that neither closure, nor unity, nor autonomy are clearly defined, logically airtight features, but susceptible of degree and quite fuzzy around the edges, it becomes clear that it is no anachronism to understand music well before the nineteenth century, and for that matter, the eighteenth, within the ontology of performance and work, even in the absence of

---

[1] Leo Treitler, 'The "Unwritten" and "Written Transmission" of Medieval Chant and the Start-up of Musical Notation,' *Journal of Musicology*, 10 (1992), 131.
[2] Ibid. 132.   [3] Ibid. 133.   [4] Ibid. 132–3.

the standard terminology or the full conceptual apparatus. I think it is worth pointing out that before the sixteenth century there was no word, either in Latin or the vernacular, for composer,[5] and before the middle of the eighteenth the concept of the fine arts, with music among them, was not in place.[6] This should hardly keep us from describing Dufay as a composer or his creations as works of art.

It is one of the signal virtues of Treitler's essay that it reveals to us the diversity of purposes that early notations served, quite different from those that they serve for us, in modern times, namely, as Treitler describes the modern purposes, the encoding of works, a guide to performers, and objects of analysis and comparison for scholars and students. As Treitler puts the point: 'Notational systems emphasizing different principles of reference and different ways of conceiving the musical object—also different states of its tradition—were developed according to the needs that the notations were meant to address.'[7]

I am interested in musical notation at the point where at least one of the purposes it serves is within the framework of what I call the 'repeatable' and the 'repetition.' I propose that this framework be thought of as the absolute minimal condition for what later firms up into the ontology of work and performance. Perhaps we should think of it as the proto-work/performance stage: and so I shall call it.

In this stage there is at least the notion that a singer is singing *something* that another singer or that singer himself can sing again at some other time. And there must be criteria in place, of some intelligible kind, either written, or orally transmitted, or in some practice or tradition, or all of the above together, that can tell the singer and his audience when he has got it right.

Of course these minimal requirements for a proto-work/performance ontology can be met without any notation at all. They can be met by an oral tradition. But before I get to the role of notation in the ontology of the repeatable and the repetition, I want to take a sidelong glance at that, and in particular the role of memory, for here I think there is some confusion in what Treitler says that it would be desirable to clear up.

[5] See Rob C. Wegman, 'From Maker to Composer: Improvisation and Musical Authorship in the Low Countries, 1450–1500,' *Journal of the American Musicological Society*, 49 (1996).

[6] See Paul Oskar Kristeller, 'The Modern System of the Arts,' repr. in Peter Kivy (ed.), *Essays on the History of Aesthetics* (Rochester: University of Rochester Press, 1992).

[7] Treitler, ' "Unwritten" and "Written Transmission",' 173.

In another of his warnings to the unwary, Treitler calls attention to the dangerous assumption that, in the distinction between written and oral performance traditions, there is frequently the implication of 'a parallelism—that written and unwritten transmissions are both processes that do the same sort of thing, that is, to transmit something—and an opposition—that they do so in different, mutually exclusive ways (as one might speak of conveying a message by telephone or by mail.)'[8] The assumption, of course, embodies the work/performance ontology, or at least the proto-stage of it; and it is that ontology that Treitler is warning us against in oral traditions—at least in *some* oral traditions. He says: 'If it is a well-known hymn that is being transmitted note-for-note through a stable performance tradition, then the formulation seems perfectly apt. But if it is a trope or an organum melody that we have every reason to think was reconstructed or extemporized in performance, then the object has not been *transmitted through* performance, it has been *realized in* performance.'[9]

So far so good: a perfectly viable distinction is being made here between two different things—singing a melody note-for-note from memory, and reconstructing it in an imaginative process, by inference, so to speak, because it is not recallable in the other way. But where things begin to get murky is where Treitler appeals for support from the psychologists. According to Frederick C. Bartlett, in his book *Remembering: A Study in Experimental and Social Psychology*, as quoted by Treitler, 'Remembering is not the re-excitation of innumerable fixed, lifeless and fragmented traces. It is an imaginative reconstruction, or construction, built out of the relation of our attitude towards a whole mass of organized past reactions or experience . . .' As Treitler glosses the passage: 'that is, remembering is always an active synthesizing process of organizing and recognizing, not the retrieval of something from dead storage.'[10]

Now what has happened here, in appealing to the psychologists, is that the common-sense distinction Treitler has made previously between performing a chant, note for note, 'from memory,' and 'reconstructing' a trope or organum melody in performance has completely broken down. If the psychologists are right, both are 'remembering' *and* both are 'reconstructing.' Treitler recognizes this. He himself observes, on the basis of the psychologists' conclusions, that 'Both refer to acts of remembering . . .'[11]

---

[8] Treitler, ' "Unwritten" and "Written Transmission",' 135.
[9] Ibid.   [10] Ibid. 146.   [11] Ibid.

How, then, does one accept the conclusion of the psychologists *and* maintain what seems a perfectly valid, commonsensical distinction between just remembering something, right off, and remembering it by imaginative reconstruction, if *both* are supposed to be the latter? Let me begin by suggesting that the question is illegitimate, and arises out of what Alfred North Whitehead referred to as the 'fallacy of misplaced concreteness.' It frequently happens that scientists redefine an ordinary word or phrase for theoretical purposes: for example, the physicists' definition of 'work.' There is nothing in the world wrong with that. The problem comes when one starts to use the scientists' redefined, usually more precise meaning where one used to use the ordinary one. So, for example, if I complain that I did not get any work done yesterday, and you reply that of course I did, since 'work' simply means the expending of energy and that is done just by breathing, it is nonsense, due, of course, to an equivocation on the word 'work,' by which I mean something like accomplishing my assigned tasks, and you mean that precise thing that the physicists mean and that everyone accomplishes all the time just as long as he or she is alive.

I hope Treitler will forgive me for suggesting that he might have fallen into the fallacy of misplaced concreteness. Perhaps I am wrong. But in any case, let me point out that what the psychologists have done is to redefine the notion of imaginative reconstruction in such a way that what we used to call immediate recall, and, as distinct from that, remembering by imaginative reconstruction, are, under the new definition, *both* remembering by imaginative reconstruction. This, however, cannot obliterate our pre-systematic, commonsensical distinction between remembering by immediate recall and remembering by imaginative reconstruction; and to think that it does is to commit that loathsome fallacy that I will not name again.

So let me now say how I, a commonsensical fellow, understand these matters. If someone should ask me, 'Do you remember how Mozart's Fortieth Symphony begins?,' I reply: 'Of course,' humming the opening theme straightaway. I have just remembered it by what I term 'immediate recall.' If, on the other hand, I should be asked, 'Do you remember how the countersubject goes to the *Et in terra pax* fugue in the B-minor Mass?' I may have to say something like this: 'Well, let's see. I can't hum it right off. But I can sing the subject. And if I do that, then, since the countersubject is sung as a continuation of the subject, I think it will come to me.' And I do; and it does; and this, I think, can properly be called an example of recall by imaginative reconstruction (of a very simple kind).

This, then, in elementary terms, is how, on the common-sense, pre-systematic level, I see the distinction between remembering by immediate recall and remembering by imaginative reconstruction. And what I want to conclude is that, first, the psychologists have not destroyed this distinction and, second, that even where remembering melodies is by imaginative reconstruction rather than by immediate recall, we may still have a musical tradition that enfranchises the proto-work/performance ontology, which I have described as the ontology of the repeatable and the repetition.

But having got so far, I want to go on to what is my major concern, namely, the evolution of musical notation from the earliest examples understandable as assuming or embodying the proto-work/performance ontology to modern notation, where, of course, the full-scale work/performance ontology is in place. How is it philosophically useful or enlightening to look at it?

One way we are well-warned *not* to look at the evolution of musical notation is as, necessarily, technical progress. As Treitler put the point in an earlier article, 'it is generally not good practice to say that a thing has the characteristics of its successors, but has them in different measure . . .'[12] Thus even if the general aim of notation, after a certain point, is to facilitate the repeating of the repeatable, it is not a good idea to see notations as getting better and better at doing this. For what each notation is supposed to facilitate the repetition of may be both artistically and aesthetically very different in each case; and it would be nonsense to think that nineteenth-century notation would necessarily be better at doing that particular job, for those particular musics, than their own particular notations do (or did) it. This much is abundantly clear.

But there is another way of looking at the evolution of musical notation, from the earliest examples of proto-work/performance scripts, to modern work/performance scores, that seems far more promising. It does not commit the sophomoric fallacy of thinking that later notations must be better at enabling us to realize in performance what *they* were evolved to realize but what early notations were evolved to realize as well: in other words, the fallacy of the

---

[12] Leo Treitler, 'The Early History of Music Writing in the West,' *Journal of the American Musicological Society*, 35 (1982), 264.

better mousetrap. It is far more like, one would think, being better adapted to one's own environment than to any other.

So what is this way of looking at the evolution of notations whose purpose is the repeating of the repeatable? Perhaps one might think of it as an evolution towards a determination of more and more of the performance sounds. That is to say, the modern score determines more precisely than, say, Bach's score of a sonata for violin and continuo, the sounds that will be produced in performance. The sounds that the keyboard player will produce in Beethoven's Kreutzer Sonata are more precisely and more fully determined than those that the keyboard player will produce in a sonata for violin and figured bass. This appears a reasonable way of looking at the evolution of musical notation, and makes no value judgements. It is non-normative, since it does not imply the notation that it is *better* to determine the sounds of the performance more fully and precisely (although it is easy to slip into the normative mode even here).

But in spite of the initial plausibility of this suggestion, and its improvement over the simple-minded, later-therefore-better view, I think it is not the right way to look at things. That is because all successful notations, from the proto-work/performance period, to the full-blown Romantic work/performance score *fully* determine the performance: do, in fact, give full instructions for sound production. The notion that a Medieval notation, even in the earliest period, underdetermines what sounds will be produced in performance, as opposed (say) to the score of a Brahms symphony, is due, I think, to a deep misunderstanding of what kind of document a musical notation is.

Suppose one says, 'Well, the reason I insist that a nineteenth-century score determines performance sound more fully than a Baroque figured bass notation, or an early notation that does not indicate exact pitches or intervals is that in the former case the score tells you exactly, note for note, what will sound in the performance, while the Baroque or early Medieval notation does not, but leaves many of these determinations open.'

But what does it mean to indicate *note for note* what is to be sounded? Any notation, *in vacuo*, is just a bunch of physical scratches on paper or parchment. It is only a notation within a musical practice that contains the rules and conventions, whether formal or informal or both, that enable the musician to interpret it. In that case, *any* correct interpretation of that notation is, by the only standard that makes sense, a note-for-note rendition.

This point seems to me of such philosophical and aesthetic importance that I want to put real emphasis on it, and try to make it unmistakably clear. Someone may say to me: 'What you are arguing for is absurd. How can you seriously suggest that a Medieval notation in which neither absolute pitches nor discrete intervals are indicated, but merely higher and lower, or the score of a Baroque sonata movement where the harpsichordist improvises the right-hand accompaniment, and the violinist elaborately embellishes the melody, is determining a sound occurrence note-for-note, the way the score of a Brahms symphony does? There is only one correct realization of the Brahms score, but many in the other cases. In the Brahms score every pitch, rhythmic value, and interval is exactly determined; however this is clearly not the case either in the Medieval or Baroque notations.'

Of course we know that that is not even the case in the Romantic score, since Toscanini's performance is going to be very different, in sound occurrence, from Bruno Walter's. But what if it were true? What difference would that make? It would still be the case that any performance of any notation would be a note-for-note one, if it followed the rules and conventions, whether formal or informal or both, within the musical practice of which that notation was a part.

Now it might be objected, at this point, that my position on the adequacy of notation, at any given historical time, forecloses on the possibility of musical notation evolving or changing, which it obviously does. For what else could drive the change, the evolution of notation, but its inadequacy—its failure to meet the needs of the composers and performers who use it? It appears as if my view implies notational gridlock.

That objection, I think, comes from overstating the case. At any given time, it might be replied, musical notation is for the most part adequate to its task of determining performance, in its historical way, note for note, else why does it exist in that form at that time? However, at any given time there will always be tensions: there will always be demands on it that it cannot meet, or cannot meet well. (In 'revolutionary' musical times, of course, the tensions will be greater, the needs more difficult to meet.) That is what drives the evolution of musical notation (or, I suppose, the evolution of anything else). So the correct way of stating my position is that musical notation, at any given time, both is and is not adequate to answering the composer's demands (if there is a composer), and determining performance note for note. But it *is*, of course, to a far greater extent than it *is not*—because *it* is there, and not something else. The pressure to evolve is always there, but relative stability is there as well.

Treitler offers many fascinating examples, in the article on the start-up of musical notation, of the various practices in which memory, notation, language and improvisation play a part. Figure 1 illustrates one that particularly intrigued me.

Treitler writes of this example:

The interpretation is clear: each marginal note [in arrow-shaped boxes] is an instruction to the singer to sing this text to the well-known tune of such-and-

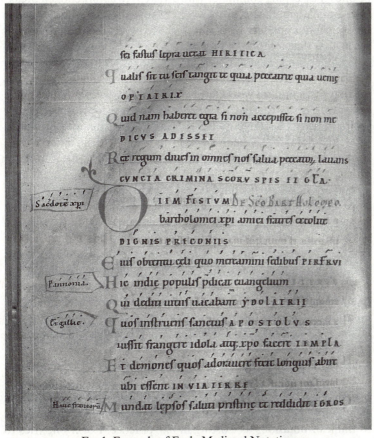

Fɪɢ 1. Example of Early Medieval Notation
(Source: Kremsmünster, Stiftbibliothek codex 309 f.214 verso.)

such. It puts him on the track of the melody, and his remembering of the melody guides him in the reading of the notation, which is also an act of reconstruction. But at the same time the notation supports him in his remembering of the melody. This interesting phenomenon of written transmission points to what must have been a fundamental relation of mutual support between reading and remembering in the performance of music after the entry of music-writing into the picture.[13]

Perhaps one's first reaction to this notation, if he or she is old enough to remember, is that it is like a Rube Goldberg invention, where through a vast complication of pulleys and strings, alarm clocks and popping toasters, eventually the dog's tail gets pulled, and he bites the sleeping commuter who awakens to a fully cooked breakfast. But, after all, a Rube Goldberg invention, we know in our hearts, cannot possibly work if it were physically realized; whereas it seems that this notation did work.

Is it, then, an inelegant notation compared to our own? Well, elegance is as elegance does, so far as I'm concerned. And if Treitler tells me that this notation worked, who am I to condemn it as lacking in elegance? Anyway, what is so elegant about a nineteenth-century score? It seems a hodge-podge to me—a weird mixture of words, signs, and notes that, when you really look at it with an innocent eye, is every bit as clumsy as any early notation Treitler offers up in his article, which is why, no doubt, it defeated Nelson Goodman's valiant attempt to make hard-edged, logical sense of it.

So what I am trying to emphasize, and to convince the reader of, is that whatever else one may think of this nearly 900-hundred-year-old notation, it did not, in contrast to ours, underdetermine performance. If there was in place, in the musical practice of which this notation was a part, a notion of correct and incorrect readings of it, if there was in place at least the proto-work/performance schema, the minimal concept of the repeatable and the repetition, then this notation fully determined within its own musical practice what *that practice* saw as a correct sonic realization of it: if you will, a note-for-note realization.

What, then, draws one so strongly to the belief that this notation, or (say) a figured bass notation, are less exact in their determinations of sonic realization than a score of a Beethoven sonata or a Brahms symphony? Let me suggest that it is the tendency unconsciously to think of notations as existing in *our* practice. For if one tries to

[13] Treitler, '"Unwritten" and "Written Transmission",' 160–2.

realize a performance of the Medieval notation or a sonata for violin and figured bass by employing the rules and conventions of nineteenth-century musical practice, then, of course, both notations will be seen as underdetermining sonic occurrence to varying degrees. But that is like putting a dinosaur in Times Square and concluding that it is ill-adapted for survival. Under the rules and conventions of modern musical practice, *of course* the early twelfth-century notation does not fully determine a performance, note-for-note. In that conceptual scheme it appears hopelessly vague in comparison with the score of a Brahms symphony. In its own practice, however, it is neither vague nor imprecise. Within the conceptual apparatus of musical institutions which it served, it provides just what the modern symphonic score does for ours: it gives all of the information a musician sees himself as requiring for a correct sonic realization. In his eyes it fully determines performance.

'But look,' one may say: 'it is clear that the twelfth-century notation does not uniquely determine performance, because the sounds it determines, on two separate occasions, will be so different, compared to the sounds produced by two different performances (say) of Brahms's Fourth Symphony, that it is senseless to call the former two performances of the same "work" at all, or in the proto-work/performance stage, two repetitions of the repeatable.'

The very same mistake, however, is being made here that we have already uncovered, of unconsciously applying our own musical practice to the early notation. For why else should we not think that within the conceptual apparatus in which the twelfth-century notation flourished the two sound occurrences *were* thought of as two repeats of the repeatable, even though within our conceptual apparatus they seem too disparate to be so taken? The facts seem to be that if the twelfth-century notation operated within constraints of correctness and incorrectness, and if the proto-work/performance ontology was in place, then each sonic occurrence *was* a repetition of the repeatable, assuming the musicians were competent users of the notation.

Why, one might wonder, have I been so aggressively insistent on the notion that early notations, and pre-Romantic ones, must not be seen as in any way necessarily underdetermining performance? Here is one reason. It leads to the claim, which may be true of some early notations but by no means of all, that it is anachronistic to ascribe to them the work/performance ontology. For if that ontology depends upon a notation fully determining performance, and if a notation cannot do that, why then the work/performance ontology cannot hold for that notation. But I have argued that, in many cases, the notation does fully determine performance, note for note, if you will, seen within the conceptual scheme of its own musical practice. And, so it seems to me, there is an unsuspected commonality between our musical world and some of the earliest notational worlds of the Western musical tradition—and, indeed, between our musical world and some scriptless ones as well.

But it needs pointing out that there may also be a wide conceptual gulf between modern notation and early ones even where the proto-work/performance ontology is in place. In other words, they may be incommensurable with ours: untranslatable, the one into the other, very much in the same way in which poetry is said to be untranslatable from one language to another. It is not that it cannot be done at all; but something important must always be lost. (Robert Frost I think said that *poetry* is what the translation leaves out.)

An obvious, recent example is figured bass notation, as it was used in the Baroque period. I am, I confess, an amateur oboe player; and, of course, I play a great deal of Baroque music. My accompanists can seldom realize a figured bass in performance, so we use the many fine modern editions with the figured bass realized by the editor. But what this really amounts to is the translation of one notation, figured bass, into another; and some things aesthetically important are compromised in the process, the sense of improvisation, for one, and the variety of realization for another. For whether Tom, Dick, or Harriet is my accompanist, the texture and voice-leading in the right hand are always the same; whereas if they were realizing from the figured bass, these would be different in aesthetically significant ways. Something serious is lost in the translation from one notation to another.

However, if so recent a notation, still after all used in teaching harmony and analysis, is, in a deep sense, incommensurable with modern notation and performance practice, how much more so must be the notation of the early twelfth century. One can, indeed one must, try to give one's reader an idea of what the early notation is doing by putting it, as best one can, in modern notation, particularly if the reader is a lay person such as myself. But in doing so, one is, of course, making the same old error of interpreting the early notation as governed by modern practice.

Perhaps what this reveals is that a musical notation is not separable from the music it notates. There is not the music on the one hand and the notation on the other, the way there is the hammer and the nail. Rather, the two interpenetrate one another in such an intimate manner as to make them both parts of the work of art, rather than the notation in service, so to speak, to the artwork. It is not, in other words, a means/end relationship.

In one place Treitler makes this intriguing suggestion with regard to a certain kind of early notation: 'In such a tradition musical items could be realized in writing as well as in performance; writing down *was* a kind of performance.'[14] It is an intriguing suggestion, for me, just because if notating is a kind of performance, then, as I see performance (and explicated that perception in *Authenticities*, 1995), notation *must* be part of the musical work. Perhaps all musical notation is a kind of performance. It is a notion worth exploring. In that case it would give us an explanation of the intimate relation that musics and their notations have: a relation that makes the notation part of the artwork itself, rather than an instrument to some artistic end. But such speculation would take me far beyond the modest pretensions of this chapter to a real philosophy of musical notation, something that, in spite of the pioneering attempt of Nelson Goodman, we do not yet possess.

If I am right in what I have said so far, then it turns out that playing the music note for note is a more expansive concept than might heretofore have been thought. And so it might appear that my analysis has gone astray in failing to capture our intuitions in this regard. I am not sure. But I think someone who thinks her intuitions are being violated might be confusing the note-for-note concept with another expression, an expression of dissatisfaction with a performance to the effect that 'he merely played the notes.'

When musicologists establish the 'text' of a musical work they frequently produce what has come to be called an *Urtext*. This is supposed to reproduce, 'unedited,' exactly what the composer wrote. If, to take an obvious example, one makes an *Urtext* edition of a composition by J. S. Bach, it may contain neither tempo indications, phrasing, nor dynamics of any kind. For to produce the *Urtext* is merely to reproduce in a printed version what the best, most authoritative manuscript or combination of manuscripts contains, and Bach's manuscripts are very spare in these regards.

---

[14] Treitler, ' "Unwritten" and "Written Transmission",' 167.

What would it mean to 'merely play the notes' in such a case? Well, of course, the performer would play the piece at some tempo or other, and what that tempo was would of course be the performer's decision to make. But the performer would not do anything in the way of phrasing except to articulate each note. Nor would he play crescendos or decrescendos, or even simple contrasts between piano and forte, because there would be no such indications in the *Urtext*. He would have to pick a dynamic level and stick with it throughout. To do otherwise would be to do more than merely play the notes.

Such performances as the one I am describing above were actually common in what might be called the early period of the early music movement, in the 1950s and 1960s; and they were justly cried down as, indeed, 'merely playing the notes,' with no musicality whatever in evidence. They were bad performances, nor did they serve any useful musical purpose. They were, essentially, sonic *Urtexts*. But they served neither of the three musical purposes that printed *Urtexts* are meant to serve, which are, I take it, to provide texts for the use of musical scholars, to provide reliable textual bases for performing editions, and to provide such performers who do not wish to use performing editions themselves the texts from which they can realize performances that are not unmusical, that are not merely playing the notes.

Now it should be perfectly clear that what I have described at some length as realizing the score note for note is definitely not the same thing as merely playing the notes. For playing the score note for note involves being governed in one's realization of it by all the customs, conventions, and practices, written and unwritten, of which that score is a functioning part. And, of course, to stick with Bach as our example, much of what the *Urtext* lacks, in writing, that is necessary for a musical performance is supplied by the customs, conventions, and practices in which the direct source of that *Urtext* is embedded.

Thus, if it may seem that what I am calling a note-for-note rendition of a score, or a score determining a performance note for note, leaves more leeway than that phrase suggests to the ordinary language ear, or seems to apply to notations that have more 'gaps,' so to speak, than would be consistent with its determining a performance note for note, I suggest, first, that we must beware of the potential confusion between merely playing the notes (the narrow, *Urtext* concept), and playing or determining note for note (the rich, musical one). But which *should* apply to a notation?

Well here, perhaps, some stipulation may be lurking in the background. But let me just suggest the following considerations. If one means by playing the notation note for note, not adding anything that is not at least implicitly there, and if one means by a notation determining a performance note for note that the notation provides all the materials necessary for the adequately trained musician to realize a performance of the work, then the *Urtext* concept of playing merely the notes does not fill the bill. An *Urtext* is not a real, living notation, but a scholar's construct; and using it as the basis for a performance, playing merely the notes, is *not* a correct, accurate realization of the work. Furthermore, treating a notation, particularly an early one, *as if* it were an *Urtext*, by playing merely the notes there written, is not a correct, accurate realization of the work either. Thus, I suggest, the way I have characterized the score, whether an early medieval notation where absolute pitches are not determined, or a nineteenth-century score of a Romantic symphony, as determining the performance note for note, although it may have some surprising results, really does capture what we essentially mean by note-for-note realization and determination.

Performing music is, of course, playing (and singing) the *notes*. What I hope to have shown, with the help of Treitler's intriguing work on early notations, is that 'the notes' are more than meets the eye. Or, rather, *just* what meets the eye, when it sees within a practice. And without a practice there are no notes at all.

2

Music, Will, and Representation

Music has perennially, most of the time peripherally, figured in the writings of the great philosophers. In antiquity, Plato and Aristotle wrote at some length about something our translators render as 'music,' but what it sounded like—whether music in our sense of the word—is difficult, if not impossible to determine. In the early modern era, Descartes, Leibniz, Thomas Reid, and Kant treated music seriously if not at length. But it is Arthur Schopenhauer who first among the first rank of modern philosophers gave music a prestigious place in a philosophical system. For that reason alone, if for no other, what Schopenhauer said about it deserves our attention as philosophers of art.

The value of what Schopenhauer said about music, for our own times, is debatable. But it is a debate well worth entering into, and I shall do so in the second half of this chapter.

The historical significance of Schopenhauer's accomplishment in the philosophy of music is both prophetic and backward-tending: prophetic in that, in contrast to Kant and Hegel, he saw music as unequivocally one of the fine arts; backward-tending because, unlike Hegel, he remained with a foot firmly planted in the eighteenth century, seeing music as still (if peculiarly) representational, while his great contemporary pushed ahead with what I take to be the first fully worked out 'expression theory' of the arts (although Reid came pretty close).

There is, then, a historical theme and a contemporary theme to be played out in Schopenhauer's philosophy of music. To the historical theme I first turn my attention.

The State of the Arts

The story we have all more or less accepted, as told in Paul Oskar Kristeller's comprehensive essay, 'The Modern System of the Arts,' is that the fine arts as we know them, as a system of related practices, came into being in the first half of the eighteenth century.[1] But the story has a crucial blind spot. For although 'music' had indeed made it into the club, it was vocal music that the word almost always connoted when music as a fine art was being discussed. And it is easy to see why. For what bound the fine arts together was the ancient doctrine of *mimesis*; and it was already a commonplace in practical music aesthetics—had been since the close of the sixteenth century—that the singing voice, in well-composed music, was a representation, an imitation, of passionate human speech.

Vocal music, then, was no problem for Enlightenment aesthetics in its major project: the definition of the fine arts. For the binding principle was imitation; and the singing voice as an imitation of the speaking voice was established doctrine. It was the growing genre of pure instrumental music that put a strain on the system. The analogy with speech or song, although it was suggested, often, is remote at best; and the absence of a text made it all the more difficult to give what the nineteenth century later called 'absolute music' any kind of respectable mimetic or representational content.

In the early part of the century, the problem of absolute music had not become acute, because the balance was still heavily weighted towards vocal music, either for the church or the opera house, in the composer's professional life; and it was certainly the almost exclusive subject to which those who might plausibly be described as engaging in philosophical discussion of music applied themselves. Instrumental music could be easily either dismissed with a nod in the direction of mimesis, put down as decorative art of no consequence, or simply ignored.

But by the last quarter of the eighteenth century, instrumental music, particularly in Germany and Austria, had arrived at a level of social esteem and importance as to be no longer beneath notice by those who theorized in a philosophical way about 'music,' *sans phrase*, to the end of making accommodation for it in the modern system of the arts. It had, indeed, become the difficult case, the crucial test. If your theory of the fine arts could not include absolute music, or at least give a philosophically convincing reason why it should not, it was a failed theory on those grounds alone.

---

[1] Paul O. Kristeller, 'The Modern System of the Arts: A Study in the History of Aesthetics,' Part I, *Journal of the History of Ideas*, 12 (1951), and Part II, 13 (1952).

The puzzle of absolute music can be seen played out in scores of minor musical writers and aestheticians of the late eighteenth century, but nowhere more clearly, or more influentially, than in Kant's *Critique of Judgement.* And because it goes without saying that Kant, in every department, was a powerful influence on Schopenhauer's thought, it is there that we can most clearly see the problem of absolute music's right to the status of fine art, as it presented itself to Schopenhauer, in working out the status of absolute music in his own aesthetic system.

The Kantian Dilemma

The section of the third *Critique* most familiar to those interested in the question of whether or not Kant thought absolute music one of the fine arts is §14, where the status of 'Euler's vibrations' is hostage to a presumed misprint in the first and second editions, corrected finally in the third—the last edition to appear under Kant's supervision. At least the current consensus is for the reading of the third edition, and I shall acquiesce in it as the most plausible.[2]

The passage, as rendered by J. H. Bernard, in 1892, with the misprint in place, reads:

If we assume with Euler that colors are isochronous vibrations (*pulsus*) in the ether, as sounds are of the air in a state of disturbance, and—what is more important—that the mind not only perceives by sense the effect of these in exciting the organ, but also perceives by reflection the regular play of impressions (and thus the form of the combination of different representations)—which I very much doubt—then colors and tone cannot be reckoned as mere sensations, but as the determination of the unity of a manifold of sensations, and thus as beauties.[3]

Read with the third edition, the crucial phrase, translated by Bernard as 'which I very much doubt,' is rendered some years later by J. C. Meredith, as 'which I, still, in no way doubt.'[4]

---

[2] For a good, brief account of the misprint, and the argument for the reading of the 3rd edn., see Theodore E. Uehling, Jr., *The Notion of Form in Kant's Critique of Aesthetic Judgment* (The Hague: Mouton, 1971), 22–6.

[3] Immanuel Kant, *Critique of Judgement*, trans. J. H. Bernard (New York: Hafner, 1961), 60.

[4] Immanuel Kant, *Critique of Aesthetic Judgement*, trans. James Creed Meredith (Oxford: Clarendon Press, 1911), 66.

If we credit the third edition of the third *Critique*, then, Kant is saying that the intentional object of musical perception, namely sound, is an intentional object that presents itself to us as *form*, consciously so taken—the form, that is to say, of Euler's vibrations. And this, for Kant, is crucial to music's status, as becomes apparent in §51. For if we are conscious of the form of Euler's vibrations, then 'would music be represented out and out as a fine art . . .' But if, on the other hand, Euler's vibrations were not so presented, as consciously perceived form, then 'it would be represented as (in part at least) an *agreeable* art.'[5]

So, what we seem to get, putting together what Kant says in §§14 and 51 of the *Critique of Judgement* is that music *is* a fine art, not an agreeable art, because—and only because—Euler's vibrations are consciously perceived as form. And this sounds right, does it not, if one is already predisposed, as many people are, to think that Kant is a formalist with regard to the fine arts.

However, we are brought up short if we believe that §§14 and 51 establish music as a fine art in virtue of form, by the following remark in the *Anthropology*, first published in 1798, eight years after the third *Critique*: 'it is only because music serves as an instrument for poetry that it is *fine* (not merely pleasant) art.'[6] What else can this mean but that Euler's vibrations to the contrary notwithstanding, music only becomes fine art when it acquires conceptual content, which poetry traditionally provides, leaving absolute music still in outer darkness?

Now to this it might be replied that the *Anthropology* represents an earlier stage of Kant's thought, recording, as it does, lectures that Kant had been giving for many years previous to the publication of the third *Critique*. But I for one find it difficult to believe that Kant would continue to tell his students things he did not believe, and then, to compound the felony, to *publish* them as well. Nor need we, in the end, ascribe such intellectually shoddy behavior to Kant. For in §§53–54 of the *Critique of Judgement* considerations surface that reveal that Kant's view there on whether or not music is a fine art is consistent with itself as well as with the statement in the *Anthropology* quoted above.

How does 'content' manifest itself in the fine arts, on Kant's view? Not through the manifest content—the statable matter—but

---

[5] Ibid. 190.

[6] Immanuel Kant, *Anthropology from a Pragmatic Point of View*, trans. Mary J. Gregory (The Hague: Martinus Nijhoff, 1974), 114.

through the ineffable 'aesthetic ideas' that such manifest content occasions. The presence of the aesthetic ideas, as I read Kant, is a necessary condition for something's being fine art, but only, it turns out, if the aesthetic ideas are cashed out in the appropriate way, which is to say, in engaging the free play of the cognitive faculties of reason and imagination. And it is obviously no coincidence that that is the very same pay-off of *form*, in the pure judgement of taste.

The problem with music is not that it fails to occasion the aesthetic ideas. Absolute music, 'as a language of affections . . . universally communicates the aesthetic ideas that are naturally combined therewith.'[7] But unlike the aesthetic ideas of poetry and painting, the aesthetic ideas of music fail to engage the free play of the cognitive faculties. The pay-off is in merely bodily satisfaction—the feeling of bodily well-being. 'In music the course of this play is from bodily sensations to aesthetic ideas (which are the Objects for the affections), and then from these back again [to bodily sensations], but with gathered strength of the body.'[8] And because of this failure on the part of the aesthetic ideas in music to engage the cognitive faculties in free play, it 'deserves to be ranked rather as an agreeable than a fine art.'[9]

What then should we make of Kant's two apparently contradictory thoughts that since Euler's vibrations are consciously perceived as form, music *is* a fine rather than an agreeable art, and (conversely) that since the aesthetic ideas it occasions do *not* engage the free play of the cognitive faculties but merely result in a feeling of bodily well-being, music must be agreeable rather than fine? I think the most charitable (and not unsupported) interpretation we can put on Kant's text is to suggest that Kant is declining to answer categorically the question of whether or not *absolute* music is a fine art—and that not because he is undecided or confused but because the answer really is 'yes' *and* 'no.' Or, rather, absolute music is fine art-like in two respects, agreeable art-like in a third.

Absolute music is, indeed, like the fine arts in that musical sound is not merely capable of charm but of beauty, since it presents itself to our cognition as form—the form of Euler's vibrations. And it is like the fine arts too in that it occasions a train of aesthetic ideas. But because the pay-off of these aesthetic ideas is bodily, whereas in poetry and painting its pay-off lies in the free play of the cognitive

---

[7] Kant, *Critique of Aesthetic Judgement*, 194.   [8] Ibid. 199.   [9] Ibid.

faculties, in that respect it is like the agreeable arts, rather than the fine arts—Kant, indeed, compares it, in function, to 'jest.'

What I want to suggest—and I think it is an eminently reasonable suggestion—is that the problem of music as a fine art presented itself to Schopenhauer in its Kantian form. Schopenhauer looked to the most philosophically penetrating answer around—the Kantian answer—and found not an indecisive answer but, rather, a decisive compromise: absolute music as fine art-*like* but not fine art—failing, indeed, just where one would expect it to fail, *if* one were still committed to mimesis, namely, in lack of 'content.' For even in Kant's sophisticated version of artistic content, conceived in terms of the aesthetic ideas, absolute music fails to come up to the mark.

The philosophical choices were clear. At the one extreme was the denial that absolute music is a fine art, at the other, to find a new, non-mimetic theory of fine art that would encompass poetry, painting, *and* absolute music. The middle way was to tinker with the mimetic theory so as to accommodate absolute music. It was the middle way, the philosophically conservative way that Schopenhauer took. But in taking that conservative, middle way, Schopenhauer achieved the revolutionary conclusion that music is not merely one of the fine arts; indeed it is the most exalted of them: *the* fine art *par excellence*, towards which in a way (to anticipate Walter Pater), all the other arts aspire. To this conservative yet at the same time revolutionary view of music, Schopenhauer's view, we must now turn our attention.

Music as Representation

Let me begin my discussion of Schopenhauer by emphasizing that I have nothing really to add to the general understanding of his philosophical position with regard to absolute music's standing as a fine art. What I hope I can add, or at least supplement, in this section of the chapter, is an understanding of its historical context and origins. I want to begin by seeing Schopenhauer on music not so much as a new, nineteenth-century phenomenon but, rather, as the culmination of an eighteenth-century one.

The argument that leads Schopenhauer to the conclusion that music is one of the fine arts strikes one not so much as an argument at all but, rather, a begging of the question. As an argument properly so called, it is, really, an argument *from* the assumption that music is a fine art to the conclusion that *therefore* it must be mimetic. Schopenhauer says:

That in some sense music must be related to the world as the depiction to the thing depicted, as the copy to the original, we can infer from the analogy with the other arts, to all of which this character is peculiar; from their effect on us, it can be inferred that that of music is on the whole of the same nature, only stronger, more rapid, more necessary and infallible.[10]

The argument, then, seems to be this. Music has the same effect on us as the 'other' (*übrigen*) fine arts.[11] They gain their effect through 'representation' (*Darstellung*) of the world. Therefore, music must also do so by representing the world in some sense. That music is compared to the 'other' arts implies that Schopenhauer has already made up his mind about music. It is a fine art; that is one of the premisses of his argument, not its conclusion.

Be that as it may, there is still, implicit in the above argument, at least what might be thought of as the adducing of evidence and support for the status of music as a fine art. For one thing, Schopenhauer states that music has the same 'effect' on us as the other fine arts (just the opposite of Kant's conclusion). That at least suggests it might be one of them. But because the other fine arts gain their effect through representation, through mimesis, it sees to follow that music also must be a representational, a mimetic art. And this is the stumbling-block. Because it seems clear *what* and *how* the other fine arts represent; whereas, as the eighteenth century found out, absolute music fails badly when one tries to apply that same 'what' and that same 'how' to it. It is Schopenhauer's ingenious new speculations on the 'what' and the 'how' that seem to get the representational theory of music out of its eighteenth-century impasse, that provide more 'evidence' and 'support' for music as a fine art. I turn now to that aspect of Schopenhauer's thought.

---

[10] Arthur Schopenhauer, *The World as Will and Representation*, trans. E. F. J. Payne (Indian Hills, Colo.: Falcon's Wing Press, 1958), i. 256. Cf. Arthur Schopenhauer, *The World as Will and Idea*, trans. R. B. Haldane and J. Kemp (Garden City, NY: Dolphin Books, 1961), 267.

[11] Arthur Schopenhauer, *Die Welt als Wille und Vorstellung* (Stuttgart: Suhrkamp Taschenbuch Wissenschaft, 1993), i. 358.

Music as Will

Schopenhauer's problem with regard to music's proposed representationality is this. He well knew that the eighteenth-century composers had exploited 'tone-painting' in a systematic way. The
Baroque composers, most notably Bach, were fond of representing
sounds, motions, and even concepts (e.g. the Trinity, or the Christian
'following' Jesus) in musical tones. Whether or not he knew this technique through acquaintance with Bach and Handel, Schopenhauer
certainly knew it, and deplored it in the tone-painting that Haydn
had foisted upon him by Baron van Swieten, in *The Creation* and *The
Seasons*, where, Schopenhauer wrote, 'phenomena of the world of
perception are directly imitated . . .' 'All this,' he urged, 'is to be
entirely rejected.'[12]

It is this marginal, trivial, if you will, representation of the sensible
world that was agreed on all hands to be possible for vocal music, at
least, to accomplish. But on it one can scarcely build a theory of
absolute music as a fine art of representation. That Schopenhauer
surely knew. His solution was not to give up the theory of mimesis or
of music as fine art but to find more impressive representational work
for music to do, more impressive, indeed, than that of the other fine
arts which, themselves, were seen by Schopenhauer as representations not of the world of sense but of the Platonic ideas. In one of the
most well known, and most pithy statements of this position,
Schopenhauer wrote:

Thus music is as *immediate* an objectification and copy of the whole *will* as the
world itself is, indeed as the Ideas are, the multiplied phenomenon of which
constitutes the world of individual things. Therefore music is by no means
like the other arts, namely, a copy of the Ideas, but a *copy of the will itself*, the
objectivity of which are the Ideas. For this reason the effect of music is so very
much more powerful and penetrating than is that of the other arts, for these
others speak only of the shadow, but music of the essence.[13]

This is a philosophically rich passage, a dense passage, and, for a
so-called 'analytic' philosopher, which I suppose I am, an obscure
passage. I shall spend some time delving into it somewhat, but before
I do, before I start trying to see through these muddy waters, I want

---

[12] Schopenhauer, *The World as Will and Representation*, i. 264.
[13] Ibid. 257.

to remark here and now what this passage, and others like it in §52 of *The World as Will and Representation,* mean for the philosophy of music as an enterprise in its own right. Their importance cannot be too strongly emphasized. At a stroke Schopenhauer both enfranchised absolute music as a fine art, and elevated it to pride of place. If any one thinker is responsible for making music *the* Romantic art *par excellence,* in short, the art of the times, at the cutting edge, it was Schopenhauer, in this passage and ones like it. Schopenhauer singlehandedly put absolute music on the philosophical and aesthetic map.

What is the exact nature, then, of music's mimetic function? Its object of representation is the metaphysical will. But what exactly *is* this representational relationship of music to the will?

In the passage quoted above Schopenhauer expresses the relationship of music to the will in two ways: as an 'immediate objectification' and as a 'copy'; in German, *unmittelbare Objektiviationen,* and *Abbild.*[14] In another passage, already quoted, he uses *Darstellung* and *Nachbild* to describe the same relationship.[15] *Abbild,* *Darstellung,* and *Nachbild* seem of a piece, and all hover around the concept of representation. But *Objektiviationen* is another animal entirely. So there seem, then, to be two concepts at work here.

The ordinary English synonyms for *Abbild* are copy, image, likeness; for *Darstellung,* description and representation; and for *Nachbild,* copy and imitation. All of these meanings are well within the eighteenth-century understanding of mimesis as the underlying principle of the fine arts. And all of these meanings carry with them the implication of human intention and execution. That is to say, copies, images, likenesses, descriptions, imitations, representations do not just happen, like earthquakes or hurricanes. They are productions of human thought leading to human action eventuating in a crafted product. So although the object of musical mimesis that Schopenhauer proposes, the thing in itself as metaphysical will, would have puzzled Enlightenment aesthetics mightily, the mimetic relationship itself that these words seem to imply would be familiar territory.

But *Objektiviationen* is, for Schopenhauer, a term of art: and it has neither the implication of human intention, nor of human action, nor of human product. The world, our world, is an 'objectification' of the will; and 'music is as *immediate* an objectification and copy of the

---

[14] Schopenhauer, *Die Welt als Wille und Vorstellung,* i. 359.   [15] Ibid. 358.

whole will as the world itself is . . .' To call music an objectification of the will, then, is to suggest that it is a natural metaphysical phenomenon, as it were: it is an emanation, an effulgence, *not* a human artefact. What could this mean?

Schopenhauer refers to music in the abstract. And one thing that is not clear is whether he is saying that music as a whole—what ever *that* means—is an objectification of the will, or whether each individual piece of music is. But most puzzling is what it can mean to say that a human artefact, which music is *either* in the abstract, *or* as individual musical compositions, is a natural emanation or effulgence of metaphysical reality. Needless to say, the notion of the phenomenal world being the way reality appears to us is itself a philosophical problem. But we do have some kind of intuitive grasp of that notion; we have a handle on it. The thing in itself presents itself to us in a certain way. That we grasp, if only because of the familiarity of the language since Kant. How music, however, stands to the thing in itself in just the same way is extremely puzzling—at least to me. I shall return to this question in the next section but first I want to go back for a moment to the more intelligible ways Schopenhauer represents the relationship of music to the will, to examine again his connection to the more traditional view, out of which his theory emerges, of music as a representational, mimetic art. (That there are problems here as well goes without saying.)

As I said earlier, the notions of *Abbild*, *Nachbild*, and *Darstellung*, for which I will simply use the English word 'representation,' right now, all suggest a conscious effort to produce a 'musical picture,' i.e. a representation. In this respect Schopenhauer can be seen still to be pursuing the Enlightenment program of mimetic art theory. But it should be perfectly clear that, given the peculiar nature of the *only* object music can properly be said to represent, on Schopenhauer's view, this analogy between traditional theories of mimesis, and Schopenhauer's, is only superficial.

Imagine a painter working at her easel. She looks at the flowers and fruits before her, turns back to her canvas, looks again at her subject, turns again to her canvas, until, by a process of looking and painting, painting and looking, she finally satisfies herself that her rendering of the flowers and fruits is as it should be. But the composer making *his* representation of the will can do no such thing. For the will is not there for him to observe; and Schopenhauer does not omit remarking on this. 'I recognize, however,' he says, 'that it is essentially impossible to demonstrate this explanation [of music's representational nature], for it assumes and establishes a relation of music as a representation of that which of its essence can never be representation, and claims to regard music as a copy [*Nachbild*] of an original that can itself never be directly represented.'[16] In other words, there can be no 'back and forth' looking between the musical 'canvas' and the object of musical representation, because the object of representation, the will, cannot be an object of perception at all. *That* music is a representation of the will, as Schopenhauer says outright, is an article of philosophical faith, 'essentially impossible to demonstrate.'

Furthermore, there seem to be two senses in which the composer cannot be aware that he is, in composing his music, representing the will at all. As we have just seen, he cannot be aware in the sense that he cannot be 'observing' the will and then fashioning the music to represent it, the way the painter can observe the fruits and flowers and then fashion her canvas to represent *them*. And, second, presumably, until Schopenhauer came along to reveal the truth, *nobody* was aware that the music he or she was composing *is* a representation of the will. Again, Schopenhauer does not omit remarking on this implication of his view. So he writes, of the composer's setting of texts, but which applies, with appropriate modifications, to absolute music as well, that

when the composer has known how to express in the universal language of music the stirrings of will that constitute the kernel of an event, then the melody of the song, the music of the opera is expressive. But the analogy discovered by the composer between these two must have come from the immediate knowledge of the inner nature of the world unknown to his faculty of reason; it cannot be an imitation brought about with conscious intention by means of concepts, otherwise the music does not express the inner nature of the will itself, but merely imitates its phenomena inadequately.[17]

But if such words as *Abbild*, *Nachbild*, and *Darstellung* are taken by Schopenhauer to mean an object that is produced without the agent being aware *that* he or she is producing such a thing, then there seems little difference between the relationship of that object to the object of representation, the will, and the relationship of natural emanation or effulgence implied by the word *objektiviationen*. The concepts seem to

[16] Schopenhauer, *The World as Will and Representation*, i. 257; *Die Welt als Wille und Vorstellung*, i. 358.
[17] Schopenhauer, *The World as Will and Representation*, i. 263.

just about collapse into one another and result in a relationship very different from what we take such words as 'copy' or 'representation' to connote, namely, a consciously fashioned representational artefact.

We seem to be driven, then, to the conclusion that whatever the various ways Schopenhauer employs to describe the relation of music to the will, the relation turns out *not* to be any of the familiar artefactual ones that we understand under the heading of 'representation,' but, rather, some kind of 'natural' relation which, nevertheless, is a relation of representation: a relation of representation that metaphysical reality produces without the hand of man.

I shall have some more to say about this relation in the next section, where I examine the relevance Schopenhauer's theory of musical representation might have for contemporary thought on the subject of absolute music's significance. In the penultimate section I shall move on to a consideration of what I myself find valuable for my own work on the problem of absolute music.

Schopenhauer and They

I think it fair to say that music first became a special, serious topic for contemporary aesthetics in the work of Susanne K. Langer, specifically, in 1942, in her highly influential book, *Philosophy in a New Key*, ch. 8. So influential, indeed, was that chapter, called 'On Significance in Music,' that until about ten or fifteen years ago, if someone in the musical world knew *anything* that a twentieth-century philosopher had said about music, it would be what Susanne K. Langer had said. And among musicians and musicologists who knew what Langer had said, many thought she was basically correct. For many of them, the 'philosophical' question of absolute music's significance was settled: Susanne K. Langer had settled it.

It is, therefore, of some importance to the evaluation of Schopenhauer's influence in our own times, as a philosopher of music, that Langer seems to place the real beginnings of modern philosophy of music with him. That, at least, is how I take her remark that: 'A great deal of philosophical thought has been bestowed on this subject [of music], if not since Winkelmann and Herder, at least since Schopenhauer . . .'[18] And if one considers only

---

[18] Susanne K. Langer, *Philosophy in a New Key: A Study in the Symbolism of Reason, Rite, and Art*, 3rd edn. (Cambridge, Mass.: Harvard University Press, 1978), 210.

the fact that Schopenhauer was perhaps the first major philosopher to emphatically place music in the modern system of the fine arts, and high man on that totem pole at that, Langer's suggestion—if that is what it is—that the origins of modern music aesthetics lie in Schopenhauer is not an indefensible one, even though there might be other candidates in the running.

But more significant still for present purposes is Langer's conviction that Schopenhauer, in his notion of music as representation of the will, is an advance in the direction of her own notion of music as 'unconsummated symbol' of human consciousness. Her evaluation of Schopenhauer's accomplishment, in this regard, is worth quoting and considering, at least briefly. She writes:

The assumption that music is a kind of language, not of the here-and-now, but of genuine conceptual content, is widely entertained, though not perhaps as universally as the emotive-symptom theory. The best-known pioneer in this field is Schopenhauer; and it has become something of an accepted verdict that his attempt to interpret music as a symbol of the irrational aspect of the mental life, the Will, was a good venture, though of course his conclusion, being 'metaphysical,' was quite bad. However that may be, his novel contribution to the present issue was certainly his treatment of music as an impersonal, negotiable, real semantic, a symbolism with a content of ideas, instead of an overt sign of somebody's emotional condition.[19]

Two persistent themes of *Philosophy in a New Key* are clearly apparent in this appreciation of Schopenhauer's contribution to the aesthetics of music. The first is Langer's *bête noire*, what she calls here (and elsewhere) the 'emotive-symptom' theory, the second, her favored theory of music as symbol, 'an impersonal, negotiable, real semantic, a symbolism with a content of ideas, instead of an overt sign of somebody's emotional condition.' Schopenhauer, she argues, rightly rejects the former and endorses the latter.

It is unfortunate that Langer fails here to distinguish between music as emotive symptom and as emotive expression. For there is obviously a big difference between my anger (say) evincing itself in the reddening of my neck or in a carefully written letter to *The Times*, the former being properly a 'symptom' of my anger, but hardly the latter, more properly described as an 'expression' of it. And, presumably, those who have held that the sadness of composers evinces

[19] Susanne K. Langer, *Philosophy in a New Key: A Study in the Symbolism of Reason, Rite, and Art*, 3rd edn. (Cambridge, Mass.: Harvard University Press, 1978), 219.

itself in the sadness of the music have frequently meant the letter to *The Times*, not the reddening of my neck. Nevertheless, Langer is quite conversant with the so-called self-expression theory of music, and a charitable interpretation of the above-quoted passage would be that Schopenhauer is to be praised as a 'pioneer' in his rejection of self-expression theories as well as emotive-symptom ones, and his endorsement of representational, or, as Langer would have it, semantic theories. And Langer, it is fair to say, was a pioneer in her recognition of Schopenhauer as a philosopher of music to be taken seriously by the contemporary practitioner, whatever one might think of the theory which Langer herself constructed on what she took to be Schopenhauer's foundation.

Having given credit where I think it is due, to Susanne K. Langer, for bringing our attention to Schopenhauer as a possible source for contemporary philosophy of music, albeit her interpretation seems to be problematic and her own theory brilliant but wrong-headed, I want now to move on to a rather daring new proposal about what Schopenhauer might have meant by music's representing the will, and what use might possibly be made of it, so interpreted.

Laird Addis, a philosopher of mind, has recently tried to reintroduce into philosophy the notion of the 'natural sign,' which he traces back to William of Occam. As Addis understands the notion, 'A natural sign is an entity that by its very nature represents something else,'[20] as opposed to the more familiar notion of a sign as something made by human beings to represent something else. It is his claim that 'states of consciousness are or contain natural signs of those things they are said, pre-analytically, to be states of consciousness *of*.'[21]

Addis's application of the natural sign concept to the nature of human consciousness is not, of course, our concern here. What is relevant for our purposes is his suggestion that the concept might be applied to music as well, and his allusion, in making it, to the very point in Schopenhauer—the representation relation between music and the will—that we were having so much trouble understanding in the previous section.

Addis writes of Schopenhauer's representational theory of music:

Does Schopenhauer mean that music, by its very nature and therefore independently of human or any other minds, represents the striving of the will

[20] Laird Addis, *Natural Signs: A Theory of Intentionality* (Philadelphia: Temple University Press, 1989), p. ix.
[21] Ibid.

and so consists of natural signs as I originally defined the notion thereof? Perhaps he does, but more likely he means that music represents the striving of the will *to the human mind*, music itself being a product of the human mind.[22]

Addis thinks it unlikely that Schopenhauer could have thought music a natural sign in the strong sense, that 'by its very nature and therefore independently of human or any other minds, [it] represents the striving will . . .' And the reason for his reluctance to ascribe such a view to Schopenhauer is clear. It seems to him, as it does to me, a monstrously implausible view. But I rather suspect he dismisses this interpretation of Schopenhauer too quickly. Certain considerations suggest that this might well have been what Schopenhauer was claiming, as implausible a view as it may seem to us.

It is of course true that *works* of music are products of the human mind, not of natural or metaphysical causes. And *to us* it seems obvious that this is true of music as a whole, the system of music as well.

Let me suggest, however, that there is a way of looking at music as a whole, and so the individual works within the system, which was known to Schopenhauer, and which there is some reason to believe informs his theory of musical representation, in spirit. It is the Pythagorean way.

By the Pythagorean way I mean the way of seeing musical sound as a function of the mathematical proportions of the octave, which is a mathematical 'law of nature.' This law of nature, the Pythagorean believes, is the basis, the material, if you will, of musical works. And this law, this musical material, reflects the structure of the universe itself. Thus, both the materials of music, and individual musical works themselves, bear a natural relationship of representation to the structure of the universe, on the Pythagorean view: they come close to being, indeed I think are, natural signs of the universe, in Addis's sense of 'natural sign.' Schopenhauer, I suggest, is a kind of metaphysical Pythagorean. His universe is the will; and music is its natural sign, as, for the Pythagorean, the 'numbers' of the intervals, both as a system and as individual musical works, are a natural sign of the structure of the world. His is the metaphysical version of the music of the spheres.

Is it plausible to attribute a kind of Pythagoreanism to Schopenhauer? Why not? He made the allusion himself. Of Leibniz's

---

[22] Laird Addis, *Natural Signs: A Theory of Intentionality* (Philadelphia: Temple University Press, 1989), 31.

deeply Pythagorean notion of music's being 'an unconscious exercise in arithmetic in which the mind does not know it is counting,' Schopenhauer wrote that 'it is quite correct from a lower point of view,' and paraphrased it for himself as: 'Music is an unconscious exercise in metaphysics in which the mind does not know it is philosophizing.' He continued: 'by union of these two very different yet correct views of music, we can now arrive at a conception of the possibility of a philosophy of numbers, like that of Pythagoras and of the *I Ching* . . .'[23]

Thus it appears to me that, viewed as a sort of metaphysical Pythagoreanism, as Schopenhauer certainly invites us to do, his strange notion of music as a kind of emanation of the will, much in the way that the world of representation is, is well captured by Addis's notion of the natural sign, and that Addis was too quick to reject the possibility. But, furthermore, what is of particular interest in Addis's discussion of Schopenhauer's musical representationalism is his attempt to use it, in a modified form, for his own very ingenious account of music's significance and effect. It is, I think, well worth examining as an indication that there may be unlooked for and unsuspected possibilities yet in Schopenhauer's strange notion of music as 'objectification' of the will. It may not, perhaps, be as embarrassingly implausible as it sounds.

Addis states his project of eliciting from Schopenhauer a viable theory of musical 'representation' as follows. 'But I wish now to modify the theory in a way that makes it one that I myself am disposed to believe, but, more important, relieves us of Schopenhauer's suspicious notion of a universal will and makes it easier to clarify the notion of representation that may here be involved.'[24] Among other things, then, Addis would, quite understandably, like a Schopenhauerian musical aesthetics without a Schopenhauerian metaphysics.

Here, then, is Addis's variation, *sans* metaphysics, of Schopenhauer's theme. 'It may well be that *given the nature of the human mind* (and possibly of all minds or even all lawfully possible minds or all actual or possible minds to which music has any meaning at all), a particular piece of music or part of it represents *to* the mind a *possible state of mind*.'[25] In other words, 'whether we know it or not, certain

---

[23] Schopenhauer, *The World as Will and Representation*, i. 256, 264–5.
[24] Addis, *Natural Signs*, 31.   [25] Ibid. 32.

possible states of mind are represented to us by music, which may or may not cause us to think of or to be in that state of mind.'[26]

Addis is well aware, as anyone would be, reading his proposal for the first time, that, as he himself says, 'it has many obvious difficulties . . .'[27] He is now in the process of working out his intriguing notion in greater detail.[28] And although I have reservations of my own with regard to his proposal, I await a more elaborate version with great expectations. Be all that as it may, the suggestion Addis has advanced constitutes a genuine attempt to make something of Schopenhauer's musical speculations for a contemporary philosophical audience. I now want to go on to another such attempt, in this instance my own. It mines a totally different vein of Schopenhauer's thinking about music, not yet discussed or even mentioned.

Schopenhauer and I

Even the reader but casually acquainted with Book III of *The World as Will and Representation* will have realized by this time that I have as yet omitted discussion of one of the most distinctive and memorable aspects of Schopenhauer's philosophy of art, what might be called the fine arts' *liberating* power.

As is well known, Schopenhauer believed that we—all of us, no matter what our calling—are dominated in our lives by what he calls the fourfold root of the principle of sufficient reason. We are driven, indeed compelled, to view the world under the categories of cause and effect, premiss and conclusion, motive and action, space and time. We labor under the baleful influence of these categories as slaves to a tyrannical master, the striving will, seeking but never finding peace of mind or rest from our intellectual and practical endeavors. But in art, either as creators or appreciators, we are set free. It is art that

raises us out of the endless stream of willing, and snatches knowledge from the thraldom of the will . . . Then all at once the peace, always sought but always escaping us on that first path of willing, comes to us of its own accord, and all is well with us. It is the painless state, prized by Epicurus as the highest good and the state of the gods; for that moment we are delivered from the miserable pressure of the will. We celebrate the Sabbath of the penal servitude of willing; the wheel of Ixion stands still.[29]

---

[26] Addis, *Natural Signs*, 32 .   [27] Ibid.   [28] See n. 37.
[29] Schopenhauer, *The World as Will and Representation*, i. 196.

Schopenhauer had a very deep insight, it seems to me, when he stated boldly that absolute music, as an art, 'stands quite apart from all the others.'[30] But he did not cash out that difference in any radical way. Rather, being committed to a generally representational theory of the fine arts, he made out music's difference, as we have already seen, in terms of the *what* and the *how* of its representationality. Unlike the other fine arts music may have been what Laird Addis calls a 'natural sign.' Representation, in any case, it remains. Apparently Schopenhauer saw no other option, although his great contemporary, Hegel, did, launching what I take to be the first fully fledged 'expression theory' of art.[31]

I believe that the clue to at least one of the things that distinguishes absolute music from the other fine arts, or perhaps even separates it from the fine arts altogether,[32] can be found in the liberating quality, just alluded to, that Schopenhauer ascribed to *all* the fine arts, music among them. What Schopenhauer did *not* see, and what I believe to be the case, is that music, alone of the fine arts, pre-eminently provides this liberation. The others of them, what I shall call the arts of *content*, the 'contentful' arts, do not provide this liberation but, on the contrary, veritably rub our noses in the very thing which they, along with music, are supposed to liberate us from.

I must, then, argue for two points in what now follows. I must show why I think the contentful arts do *not* liberate, and why I think music does. But I shall *assume* and not try to argue for the contention that music is *not* an art of content. I shall assume that it is an art of pure structure and sensuous aesthetic qualities, although unlike others called 'formalists' who also hold this view, I include as part of music's structure and sensuous aesthetic qualities expressive qualities as well: happiness, sadness, and the like. I have argued for all of these points on numerous occasions before, and will not, cannot, rehearse those arguments here.

Why are the contentful arts *not* liberating arts? Simply because at their best and most profound, they raise all those questions of philosophical and moral import that bring us face to face with the world of cause and effect, space and time, motive and action, premiss

---

[30] Ibid. 256.

[31] There were glimmerings of an expression theory in Thomas Reid. See my 'Thomas Reid and the Expression Theory of Art,' *The Monist*, 61 (1978).

[32] See my 'Is Music an Art?' in Peter Kivy, *The Fine Art of Repetition: Essays in the Philosophy of Music* (Cambridge: Cambridge University Press, 1993).

and conclusion, just that world of restless willing from which Schopenhauer looks to the fine arts for surcease. Far from liberating us from the problems of the world of the striving will, the contentful arts immerse us in it. This is not a defect in them but part of their very purpose a good deal of the time. They *are* the *contentful* arts; and so they must give us that pain along with their gifts of aesthetic satisfaction. They give us *our world*, albeit transformed and transfigured in the manner of the fine arts.

It is in *absolute music* that we seek and find liberation. It is absolute music that gives us a world, but not *our* world. Many people have instinctively felt this. It was Schopenhauer, I suggest, who first gave us the concepts and the language to express this intuition adequately.

But though I think that Schopenhauer's idea of liberation is the very thing to describe one of the distinctive features of absolute music as a fine art, I find his description of what that experience is like unsatisfying. Let me remind you of what it is. He says that 'It is the painless state, prized by Epicurus as the highest good and as the state of the gods; for that moment we are delivered from the miserable pressure of the will.'

Far be it from me, at my age, to underestimate the blessing of the painless state. The absence of pain, God knows, is blessing indeed. But it is a negative state, an absence; and it fails to capture the positive state, certainly an intense pleasure, broadly speaking, which the liberation of absolute music imparts to its devotees. How can Schopenhauer's concept of liberation be accommodated to this intuition?

It seems to me we can do this by distinguishing between the absence of pain, a 'steady state,' with the release from pain, a process, and observe that the latter, the experience of being released from pain, is, as Socrates observed long ago when released from his shackles on the last day of his life, a palpable form of intense pleasure.[33] What I am saying can, I think, only be appreciated by someone who has had the experience, as I think most of us have had by the time we reach adulthood, of being in severe pain and being released, in a fairly brief space of time, from it. Anyone who has had that experience will, I think, feel as I do that that experience is one of an intensely pleasurable kind. And that experience, it seems to me, comes close to being the *kind* of experience the musical liberation

---

[33] See Plato, *Phaedo*, 60b–c.

from our world appears to be, when it is the world of anxious thought about the deeply painful and perplexing problems of the human condition. I have written of this experience of musical liberation at greater length elsewhere,[34] and cannot go into it any further here.

But I must add, nevertheless, that I am not suggesting the idea of musical liberation I have extracted from Schopenhauer is by any means the full answer to the question of what it is about absolute music, about pure, contentless structure that so captivates its devotees.[35] I do suggest that there is a deep chasm between absolute music and the contentful arts, as well as close affinities. The affinities are all those features of aesthetic and artistic structure that finally drove the Enlightenment to at least consider the possibility of absolute music's being of a piece with poetry, painting, and the rest. The chasm is that between arts that give us our world, albeit transformed in the myriad ways of such arts, and the arts that give us *a* 'world' of *their* material alone. Absolute music is, in the West, the pre-eminent art of the latter kind. And one of its charms, one of its seductions, I strongly feel, is just that sense of liberation from the wheel of Ixion that Schopenhauer spoke of for all the arts, but which seems so particularly pertinent to the art of absolute music, as it was passed into the hands of the Romantic composers by Haydn, Mozart, and Beethoven. For me, at least, that idea of artistic liberation was Schopenhauer's greatest contribution to current debate surrounding the nature and significance of what I have called elsewhere the 'pure musical experience.'[36] It has motivated my own work, recently, and I have hopes, if not expectations, that it will motivate the work of others as well.

Schopenhauer's Contribution to the Philosophy of Music

This chapter has concerned itself with two aspects of Schopenhauer's musical philosophy, his notion of music as representation and his notion of music as liberation. And I have tried to evaluate

---

[34] See the last chapter of my *Philosophies of Arts: A Study in Differences* (Cambridge: Cambridge University Press, 1997).

[35] For more of what I have to say on this perplexing matter, see my *Music Alone: Philosophical Reflections on the Purely Musical Experience* (Ithaca: Cornell University Press, 1990), and 'The Fine Art of Repetition,' in *The Fine Art of Repetition*.

[36] *Music Alone, passim.*

Schopenhauer's musical philosophy from two different perspectives, its importance for *his* time and its importance for *ours*. It is appropriate now for me to briefly summarize my conclusions.

For his own age, Schopenhauer's great accomplishment—and it is not to be underestimated—was both to elevate absolute music to full status as a fine art and, in the process, to elevate it above them all, no longer a poor relation but lord of the manor. Schopenhauer, surely, helped in large measure to make absolute music *the* Romantic art, *the* art of its times.

For us, Schopenhauer's legacy is more obscure and difficult to assess. However she used, or *mis*used Schopenhauer's notion of music as representation, Schopenhauer was surely an inspirational figure for Susanne Langer, and she for us. And if the work of Laird Addis comes to fruition, Schopenhauer's theory of musical representation may yet have a new life in the notion of music as a 'natural sign.'[37]

My own work, until very recently, had been completely unaffected by Schopenhauer's aesthetics. But I now see his notion of art as liberation as at least a partial explanation for our attraction to absolute music, an attraction that I have thought for years, and still do, is one of the most difficult and neglected problems in contemporary philosophy of art.

A final assessment of *any* great philosopher is, of course, quite impossible. As soon as one thinks that some great figure in the philosophical past has nothing more to say to us, along comes someone to prove the opposite. For this reason I shrink from passing a final sentence on Schopenhauer as philosopher of music. A very short while ago I would have scoffed at the idea of finding anything useful for my own work in Schopenhauer's musical speculations. Now I find inspiration there, as Susanne Langer did before me.

---

[37] When the above was written, Addis's full-scale presentation of his view on music was in process. It is now published as *Of Mind and Music* (Ithaca: Cornell University Press, 1999). It is still too early to judge the success of his enterprise.

On Hanslick's Inconsistency

In an essay of mine called 'Something I've Always Wanted to Know about Hanslick,' I wrote about an inconsistency I thought I detected in Hanslick's famous little book, *Vom Musikalisch-Schönen*, between what Hanslick calls his 'negative thesis'—namely, the thesis that music cannot represent or embody in any way the ordinary, garden-variety human emotions—and a passage concerning Gluck's aria, 'Che farò senza Euridice.'[1] At the end of that essay, I suggested, very briefly, that there was an inconsistency, as well, between the negative thesis, as a theoretical pronouncement, and Hanslick's practice as a critic of music. Because it was a brief coda to an essay on another subject, I did not amplify my views on this latter inconsistency, or make them as clear as I would like to have done. I would now like to take the opportunity to repair this defect.

Let me begin by distinguishing three different senses of 'inconsistency.' The most obvious kind of inconsistency, perhaps, the hard-nosed would say, the only literal one, is where there is genuine logical contradiction. The proposition, 'The cat is on the mat,' thus, is inconsistent with 'It is false that the cat is on the mat,' or any proposition that logically implies the latter. Call this 'formal inconsistency,' or 'formal contradiction.'

But suppose I should say, 'The cat is on the mat but I don't believe it.' Now this is not a formal contradiction. For the propositions, 'The cat is on the mat,' and 'I don't believe the cat is on the mat,' are logically consistent. It is the *utterance* of them both together that is odd, because self-defeating, since one is a speech act affirming, the other denying, the same proposition. I think (but am not sure) it was G. E. Moore who dubbed this kind of thing 'pragmatic contradiction'; and so I will call it as well.

[1] Peter Kivy, 'Something I've Always Wanted to Know About Hanslick', *Journal of Aesthetics and Art Criticism*, 46 (1988).

A third kind of inconsistency might be called 'contradiction in practice,' or 'practical contradiction.' It is this kind of inconsistency that Hume, I take it, was talking about when he remarked that the skeptical doubts embraced in the philosopher's 'closet' fail to govern the philosopher outside it, facing the everyday occurrences of the workaday world. One may doubt induction on paper, but one is still governed, in spite of that, in avoiding fire and eating bread, by the fact that the former, in the past, has burned, and the latter nourished. One cannot seem to help it. It is this practical inconsistency that, however imprecisely in my earlier essay, I described as holding between the negative thesis in what Hanslick calls his 'little book' and his conduct as a professional critic of music. It was the Humean image, then as now, that I had before my mind. I will take the liberty of quoting myself; 'To put the thing directly, Hanslick is like a solipsist who can't help writing letters. He argues that music has no expressive qualities. But when he steps out of the philosopher's closet to face the music, he sings a different tune.'[2] It is, then, what I have been calling 'practical contradiction' that I claimed, in my earlier article, was evident between Hanslick's theory, and his practice; and I still think that is right. For whereas in the little book, Hanslick, in the negative thesis, mounts an elaborate series of arguments to the effect that, properly speaking, music cannot be 'happy' or 'angry,' 'melancholy' or 'yearning,' or the like, he uses such emotive descriptions of music liberally and apparently without qualms in his musical criticism.

Two possible objections that might be brought against my claim of Hanslick's inconsistency are these. First, there are just too few examples of emotive description in the musical criticism to amount to much more than a *lapsus linguae*. And, second, even when he does describe music emotively, there is nothing contradictory in it since he endorses the 'figurative,' non-literal uses of emotive description in the little book, there being, clearly, no contradiction in denying, for example, 'The music is sad' at the same time as saying 'The music is "sad," figuratively speaking.'[3]

Now with regard to the second objection, it ought to be clear, straightaway, that it is good against formal contradiction and

---

[2] *Journal of Aesthetics and Art Criticism*, 46 (1988), 416.

[3] Both these objections have been suggested to me informally, over the years, by various people, but most recently in a more formal manner by Robert Hall in a contribution to a symposium on Hanslick, at a meeting of the Canadian Society of Aesthetics, 3 June 1995, in Montreal.

pragmatic contradiction. For there is no logical inconsistency in say-ing 'S is not-p' and 'S is (figuratively) p,' since p and '(figuratively) p' name two different properties of S. And for the same reason, there is nothing strange in 'S is p but I don't believe it,' if that is glossed as 'S is p but I don't believe it's literally p.' But it is not good, as we shall see in a moment, against what I am calling 'practical contradiction' or 'contradiction in practice.'

The first objection, however, *is* good against the claim of practical contradiction, if it is good at all. But it is not good at all because predicated on a premiss that is false. It is just not the case that, in his practical criticism, Hanslick is sparing in his use of emotive language. For Hanslick regularly, avidly, systematically uses emotive terms to describe the works of music he criticizes. I cannot prove that here, for that would require canvassing the criticism of a fifty-year career in professional journalism. All I *can* do is to point out that, like many of my readers, I have become acquainted with Hanslick's music cri-ticism through Henry Pleasants' anthology of Hanslick's reviews;[4] and I have no reason to believe that Pleasants has not given us a fair, unbiased sample of the material. And if one, for instance, merely read the reviews that concern absolute music, the worst case, one would presume, for emotive criticism, one will find that there is not a single one in which expressive epithets not only figure, but figure *importantly*.

This is not to say Hanslick uses expressive talk to the exclusion of other kinds. Each review is a mixed bag where descriptive language is concerned. Nevertheless, he never fails to make use of emotive descriptions; and they are always used seriously and centrally, not just as afterthoughts, or in passing. This, I say, is the practice that is inconsistent with theory—inconsistent, that is, in the sense of practi-cal inconsistency. But exactly wherein that inconsistency lies requires that we answer a question as yet unasked, namely, what does Hanslick *mean* by 'figurative' when he says that emotive epithets are not literally, but figuratively used?

There are, of course, many figurative uses of language. The two figures that immediately come to mind in the present context are metaphor and simile. Simile, I think, is something like what Hanslick has in mind. Here is why.

---

[4] Eduard Hanslick, *Music Criticism 1846–99*, ed. and trans. Henry Pleasants (Baltimore: Penguin, 1950).

Hanslick says, in the little book, that music cannot embody emotions but *can* embody what he calls their 'dynamic.' Thus a piece of music cannot be angry, but it can possess the dynamic of anger: it can be vigorous or turbulent, or something of that kind. So we can say that music is anger-like in being vigorous or turbulent; and when we say it is angry, then we are saying that it is anger-like, intending by the use of that simile to pick out, for readers, the vigorousness or turbulence. I suggest that emotive terms are, for Hanslick, the linguistic figures called 'similes.' And it is characteristic of similes but *not*, let me add, metaphors, that they can always be translated without remainder. All that it means, in a given context, to call music angry, on Hanslick's view, is to call it turbulent or vigorous, or whatever— whatever, that is, the dynamic the simile was meant to pick out. The significance of this last remark will become apparent in a moment.

It may, however, be feared here that I am going against received opinion in claiming that similes can be successfully translated or paraphrased. But, I must emphasize, it is metaphor, not simile, that received opinion is all about. It is one thing to say 'X is *like* Y,' quite another, deeper and more mystifying thing to say that 'X *is* Y.' It is 'Juliet *is* the sun' not 'My love is *like* a red red rose' that has caused most of the philosophical trouble and inspired most of the philosophical analysis, from Max Black to Donald Davidson. So if you believe it has been conclusively shown by philosophical analysis that metaphors are untranslatable, or cannot be paraphrased, it does not commit you to a similar conclusion about similes. I do not say that simile adds nothing to meaning. As I think Stanley Cavell once said, if metaphor is pregnant, simile is a little bit pregnant. I cannot do better than to leave it at that.

If a simile can always be replaced with a literal description, why should one use similes at all, one may ask? The obvious answer is, for stylistic reasons. It just becomes boring to always say straight out what something *is*; so we sometimes, for the sake of variety and richness of language, say *what it is not* but *what it is like*.

The problem with Hanslick, then, is not that he uses emotive similes, even though they are always translatable into literal descriptions.[5] The problem is that he uses them all the time; that they crop

---

[5] One need not accept my assertion that similes can be paraphrased without remainder, or even that what Hanslick has in mind are similes and not metaphors. I think the argument is good for other views of similes, as well as for metaphors. (I am grateful to Ted Cohen for helping me get straight on the metaphor–simile thing, and for giving me the courage of my convictions, whether or not they are *his* convictions.)

up regularly, to a degree far in excess of any other kind of simile; that emotive similes almost always seem appropriate. An occasional emotive simile would not raise eyebrows, any more than when Tovey uses an animal simile, where he says that a Haydn rondo begins like a kitten but ends like a lion. But if Tovey *always*, consistently, systematically used animal similes in every musical analysis that he produced, we would then smell a rat. Why consistently use animal words to describe music unless there were something in the music that could only be described in those words and no others?

That is the question we must put to Hanslick, with regard to emotive words. Since emotive words applied to music are, on Hanslick's view, similes, they are always translatable into literal terms. An occasional use is unproblematical. But the consistent use of them, the use of them over and over again, is inconsistent with their really being similes. One way, then, of putting the inconsistency that there is between Hanslick's theory and his practice is to say that in theory Hanslick sees emotive descriptions as similes, but in practice uses them in a way incompatible with their *being* similes. That is the inconsistency in practice of which I speak.

Now if you ask me *why* Hanslick's practice is out of sync with his theory in this regard, I think the answer is obvious. The reason emotive terms when applied to music are unlikely to be similes is because they cannot be translated into non-emotive terms; and the reason they cannot be translated into non-emotive terms is because there is something in music that they and only they can literally describe, namely, *emotive properties*. Each time Hanslick confronts a piece of real music, outside the philosopher's closet, he becomes aware by direct acquaintance of what his theory tells him cannot be. And as in the case of the Humean skeptic, nature defeats theory and Hanslick becomes an emotivist *malgré lui*. He cannot but describe music in emotive terms, because the emotive properties simply will not be denied: they *will* be heard, and Hanslick has the ear to hear them.

4

Making the Codes and Breaking the Codes: Two Revolutions in Twentieth-Century Music

Introduction

The title of this chapter taps into two senses of the word 'code': the sense in which a code is a kind of language, as where one devises a code for conveying secret messages, and the sense in which a code is a prescription for behavior, as where a restaurant imposes a dress code on its patrons. Of course my subject is music, not cryptography or etiquette, so I will begin by stating briefly what it is in the musical experience that I think best exemplifies the linguistic sense of a code, and what the prescriptive sense. When I have done this I can then be more specific about the direction this chapter is going to take.

Western art music has been described as a language often enough that the idea is common coin. Of course music is *not* a language. It *is* language-like, however, in more than one respect, perhaps the most familiar being the way in which it is supposed to be a 'language of the emotions.' Music as a language of the emotions, then, is that aspect of music that exemplifies most obviously the linguistic sense of a code. Western art music, since the end of the sixteenth century, has evolved into a kind of music that might be described, loosely but not literally, as, among other things, an emotive language or code.

Of more recent origin is the sense in which music might be thought to embody or involve or imply what I have called a prescriptive code, a code of proper behavior. Of course music does not behave or mis-behave, but listeners may. The prescriptive code, then, that Western art music involves, or rather has done since sometime in the second half of the eighteenth century, is a listening code: a way prescribed in which listening is to be done. It is familiar to all philosophers of art as the so-called aesthetic attitude, or, since the time of Immanuel

Kant's *Critique of Judgement*, the attitude of aesthetic disinterested-ness. The aesthetic attitude was not, I hasten to add, an attitude pre-scribed only for listening to music. It was supposed to be an attitude required for appreciation of all of the arts, and natural beauty as well. But as I shall argue, it has particular significance for the art of music and, especially, the art of absolute music that grew to major proportions towards the end of the eighteenth century, at the hands of Haydn, Mozart, and Beethoven.

With these preliminary distinctions having been made, I can now explain what the general argument of this chapter is, and how I shall try to make it out. I will argue that music, in the modern era, roughly the late seventeenth, eighteenth, and nineteenth centuries—and I will be talking, principally, about instrumental music—evolved into a highly expressive musical structure, meant to be attended to in a spe-cial way, in, that is to say, the way of the aesthetic attitude. In part, this kind of music and this way of listening to it have prevailed into the twentieth century. But two 'revolutions,' in the music of our cen-tury, have, I shall argue further, broken with the linguistic code of expression, and the prescriptive code of the aesthetic attitude, respec-tively. Twelve-tone serialism of the Second Vienna School broke (not completely, but, I shall claim, significantly) with the linguistic code, minimalism (again, not completely but significantly) with the pre-scriptive code. And it is because of these breaks with tradition that these two musical styles, in different ways, have been difficult for lis-teners of different kinds fully to accept.

In order to make out my case, in the first section of this chapter I shall briefly sketch the history and nature of what I have been calling music's linguistic code: the code of musical expression. In the second section, I shall do the same for music's prescriptive code: the so-called aesthetic attitude. And in the final section, I shall try to show in what way twelve-tone music may be seen to have broken from the linguistic code, minimalism from the prescriptive code.

But one word of warning before I get on with my business: in this chapter I make no value judgements. I do not say it is a good thing that atonalism and minimalism have broken from the musical codes of the past in the ways specified. I do not say it is a bad thing. I merely say that it is the case, and try to understand what has happened, how it has happened, why it has happened. If what I believe has happened has evaluative implications one way or the other I leave it to others to draw them.

The Expressive Code

The expressive code of Western art music, against which certain forms of twentieth-century music have revolted, is itself the result of a musical revolution: perhaps the greatest revolution in music history, at least since the beginnings of musical notation and the advent of polyphony. It is the revolution motivated by the Counter-Reformation and the Council of Trent that propelled Western music into the early modern era.

A profound change took place towards the end of the sixteenth century in the way sacred words were set to music in the Catholic liturgy. The traditional explanation for this is that misgivings were felt, and expressed through directives of the Council of Trent, with regard to the roles played by the words and by the music in the polyphony of what we take to be the fullest flowering of the Flemish School. In general, the complaint was that the role of the music was too great, the role of the words too small; in particular, the meaning of the sacred text was made unintelligible by the overwhelming complexity and thickness of the polyphonic setting.

Polyphony in the Catholic Church was, indeed, fighting for its very life, and survived only by finding a way to accommodate itself to directions of the Council, which were, in part, that: 'The whole plan of singing in musical modes should be constructed not to give empty pleasure to the ear, but in such a way that the words may be clearly understood by all, and thus the hearts of the listeners be drawn to the desire of heavenly harmonies, in the contemplation of the joys of the blessed.'[1]

There are two precepts that bear scrutiny here: that the music of the service should not 'give empty pleasure to the ear' and that 'the hearts of the listeners' should be moved to edifying thoughts by the words thus understood. It is, let me urge, a new aesthetic of text-setting that had revolutionary implications.

The first precept, that the music of the church should not merely give empty pleasure to the ear, seems clearly to be a swipe at the very music impelling in the first place the musical reform movement of the

---

[1] Quoted in Gustave Reese, *Music in the Renaissance* (New York: Norton, 1954), 449. I am giving, in brief form, here, an account I gave at greater length in my *Osmin's Rage: Philosophical Reflections on Opera, Drama and Text* (Princeton: Princeton University Press, 1988).

Counter-Reformation, namely, the elaborate Flemish polyphony of the late fifteenth and early sixteenth centuries. This music, so rich in melodic and structural complexity, followed an aesthetic of text set-ting that I have described elsewhere as the 'principle of opulent adornment.'[2] The sacred words were, so to speak, precious gems, mystical objects, sacred relics that were to be placed in the richest, most ornate possible settings. The Flemish composers were jewelers, the liturgy their precious jewels, for which, like the makers of those fantastically elaborate reliquaries that house bits of the true cross or a saint's middle finger, they fashioned golden and crystal boxes in sound. But in so doing they made the words themselves unintelligible to the listener. The center of attraction was, clearly, the reliquary, not the relic. In the eyes of the Council of Trent, then, sacred music, at the hands of the Flemish masters and their followers, had become merely empty pleasure to the ear. For what was supposed to appeal to the religious understanding, namely, the meaning of the words, had become completely obliterated because the music had made the words themselves completely unintelligible. Listen, for example, to a mass setting by Ockeghem, and try to understand the text. By the time the long, sinuous melodic line has reached the last syllable of a word, one has lost track of what the first syllable was.

But how does one go from there to a realization of the second pre-cept of the Council's directive, to make the words clearly understood by all? Well, if one asks oneself what the best way is to convey one's meaning, in words, to one's listeners, the answer obviously will be: to speak them as clearly and distinctly as one can. Furthermore, if speaking clearly and distinctly is the paradigm of intelligibility, then what vocal music must do to make the sung text intelligible to the lis-tener is to *represent* speech, as closely as possible, in the artistic medium of musical sound. Vocal music, in other words, is, under the aegis of the Council of Trent, about to become a representational art form, joining narrative poetry, drama, painting, and sculpture in what was to become, in the first half of the eighteenth century, the modern system of the arts, the fine arts, in other words. The princi-ple of opulent adornment as an aesthetic of text-setting was to be replaced by another, the principle of textual realism.[3] It is this prin-ciple of textual realism, furthermore, that has dominated the musical setting of words throughout four centuries, and into our own, with but little dissent.

[2] Kivy, *Osmin's Rage*, 8–14.   [3] Ibid.

All would agree that the second directive of the Council of Trent to Catholic church musicians, to make the words intelligible to worshippers, was most fully realized, at the highest artistic level, by Palestrina, although his supposed role in the Council's deliberations is more fantasy than fact. And if one listens to his liturgical settings, in contrast to those of Ockeghem and his school, one cannot help but perceive how much more closely the former conforms his musical pace, length of melodic phrase, and rhythmic structure to the way the words might be declaimed. Try to speak the Latin text tonelessly, in Ockeghem's way, and then in Palestrina's, and you will see how much more closely Palestrina has kept to the spoken words. But why call what Palestrina is doing the *representation* of human speech? And what has all of this to do, anyway, with the development of an expressive musical code? In a moment the answers to both of these questions will become clear.

Were these conjectures about Palestrina's and other post-Tridentine polyphony the only evidence adduced for the notion that an aesthetic of text-setting was in the making, correctly described as the musical representation of the speaking voice, it would, quite justly, be greeted with considerable skepticism. But let us recall what other event of great moment for the art of music took place at the close of the sixteenth century, and was prepared for, in theory, during Paletrina's floruit. I am referring to the invention of opera, and the theoretical speculations of Girolamo Mei and Vicenzo Galilei that preceded it.

As is well known, the program that was laid upon the first opera composers, Peri, Caccini, and the great Monteverdi, was the representation, in musical recitation, of the passionate speaking voice. In other words, it was not merely the representation of human speech that was to be undertaken but the representation of human speech under the influence of heightened emotion. The reason for this seemed to be twofold. First, it was believed that under the influence of the emotions, the speaker's voice took on a musical quality, became toneful, if not tuneful; and such toneful speech could, it seemed apparent, be more easily and realistically represented in music. Second, it was becoming widely believed that music should be not only beautiful but emotionally moving as well. The ancient texts—in particular, Plato and Aristotle—were invoked to show that the ancient Greek music could arouse deeply emotional experiences in listeners. Plato thought this mostly a bad thing, Aristotle frequently good. The theoreticians of opera were on Aristotle's side, thought that complex polyphony could not be deeply moving, and hence urged the representation of emotive speech, in sparsely accompanied monody, as a way of recapturing the power of music over the emotions, which, on the authority of Plato and Aristotle, they believed the ancient music possessed.

But why should the representation of emotive speech, in musical tone, have the capacity to arouse the emotions so represented? In the beginning, at least, a kind of sympathy theory was proposed, which had it that just as we tend to feel with other people, to feel the emotions they may be feeling, so if we see or hear a representation of someone expressing a deeply felt emotion, we, in like manner, by a kind of fellow-feeling, will tend to feel that emotion as well. As Vincenzo Galilei summed up the whole program, the purpose of music ought to be 'to express the passions with great effectiveness . . . and secondarily to communicate these with equal force to the minds of mortals for their benefit and advantage . . .'[4] What I have been calling the emotive code of music was now fully launched, if not yet fully developed.

If you listen to the operatic monody of which I am speaking, particularly its later stages, you will read its expressive language with ease. Furthermore, this is true, I am certain, not only of the experienced listener to what I will call, as is customary, classical music (for want of a better word), but true of anyone habituated to the Western tonal system through the many forms of popular music that are ever-present in our listening space. In particular, the connection of minor mode and chromaticism with the dark emotions, major mode and diatonic harmonies with the bright ones, is firmly in place. Indeed, and this is an important point as well as an obvious one, the emotive musical language of which I speak is an inseparable part of the major/minor tonal system. At least as our music, both classical and popular, has developed, one cannot have the expressive language without the system.

I have been arguing that the program which established the emotive musical code of Western art music, in the modern era, was one of representing the human speaking voice in the musical medium. This was the program both of the post-Tridentine church composers, of whom Palestrina is the acknowledged master, and of the early

---

[4] Vincenzo Galilei, *Dialogo dell musica antica é della moderna*, in Oliver Strunk, *Source Readings in Music History* (New York: Norton, 1950), 307.

opera composers, of whom the acknowledged master is Monteverdi. Especially in monody, one can discern some of the emotive figures that have survived in tonal music in the West, both classical and popular, into our own times. Of these can be named, for example, the so-called sighing figure, the upper appoggiatura descending to resolve a dissonance; the upward leap representing a cry or exclamation; and others, familiar to the learned explicitly, implicitly to the lay listener.

But such a program of vocal representation, it is clear, cannot possibly account for the full flowering of the emotive code, as we now know it, although it was obsessively appealed to by philosophers, mostly unmusical by their own admission, through to the end of the eighteenth century, Kant included in that number. This for two reasons: first, vocal music itself, by the middle of the seventeenth century, had gone far beyond the state where it could be correlated directly with the cadence or range of the passionate speaking voice. Second, and even more important for our purposes, the development of complex instrumental forms, even further from a possible vocal model for the expressive code, forced theorists to cast about for another explanatory expedient. The early emotive vocabulary persisted even here. Instrumental music, however, by the time of the High Baroque, was enriched with a stock of expressive figures, scarcely even realizable by the singing voice, let alone the speaking voice, which demanded another model entirely. What were these non-vocal musical figures expressive in virtue of—what was *their* etiology?

It is not clear whether, in answering this question, art was imitating philosophy or the other way around. In any event, the growth and full development of the emotive musical code, in the late seventeenth century and the first half of the eighteenth, demanded some kind of aesthetic, which is to say, philosophical foundation. That it was given by the new Cartesian psychology wedded to good old-fashioned rhetorical theory.

In brief, the story is as follows. In 1649 René Descartes published his treatise on psychology, *De Passionibus Animae* (*On the Passions of the Soul*). It was a work that had profound influences on one hundred years of thinking about expression in the arts, and, most particularly, expression in the art of music, about which Descartes himself had already written in his early *Compendium Musicae*.

The basic idea of the Cartesian psychology is that the emotions are caused to be aroused in the subject's mind by particular motions of what Descartes called the animal spirits. These were imagined to be diffused throughout the nervous system, which was conceived of as a kind of hydraulic network of pipes and conduits connecting the brain with the external senses and the rest of the bodily organism. If a person, then, should perceive (say) a threat to her personal well-being, that would, through the relevant sense modality, set the animal spirits in the particular motion appropriate to fear, which emotion would thereby be aroused in the soul, motivating appropriate escape or defense behavior.

An important consequence of this theory that many contemporary philosophers find less than plausible is that the emotions—among which Descartes distinguished six basic ones—can be aroused *without* the appropriate perceptions and beliefs, merely by stimulating the animal spirits directly to move in the ways specific to them. So, for example, if I can, on this view, cause your animal spirits to move in the way specific to fear, you will feel fear in the complete absence of any perceived or imagined threat; and likewise for the whole emotive repertory and characteristic motions.

It was this consequence of the Cartesian psychology that the musical theorists lighted upon and exploited. The idea was that music, characteristically described then, as now, in terms of motion, might, with *its* so-called 'motion,' mimic the motions of the animal spirits, set them into sympathetic vibration, as it were, and in so doing arouse the emotions directly, circumventing the usual perceptual and cognitive pathways. Descartes's *Passions of the Soul*, then, gave music a new representational project: to represent, in musical tones, the motions of the animal spirits specific to the arousal of the basic human emotions. In this way, its expressive vocabulary could be amplified; for it not only still had the basic array of speech-related emotions in its 'dictionary,' but also the newly coined Cartesian ones, with the animal spirits as their representational objects. And because the animal spirits could be imagined to move in intricate, rapid, even violent ways, they provided imagined objects of imitation that comported well with the new instrumental melodic figures, intricate, rapid, violent, as the motions of human speech did not.

The Cartesian aesthetic of musical emotions reached its fullest embodiment in the writings of Johann Mattheson, and especially in his compendious *Der vollkommene Capellmeister* published in 1741, and still being recommended to students by Beethoven in the nineteenth century. Among many other things, Mattheson's text provided the fullest emotive vocabulary for what we know as the *Affektenlehre*. Nor is there any doubt as to the source of Mattheson's inspiration. With regard to 'the doctrine of the temperaments and emotions . . .' Mattheson advises his readers, 'especially Descartes is to be read . . .'[5]

Without delving deeply into Mattheson's rather verbose but in some ways insightful tome, it might be useful to quote some examples of the emotive vocabulary, as Mattheson perceived it. He writes, 'Since for example joy is an expansion of our soul, thus it follows reasonably and naturally that I could best express this affect by large and expanded intervals.' And again, 'if one knows that sadness is a contraction of these subtle parts of our body, then it is easy to see that the small and smallest intervals are the most suitable for this passion.' Mattheson concludes, after a litany of such instances, 'and in this way one can form a sensitive concept of all the emotions and compose accordingly.'[6]

At the time of Mattheson's writing, the full expressive vocabulary of Western tonal music, both classical and popular, was more or less in place. This we know because we can still 'read' the emotive language of the eighteenth century with no help from the experts. That is not to say that later composers did not add to the 'dictionary,' or that some of the more arcane figures did not fall into disuse. But in the main the expressive code had been established, which would serve Western composers as long as major/minor functional harmony was their medium. Of course the Cartesian animal spirits went the way of phlogiston and the aether. What they left behind, however, and what they were instrumental in forming, namely, the code of musical emotions, endures wherever the tools of the tonal trade are taken up.

I now must leave the emotive code temporarily, to take up the second, the prescriptive code. But I do so with two important observations. The first is that, by and large, the emotive code of which I have been speaking was applied, until late in the eighteenth century, largely to vocal music, although the notion that pure instrumental was to have, in its individual movements, a 'leading emotion' was abroad. That is to say, the main thrust of the *Affektenlehre* was as a method to make the musical accompaniment of a vocal line and the

---

[5] Johann Mattheson, *Der vollkommene Capellmeister*, trans. Ernest C. Harriss (Ann Arbor: UMI Research Press, 1981), 104 (pt. I, ch. 3, art. 51). I have given a fuller interpretation of Mattheson's position in 'Mattheson as Philosopher of Art', in P. Kivy, *The Fine Art of Repetition: Essays in the Philosophy of Music* (Cambridge: Cambridge University Press, 1993).

[6] Mattheson, *Der vollkommene Capellmeister*, 104–5 (pt. I, ch. 3, arts. 56–61).

vocal line itself congruent with the emotional tone of the text. Absolute music was not yet the issue it was soon to become. I will return to this point later on.

My second observation concerns how we are to construe the emotive code from the listener's point of view. As we have seen, both the representation of the emotive speaking voice, and the representation of the Cartesian animal spirits were understood not merely as aesthetic ends in themselves, but as means to arousal of the emotions they represented. But here I shall set the arousal question aside. For there *is* a general consensus among contemporary philosophers of art that whatever else the emotive code is, and whatever its real foundations, it is, to begin with, a code to be read *in* the music. We hear the sadness or happiness or whatever in the musical structure itself, as we hear such other phenomenological features as tranquility, turbulence, and the like. From now on, that is how the emotive code is to be understood: as a code, that is, to be read in the music, not in the listener's emotive life.

The Prescriptive Code

It is generally conceded by intellectual historians and philosophers of art that profound changes in our thinking about the theory and practice of the fine arts occurred during the eighteenth century. I am directly concerned here with three of these: the rise to prominence of instrumental music, the development of the so-called aesthetic attitude, which I have characterized for the purposes of this chapter as a prescriptive code for listening, and, in connection with both of these, the advent of the public concert and public concert space.

Much has been written about the origin and early development of the aesthetic attitude, and a good deal of heated controversy generated. But one thing seems clear: what was evolving was supposed to be a special way of attending to nature and to art that was proper to nature if it was to be perceived as beautiful rather than (say) useful, or dangerous, and proper to art if (to put it vaguely) it was to be perceived in the way proper to it as art rather than (say) a useful object or a dangerous one. And, again, to put it vaguely, the general drift of the aesthetic attitude theory as it developed from the early eighteenth century was towards the enfranchisement of *formal* properties as those attention to which essentially defined it. This tendency culminated in Kant's notion of what he called the pure judgement of taste.

The red thread that ran through philosophical speculation concerning art and beauty in the Enlightenment was the problem of what was called, in Britain, the standard of taste. It was the problem of how judgements of aesthetic taste, which were, all agreed, judgements based on subjective feelings of satisfaction or dissatisfaction, could also be objective, in the sense of there being good taste and bad taste, correct judgements and incorrect ones. How could a judgement be *both* 'subjective' and 'objective'?

In brief, Kant's answer, in the *Critique of Judgement*—the section called the 'Analytic of the Beautiful'—was that even though judgements of taste are made solely on the basis of the judge's feeling of satisfaction, when they are *pure* judgements of taste, which alone are truly judgements of beauty, there is at least the expectation of universal agreement, for it is the impurities that may creep into the judgement that account for the oft-remarked diversities and disagreements.

A *pure* judgement, Kant claimed, was one in which all else was filtered out but the awareness of form: the form, merely, of the appearance of an object, its presentation to some sense modality. If, in other words, one abstracted from perception all interest, as Kant called it, in the nature of the object of perception, even interest in whether or not the object exists as anything beyond mere sensible appearance— whether or not, to put it crudely, it is an oasis or a mirage or a dream or a hallucination—then all that is left to perceive is the form of the appearance. In Kant's words: '*Taste* is the faculty of estimating an object or mode of representation by means of a delight or aversion *apart from any interest*. The object of such delight is called beautiful.'[7] When this attitude of disinterestedness is achieved, and the pure form of the appearance is the object of perception and judgement, all cause for diversity in taste is removed, because all that is in play are the faculties of imagination and judgement, in a kind of interaction that Kant called their 'free play,' and which, he thought, for reasons we cannot go into here, must be assumed universal in the species.

Is it a coincidence that at the time the aesthetic attitude theory reached full development, in 1790, the art of pure instrumental music had reached a position of prominence in the musical world not theretofore attained? Coincidence or not, the music seems made for the attitude, the attitude for the music. Whether or not the newly

[7] Immanuel Kant, *Critique of Aesthetic Judgement*, trans. J. C. Meredith (Oxford: Oxford University Press, 1911), 50 (§5).

prominent absolute music was one of the fine arts, as texted music was agreed to be, became a point of philosophical contention among Kant and his contemporaries. Kant never quite made up his mind either way. But that, for our purposes, is irrelevant. What is relevant is that the aesthetic attitude, in something like the form I have just described it, became the prescriptive code for listening to a kind of music not only ideally suited to that code but hardly susceptible of full appreciation without it.

The aesthetic attitude as an integral part of philosophical art theory persisted well into the twentieth century, and was given a devastating critique as recently as the 1960s by the American philosopher George Dickie, who concluded that as far as he could tell, all the aesthetic attitude amounted to was a pretentious way of saying that when you experience a work of art you should pay close attention to *it*: to, that is, the features relevant to it as an artwork.[8] But at least with regard to the art of instrumental music, that prescriptive code is not as empty as it may sound, if viewed in its historical context.

In its bare, minimal sense, the prescriptive code says: 'pay close attention to this music, and to nothing else'. But why should anyone need to be told that? Isn't it too obvious to be spoken? That is what you *do* when you listen to serious music. Not at all, because the settings in which most instrumental music was performed, and listened to, before the crucial period about which I am speaking, were settings in which the listener was *not* meant to pay close and exclusive attention to the music—rather, casual and intermittent attention. The settings were social and ceremonial ones. More than music was going on, and a great deal of it more important to the participants than the music.

That brings us to a further consideration. The growth of instrumental music, and the rise of the prescriptive listening code embodied by the aesthetic attitude, coincided with a third crucial development: the institution of the public concert and public performing space (which is to say, the concert and concert hall). Is this yet another coincidence? Again, I hardly think so. For just as the aesthetic attitude and the burgeoning instrumental idiom seem made for one another, so, as well, does the setting of the concert hall seem made for *them*. Because as it is the purpose of the prescriptive code to mandate close and undivided attention to the musical work, it is

---

[8] George Dickie, 'The Myth of the Aesthetic Attitude,' *American Philosophical Quarterly*, 1 (1964).

the purpose of the concert space to provide the setting whereby that close and undivided attention is made possible. We all face front; the musicians are before us; and only one thing happens: music.

But recall, too, that the aesthetic attitude, in its most influential, Kantian formulation, tends to favor formal properties. Thus, the prescriptive code does not merely say, 'Pay close attention to the music and nothing else,' but 'Pay close attention to the formal properties of the music and nothing else,' which properties I take to be not merely those that are, literally, the formal, structural ones; rather, all of the (roughly speaking) phenomenal properties of the music of which the formal ones are a part.

By the end of the eighteenth century, then, pure instrumental music had become a major part of the serious music-lovers listening diet. It demanded a kind of listening implicitly assumed and explicitly mandated by what I have been calling the prescriptive musical code. It flourished in an entirely new setting, the public concert and public concert space, designed for just that kind of music, and just that kind of listening the prescriptive code laid down as necessary.

There is, however, one additional point to be made before we have finished with this sketch of what might be called the philosophical and institutional presuppositions underlying the modern repertory of absolute music. This point requires a brief return to the first musical code: the linguistic code of musical expression.

It will be recalled that I represented the expressive code as a vocabulary whereby the composer was enabled to choose musical materials emotively appropriate to the texts he was setting. This is particularly obvious in the case of Mattheson, who brought the *Affektenlehre* to its most elaborate form, specifically for the use of church composers, whose music he described, in *Der vollkommene Capellmeister*, as a kind of sermon, 'above all a teacher of propriety.'[9] The expressive code, in conjunction with the text, was to constitute the means of instruction.

None the less, it would be a serious mistake to think that the expressive code did not play a role—a very prominent role—in the burgeoning art of instrumental music as well. For, clearly, vocal and instrumental music in the Baroque and Classical periods did not occupy separate, hermetically sealed compartments but, quite to the contrary, were closely related and interpenetrated one another to a

---

[9] Mattheson, *Der vollkommene Capellmeister*, 104 (pt. I, ch. 3, art. 54).

high degree. Thus instrumental music too was read as, among other things, an expressive structure. So when I describe the prescriptive code as requiring of the listener close, undivided attention to the phenomenal properties of instrumental music, it must not be forgotten that expressive properties are among them, and doubtless the most readily perceived by the lay person, a point I shall return to.

Thus, the linguistic and prescriptive codes are by no means unrelated. The prescriptive code adjures the listener to concentrate, with undivided attention, on the phenomenal properties of music. Among those properties are the expressive ones, constituting the linguistic code that, by the time of the High baroque, was fully entrenched and handily read by the enculturated listener, whether or not she was musically trained. By the eighteenth century, then, the prescriptive code, the linguistic code, the now prominent genre of absolute music, and the public performance space, the concert hall, existed in one integrated package. Furthermore, this package essentially defined the experience, the institution, the repertory of absolute music from the waning years of the eighteenth century to the beginning years of the twentieth; and, indeed, still persists intact to this day, although we have seen in the twentieth century challenges to it, two of which I will be discussing a bit later. But not only does the package, if I may so call it, define our listening stance and listening place for the music that was composed, and continues to be composed, under its aegis. It defines, for better or worse, our listening place and listening stance for music that was composed for far different social settings, well before the rise of the aesthetic attitude, and in which such an attitude would be out of place as well as impossible to attain. The Brandenberg Concertos and Handel's Water Music, to instance two cases that are both in the modern concert repertory,were not written for the concert hall, and exist there, abducted from their natural habitat, much like an altarpiece or African mask in the art museum. Indeed, the concert hall might well be called a sonic museum.[10] In sum, then, the compositional, performing, and listening practices that have defined the so-called classical repertory of instrumental music from the late eighteenth century to the present day consist in a prescriptive code that demands close, undivided attention to the phenomenological properties of music, a music designed to satisfy just that listening code, a concert space designed to house just that kind of music, and

---

[10] I have written about this at some length in *Authenticities: Philosophical Reflections on Musical Performance*(Ithaca: Cornell University Press, 1995), chs. 4 and 8.

an expressive linguistic code that provides perhaps the most easily perceived of the phenomenological properties of that music, hence those properties most relied upon by the lay listener in orienting himself in his listening experience. In our century that package of musical practices has persisted—but not without challenges. To what I consider the major such challenges, atonal serialism and minimalism, I now turn my attention.

Two Musical Revolutions

I want to make some brief remarks about what many would take to be the most drastic break from our musical tradition: the twelve-tone compositions of Schoenberg, Berg, and Webern; in short, atonal serialism. One may be puzzled as to why I want yet again to go over ground that has been covered often before. But what I hope to show in this discussion is that the atonal revolution can cast some light on the minimalist revolution, and vice versa, when *both* are seen against the background of the two musical codes that I have just explained.

I begin with a familiar story that is supposed to be history. I do not know whether it is history or not, and it does not matter; nor do I remember where I first read or heard it, so I cannot attribute it to its source. But it is a useful story for making a point.

According to this supposed historical narrative, the twelve-tone system of Arnold Schoenberg is a natural culmination of the growth of chromaticism in nineteenth-century Romantic music. One can, in other words, plot a course of increasing chromaticism from (say) *Tristan* to Mahler to *Verklärte Nacht*, with but a small step from there to full-blown twelve-tone atonalism. It is a course in which the tonal center becomes more and more ambiguous, the chromaticism more and more pervasive, until no tonal center remains, all of the twelve tones, therefore, of equal importance, and the serial system exists, quite naturally, an accomplished fact, merely awaiting systematization in the familiar set of compositional rules well known to all. According to this story, then, the twelve-tone system was no more an invention of Schoenberg's than the sonata form was of its first theoretical expositors, or Greek tragedy of Aristotle's.

As history, this account is just too good to be true. For one thing, it strongly suggests a Hegelian working out of some inner musical logic that one should be very reluctant to endorse; and, for another, it is offered as a kind of slippery slope argument that is supposed to entice the skeptical listener into accepting the music on the grounds that the difference between serial atonalism and the chromaticism of Bach or Wagner is merely a matter of degree: of small incremental steps. So if you like the *Chromatic Fantasy and Fugue*, and *Tristan*, and *Verklärte Nacht* for *their* chromaticism, you are then on the slippery slope that will lead you inevitably to like twelve-tone music, which is, so the story goes, only the next step in the progress of chromaticism, chromaticism's limiting case.

But the atonalism of the Second Viennese School is not chromaticism, and the slippery-slope argument, whether historically true, or rather what philosophers call a 'rational reconstruction,' cannot show that it is. What it does show is that slippery-slope arguments can lead to changes that are, at last, not merely changes of degree but changes of kind. (A pebble is not a heap.) Such a change is the break with tonality that Schoenberg and his school made.

The chromaticism story, then, is bad history. That does not, however, make it bad analysis. As a way of looking at twelve-tone atonality, it has something to teach us. Let us, then, look at serial atonality *as if* it were the last stage in the progress of chromaticism. And let us look at it this way in relation to the linguistic code of musical expression.

Chromaticism is, of course, one of the most prominent parts of the expressive vocabulary. It is invoked for anguish, pain, foreboding, and various other dark emotions, in their most extreme manifestations, when setting texts. And it carries these emotive qualities with it into instrumental music as well. But now consider the point where chromaticism is so ubiquitous that it crowds out the rest of the emotive vocabulary. When that happens chromaticism essentially has lost its expressive power. It is rather like the way imprecations and four-letter words lose their power to shock when they are too frequently employed.

Furthermore, when chromaticism becomes serial atonality, not only is the emotive significance of chromaticism lost, but the rest of the emotive vocabulary as well, simply because the whole expressive code is framed in terms of the major/minor tonal system, and came into being, as we know it, in lock step with that system. Major/minor tonality is to the expressive code what grammar is to a natural language. Reject the syntax, and most, if indeed not all semantics departs with it. In short, twelve-tone serialism, and the later serialism that developed from it, cannot be read as an expressive language in the old sense. In breaking with major/minor tonality, it has broken the expressive code.

Now, of course, twelve-tone serialism has its own syntax, well known to all, and has maintained the whole repertory of Western musical forms, genres, and techniques: symphony, string quartet, sonata form, fugue, canon, crab, inversion, diminution, augmentation—the lot. Furthermore, in preserving these forms and techniques, frequently exploiting them in extremely complex ways, serialism has certainly *not* broken with the prescriptive code. Indeed, it is difficult to think of any music in our tradition more demanding of what it enjoins: close and undivided attention to formal structure.

Now as we all know, twelve-tone music, which has been with us for more than half a century, has failed to gain a wide acceptance among serious classical music lovers. Various reasons have been offered for this beyond the usual appeal to the time-lag between the composition of new music and its acceptance by the musical public. Leonard Meyer has suggested that the almost complete lack of redundancy in serial music simply overloads our perceptual circuits, as it were, making demands on our mental processing that cannot be met.[11] Along similar lines, Lerdahl and Jackendoff, in claiming that there is, in human beings, a deep structure innately favoring tonal music, suggest that 'listeners will find it difficult to assign any rich structure to music composed by these techniques.'[12]

I do not say that these hypotheses are wrong, nor, on the other hand, do I endorse them. But I can suggest another, not inconsistent with them. It is simply that, in breaking with the linguistic code of musical expression, twelve-tone music has denuded itself of just that aspect of classical music that is most accessible, and that the lay listener relies on most heavily. Furthermore, this explains, as well, why twelve-tone music *does* have a substantial following among musicians and musically trained listeners. For they rely less on the expressive code than the lay person and are more prepared to follow the complex formal aspects of such music, under the strict discipline of the prescriptive code.

Another point worthy of note is that where twelve-tone compositions have gained entrance into the mainstream repertory, as, for

---

[11] Leonard B. Meyer, *Music, the Arts and Ideas: Patterns and Predictions in Twentieth-Century Culture* (Chicago: University of Chicago Press, 1967), ch. 11.

[12] Fred Lerdhal and Ray Jackendoff, *A Generative Theory of Tonal Music* (Cambridge, Mass.: MIT Press, 1985), 301.

example, Alban Berg's *Wozzek* seems to have done, the expressive code *has* been preserved, and, as some have suggested, has been preserved by Berg's uncanny ability to exploit tonality within the twelve-tone system, and rescue at least some essential remnants of the traditional expressive vocabulary. (This is also true of some of Berg's instrumental works.)

But why, it might well be objected, cannot a new musical system such as twelve-tone serialism, even though it is not a tonal system, develop its *own* expressive code? Why cannot it develop its own emotive language, as the major/minor tonal system did? Perhaps it has, and we have just not yet learned to 'read' it.

I have no conclusive reply to this objection. What it claims may well be true. But there is some reason to be at least suspicious of it.

It has become increasingly clear, through recent work by psychologists, evolutionary biologists, and analytic philosophers, that at least the basic emotions, those with the most readily recognizable behavioral manifestations, are expressed in ways that are not historically or culturally imparted, but, rather, in ways universal to the species (and even to some of the lower primates). Furthermore, it is these basic emotions that, not by coincidence, the expressive code of the major/minor system has been able most successfully (and uncontroversially) to embody. Any other musical system, if it is to develop an analogous expressive code, must do it by embodying these same, universal emotive expressions. And it may well be, although I cannot say for sure, that it is the major/minor tonal system, and no other, that is peculiarly suited to the task. If that is the case, then serial atonalism will be permanently cut off from the expressive code. But, I hasten to add, this does not imply any adverse judgement upon it. There is nothing written in heaven, or carved in stone, that says great music must be expressive music or easily accessible. None the less, it is the case that, in our times, serial atonalism either lacks an expressive code, or possesses one that ordinary listeners, including myself, cannot read. That makes it a musical revolution of impressive magnitude. And if that also closes it off to some substantial part of the listening public, so be it. Everything is not for everybody.

I turn now, at last, to minimalism. I have been a long time in getting there, but I hope my previous remarks will help cast some light on the topic.

I begin my discussion with an anecdote. It was told me in conversation by a very well-known Professor of Music at an extremely prestigious American university. And because what one says at a cocktail party one does not necessarily expect to have quoted in print, I am not going to mention any names.

According to this professor, a composer of minimalist music, whose name you would all immediately recognize were I to mention it, was contemplating the composition of a work for the violin. Because he was not a violinist himself, he wisely decided to discuss his musical ideas with a distinguished performer on that instrument, to make certain that his work would be both idiomatic and playable. In a short time the composer and violinist became rather friendly. So at one point the violinist decided to venture a mild criticism of the composer's music. What he said was essentially to the effect that he thought the composer might perhaps consider not confining his palette to the longer note-values but get down as far as sixteenth-notes, and, into the bargain, exploit a few dotted rhythms for variety's sake. The composer's reaction was quick, and decisive. 'What do you take me for?' he asked, 'one of those Princeton boys?'

Now aside from the wonderfully mad assumption that the slight lapses from minimalist orthodoxy the violinist was suggesting would, at a stroke, turn the composer in question into another Milton Babbit, the composer's response has something obvious to tell us, and also something a little less obvious—both relevant to our deliberations.

The obvious moral of this tale is that, needless to say, minimalism revolts against musical complexity in its most extreme form. Of course the swing from complexity to simplicity is nothing new in the history of music. The church music of the Counter-Reformation was a reaction away from the complexity of Flemish polyphony, music of the pre-Classical period a reaction away from the complexity of the High Baroque.

But the less obvious point, which lies in the humor of the anecdote, is the extremity of the revolution that minimalism has made: the violence of the break from twelve-tone atonalism and the so-called 'total serialism' of the Princeton School. This is, I suppose, only to be expected, since atonal serialism is itself an extreme break with the tradition of major/minor tonality. To put it crudely, music written in the tradition of functional harmony strikes some sort of balance between repetition and change: between the redundant and the unexpected. Twelve-tone atonalism was, among other things, a total rejection of redundancy: the avoidance of repetition was axiomatic.

The predictable reaction away from the complete rejection of musical redundancy is the total embracing of it, hence the obsessive repetition that has become the hallmark of the minimalist movement.

More obvious still is the obsessive tonality of minimalism, again, one must suppose, a reaction from the obsession of twelve-tone serialism with avoiding the merest suggestion of any tonal center or priority, even temporarily. The reaction away from having no tonic at all is, in its most extreme form, having tonic only.

Thus, to sum up the more or less obvious points made just now, minimalism is a violent departure from the three hallmarks of twelve-tone composition and at least some of its serialist successors: it is an uncompromising rejection of complexity, and an affirmation, in the strongest possible way, of redundancy and tonality.

Now all of the above make minimalism a drastic departure from what is arguably the most talked about and controversial musical movement of the twentieth century. But this in itself hardly marks it out as *very* special, or *very* revolutionary. The artists of a new generation have usually set a course at least in some important way different from their immediate predecessors: that is a cliché of art history. What is momentous about minimalism, I want to argue, is that in at least some of its more prominent manifestations, it rejects the most basic and all-pervasive axiom of instrumental music in the modern era: *the prescriptive code of the aesthetic attitude*. In this, appearances to the contrary notwithstanding, it is an even more violent musical revolution than the twelve-tone system.

The major operator in the revolution is, of course, redundancy, although obsessive tonal monotony also plays a prominent role. To see this it would be well to remind ourselves what the traditional function of internal repetition is in the music of the seventeenth, eighteenth, and nineteenth centuries. Clearly, one major function is to create expectation, which, within a reasonable period of time, that is to say, a period commensurate with our powers of perception, memory, and mental processing faculties, will allow the outcome to make musical sense in terms of the repetition that has built up the expectation. This repetitional function relies, of course, on concentrated attention: in other words, adherence to the prescriptive code. Without that, neither the repetition nor its outcome will have its intended effect.

But suppose, now, that repetition becomes obsessive, as it does in much minimalist music. Suppose, indeed, it becomes so protracted that it defeats our powers of concentration, perception, and mental processing, thus making it impossible for us to comprehend the outcome in functional terms; or suppose, in fact, that there is *no* functional outcome at all: suppose, in other words, that the repetition is not for the sake of something else, but an end in itself. In either of these two cases it becomes clear that the prescriptive code is not merely impossible to comply with but simply irrelevant. To such music it is not even meant to apply; it has been rejected.

Leonard Meyer says something along these lines in regard to another musical phenomenon of our time that is worth quoting in this regard. He writes:

in markedly goal-directed, syntactic music such as Beethoven's, patent redundancy (such as occurs in measures 16–25 of the first movement of the Sixth Symphony) creates strong expectation of change; while contemporary, popular, 'new age' music, which is highly redundant but only weakly goal-directed, gives rise to minimal tension and expectation. . . . [S]ome listeners have learned that Beethoven's music should be given devoted attention, while aficionados of 'new age' music find that attention can be perfunctory, even sporadic.[13]

It may well be responded that new age music, which is clearly meant merely as background—Muzak carried to its ultimate extreme—cannot be taken seriously, and our attitude to it, 'perfunctory, even sporadic,' in Meyer's characterization, cannot therefore serve as any kind of analogue or model for the proper attitude to be taken in the perception of minimalist music, which *is* meant to be taken seriously. The point is well taken; and words such as 'perfunctory,' with their distinctly negative tone, are best avoided. Nevertheless, the basic contrast Meyer is making between the 'devoted attention' he describes as the favored attitude towards goal-directed, syntactic music, which is to say, what I have been calling the aesthetic attitude, and whatever other attitude may be appropriate, which the aesthetic attitude is *not*, towards highly redundant, non-goal-directed music, is a contrast that cannot be dismissed out of hand. And there *are* other analogies available.

Still remaining within the popular sphere, there is redundancy abounding, for example, in a good deal of the music associated, in the United States, with the so-called drug-culture of the 1960s. Such

[13] Leonard B. Meyer, 'A Universe of Universals,' *Journal of Musicology*, 16 (1998), 14.

music, I am told by one of the survivors, must be listened to while 'stoned,' in which state you are supposed to have something like an orgasmic (is it fair to say?) 'aesthetic' experience. Here we are far from the prescriptive code of Western art music. Are we anywhere near the experience of minimalism?

Let me adduce but one more example that, I think, cannot be dismissed lightly, as my previous two might, perhaps unfairly. I refer to the ragas of Southern India, which represent one of the richest of the non-Western musical traditions. As is well known, such music seems, at least to the Western ear, highly redundant. Furthermore, the compositions themselves, as well as the concerts (if that is the right word for them) in which they are heard, exceed in length, by orders of magnitude, anything in our listening tradition, even the *Ring*. This protracted listening time seems to preclude anything resembling what I have called our prescriptive code: the code of the aesthetic attitude. One cannot give concentrated, undivided musical attention over a period that may well exceed eight hours. Something *else* is going on here, for which the prescriptive code of Western music seems not only impossible but irrelevant.

What I am arguing, then, is that minimalism, for all of its *prima facie* simplicity and accessibility, represents an even wider break with the Western musical tradition than atonal serialism, for all of *its* complexity and inaccessibility. For if I am right in arguing that minimalist music has broken the prescriptive code, then it has broken with the most basic premiss of the modern Western musical tradition. Instrumental music, 'as we know it,' but without its expressive code, is a perfectly comprehensible possibility. Instrumental music, as we know it, but which defeats the prescriptive code, simply is not instrumental music as we know it. That is not a criticism. It is, if I am right, a plain statement of fact.

The irony is that the more drastic break with tradition has spoken to the larger lay audience, the less drastic to the audience of musically trained and learned. This is an odd result, as things tend, in the history of art, to turn out just the opposite way. Thus it appears that in yet another respect, minimalism turns out to be a drastic departure from tradition.

I have argued, then, that the most revolutionary thing about the minimalist movement is its breaking with the prescriptive code of the aesthetic attitude. But there is, perhaps, another way of construing at least some minimalist compositions that keeps them within the prescriptive code, albeit in a somewhat altered way. I want to conclude by briefly considering that possibility.

Of course no minimalist music is *completely* redundant—but all redundant to a degree, an order of magnitude beyond anything before it, that seems to defeat the attitude of close, undivided attention the prescriptive code enjoins. However, the composer of at least some of this kind of music might well reply in this wise: 'Of course I have exceeded by orders of magnitude the redundancy of traditional, goal-directed music. But the point is not to defeat the prescriptive code: the point is to push it beyond its previous limits. The more redundancy is increased, the more momentous even the slightest change will be. So the point of this music is to increase the listener's sensitivity to minute changes, by placing them within a structure of extreme redundance. And far from this defeating close and undivided attention, it *requires* such attention to a degree beyond that, indeed, required by (say) *The Art of the Fugue*, or even twelve-tone serialism. It may even require an attentiveness beyond the capabilities of the contemporary listener. But why construe that as evidence of the composer's intention to defeat the aesthetic attitude? Rather, construe it as evidence that, like all original artists, the composer of minimalist music intends to expand his or her audience's perceptual faculties. Future generations will, by listening to this music, increase their capacity to attend, become sensitive to musical change to a high degree heretofore unattainable, and reap, thereby, the benefits of a new and subtle musical experience. Minimalism, far from being a rejection of the prescriptive code is, rather, a celebration of it.'

So I imagine the minimalist composer, at least of a certain stripe, might respond to the thesis that minimalism in music eschews the prescriptive code. As I say, this is an alternative reading of the relationship of *some* minimalist music to the so-called aesthetic attitude. Whether it is a satisfactory reading of all of it I tend to doubt, although I am open to persuasion on this point. For it seems to me that at least many of the most well-known examples of musical minimalism aim at something very different to what the prescriptive code is meant to facilitate. The most frequently invoked description, I find, in speaking both to lay listeners and musicians alike—at least to those who are sympathetic to the style—is 'mood' or 'state of mind.' 'At its best,' a musician said to me recently, 'it imparts in me a kind of tranquility I do not get from other music.' Whether this is to be construed as a worthy goal or an unworthy one for music to achieve is a question I leave open, as I do all the questions I have raised. I do not offer anything I have said as more than a tentative hypothesis, to be tested by discussion and argument.

PART II

Music and the Emotions (Yet Again)

Auditor's Emotions: Contention, Concession, and Compromise

I

If a gradual move towards consensus is a sign of progress in philosophical enquiry, then there certainly does seem to have been progress, in recent years, with regard to the age-old question of what it might mean to ascribe emotive predicates to music. For more and more philosophers seem willing to accept, nowadays, that when one calls a piece of music sad or yearning, contemplative or angry, joyous or melancholy, what one must mean, *at least*, if not at most, is that that music possesses those emotions as heard, perceptual, 'phenomenological' properties of the musical surface and structure itself. As a matter of fact, the philosophical adversary with whom I will be contending in the present paper agrees with me (I think) on that, as do many others, although there is substantial disagreement about how the emotions become or are constituted perceptual properties of the music.

But when it comes to listeners' emotive reactions to music, what I alluded to in the title of this chapter as 'auditor's emotions,' the consensus breaks down. And perhaps this is to be expected. For when one goes from talk about the perceptual properties of an 'object' to talk about the emotive responses of a perceiver to those properties, it should hardly be surprising that one goes from consensus to contention. Is it not proverbial that the emotive responses of individuals to their commonly perceived world are very personal and idiosyncratic? It would, therefore, be irrational to hope for or aim at a consensus here. There have to be important differences in the ways auditors react emotionally to music, as there must be important differences in the ways people react emotionally to various other aspects of their surroundings.

I have grown increasingly tolerant, as the years go by, of ways of listening to music that differ from my own. I have ceased to claim (or to think) that the way I listen to music is the only way, the best way, or a privileged way of listening. What I *do* claim is that it is a way of listening I share with a substantial number of other people, similarly trained in music and musicianship, and that, with regard to this way of listening, I have a thorough, fully satisfactory account, at least in outline. In particular, and particularly relevant to present concerns, it is an account that explains how the expressive properties of music are perceived, how music is deeply moving emotionally, and what role the expressive properties can play in that deeply moving experience.

But if one is fully to understand my view, one must also fully understand over what the word 'music' ranges when I make claims about music's emotive powers. I have had thrown up against my claim that 'music' does not arouse what I call the 'garden-variety' emotions—joy, anger, melancholy, yearning, and the like—the most bizarre and outlandish counter-examples: bizarre and outlandish not because they fail to be cases in which music contributes to the arousal of the garden-variety emotions, but because the kind of music adduced, and the contexts in which it flourishes, are both far removed from the music and the context to which my analysis is directed. So I must first make clear what that music is, and in what context it operates. Perhaps I should have made this clearer a long time ago, but I suppose I thought it was obvious.

In the mid-eighteenth century two obviously related musical phenomena occurred: the institution of the public concert and the rise, both in social status and production, of pure instrumental music— what the nineteenth century called 'absolute music,' and what I have become in the habit of calling 'music alone.' It is, I am sure, no accident that the public concert and its setting, the modern concert hall, came into being at about the same time as another great public institution devoted to the propagation of the fine arts, namely, the museum. And it seems altogether appropriate, upon observing this far from coincidental set of events, to think of the concert hall as a kind of 'sonic museum.' It is absolute music, in the setting of the sonic museum, that is, and always has been the sole object of my enquiry and over which my theory of music and the emotions ranges. I make no claims for other musics, in other settings, except for the obvious case of recorded music, which has transferred, as it were, the public concert and its music to private space.

To be sure, this does not mean to imply that I confine my theorizing to absolute music written after the 'great divide' between public music-making in the sonic museum and its earlier manifestations, any more than does the sonic museum confine *itself* to exhibiting only music written since its inception. Indeed, it is a valuable function of the sonic museum to make available, for our appreciation, musical works of earlier times that were composed with very different settings in mind, religious and state ceremonies, domestic and aristocratic music-making, dances, dinner parties, weddings, and so on, just as it is the function of the fine arts museum to show such objects as African masks and altar paintings, which have, like their musical counterparts, been wrenched from their intended places in the world. But just as an African mask or an altar painting may have very different effects on viewers when experienced in its original setting from the effect it has in the fine arts museum, viewed as a purely aesthetic object, so too the minuet or military march may well have a very different effect, the former in the ballroom, the latter on the parade ground, from the effects that they will have in the concert hall. And it is only music in the context of the concert hall, or its surrogate, the home, by way of the record player, about which I speak; only that music in that context that I attempt to characterize.

These limiting conditions having been laid down, let me now state, in the briefest possible way, what my view is regarding the emotions we perceive in music, and the emotions we feel for it. It is my view, then, that when we characterize music as yearning or angry, joyous or melancholy, we are identifying heard qualities of the music, as we do when we characterize it as tranquil, dissonant, chromatic, major, minor, modal, diatonic, or whatever. We are not saying, at this point, that the music makes us yearn, or be angry, joyous, or melancholy, but that it *is* those things.

But as a listener, I also feel deeply moved, sometimes, by the music I hear. However, it is not that I am deeply moved by music in virtue of its arousing in me the garden-variety emotions it possesses. It is rather that I am deeply moved by the beauty of the music; and I can give this emotion no other name than that. Of course this does not mean that I feel the 'same' emotion when I am deeply moved by the beauty of Bach's *English Suites* as when I am by the beauty of Schubert's Improptus, Op. 90. Because they are such different works, and because I am moved by such different musical features in them, it is no more the 'same' emotion than is the love one feels for one's golden retriever the 'same' emotion as the love one feels for one's child, except in the sense that the latter two are both 'love,' and the former two both 'the emotion aroused by beautiful music' (or whatever you wish to call it).

Nor, of course, am I making any objective claim about what music is beautiful (and therefore moving) and what is not. It is what I, or anyone else, now takes to be beautiful music that will move us; and that, of course, will be different music for different people, and different music for the same person, at different times in his or her life. This, basically—*very* basically—is my view of how I find music itself expressive, and how I find that it moves me emotionally. I think my way of perceiving the expressive properties of music, and the way I am moved by music, are also the ways a substantial group of other listeners perceive the expressive properties of music, and are moved by it. There are those, however, who say that they have a very different kind of emotional experience from mine when they listen to music. And one of these others, Colin Radford, is the subject of my discussion in this chapter—a discussion, I want to add, that is not offered in the usual spirit of philosophical confrontation and debate but, as the title of this chapter is meant to imply, in the spirit of concession and (it is to be hoped) future consensus as well.

II

In 1989, Colin Radford published an article called 'Emotions and Music: A Reply to the Cognitivists,' that intrigued me when I read it, and continues to do so.[1] The reason Radford's article intrigues me is twofold. First, it provides the only plausible account I have ever read of how the emotions in music might arouse those emotions in listeners. Second, although it seemed to me when I first read Radford's article that if he were right I must be at least partially wrong about how music moves, namely, wrong in denying that music can move by arousing the garden-variety emotions, I continued to find a hard kernel of truth in Radford's account, and yet continued to find my own experience of music completely at odds with what it should have been, if what Radford said were true.

[1] Colin Radford, 'Emotions and Music: A Reply to the Cognitivists,' *Journal of Aesthetics and Art Criticism*, 47 (1989).

In two of the supplementary chapters to the second edition of my book, *The Corded Shell*, I attempted, by something like a frontal assault, to counter Radford's arguments.[2] He has now responded with another intriguing article in support of his position.[3] It is a very short article, but in spite of that an extremely rich one. And I cannot deal with all Radford's points adequately here. What I am interested in is the basic argument itself, as to how Radford thinks music moves the emotions. However, I no longer think that any progress is to be made here by way of a frontal assault. For I now think I see why Radford is right about something very important, and yet why that is completely compatible with my own emotional experience of music and my own account of it. That, in any case, is what I wish to argue for here.

The beauty of Radford's argument is its simplicity. Accounts of how music is supposed to arouse the garden-variety emotions invariably give us ponderous or bafflingly intricate Rube Goldberg machinery that, like Ptolemy's epicycles, it is just impossible to believe have any reality in nature, and yet cannot be refuted because of the notorious impossibility of proving the negative. Radford, on the other hand, offers us no explanation at all of *how* music might arouse the garden-variety emotions. What he does do is to try to convince us that music *must* do this: it is just common sense, and there's an end on't. (At least so I interpret him.)

The argument is simple and compelling. It is a fact, Radford points out, that no one would deny, that dreary, sunless days depress people. In a word, depressing days depress us. But a depressing or dreary day *possesses* that quality as an expressive quality, in much the way that music does: it is not that we call sunless days dreary or depressing *because* they cause us to be dreary or depressed; rather, the dreary or depressing quality that we perceive in such a day causes us to feel dreary and depressed. If this is so, which it seems to be, then it also seems reasonable to suppose that anything else that possesses an emotion or mood as a perceptual quality will cause those who perceive it to fall into that emotion or mood. And since music possesses emotions or moods as perceived qualities, how can we reasonably deny that it arouses these emotions or moods in those who perceive

---

[2] Peter Kivy, *Sound Sentiment: An Essay on the Musical Emotions* (Philadelphia: Temple University Press, 1989), 157–63, 224–9.

[3] Colin Radford, 'Muddy Waters,' *Journal of Aesthetics and Art Criticism*, 49 (1991).

them? We may not be able to explain *how* the emotions or moods are aroused in any of these kinds of cases. That they are aroused, however, seems indubitable: an item of common sense. Once one accepts it for dreary days and (another of Radford's favorite examples) cheerful colors, one cannot very well reject it when it comes to sad and happy music.

The argument does seem very compelling. And it is completely at odds with my musical experience. For by the dog, I wear that sad music does not make me sad, nor happy music happy. Am I some kind of anomaly? Am I missing an important circuit? Am I an unmusical or unemotional listener? I think it would be hard to make any of those charges stick against me. So what is going on? I think I know. It is quite simple. But it did take a concatenation of circumstances to get me to see that the kernel of truth in this very compelling argument of Radford's is perfectly compatible with the nature of my musical experience. Here, in any event, is my hypothesis.

In reading Radford's most recent article, my eye fastened on the way in which he puts his position in one place. He is answering my objection, voiced to his earlier statement of his views, that there is no real empirical evidence for 'cheerful' colors having the effect of making us cheerful. He writes:

Do we really *need* sociological evidence to confirm the assertion that this light, bright, 'cheerful' color has a tendency to lighten people's spirits, make people feel 'brighter' and more cheerful? I do simply *say* that bright, 'cheerful' colors have a tendency to make me feel more cheerful, and 'assume,' on the basis, if any, of scant anecdotal evidence that others do and would say the same, or very similar.[4]

What I noticed, here, was the word 'tendency,' used twice by Radford in this passage to state his position. I doubt I would have noticed this except for the coincidental fact that I had been reading, just a week or two before, a very stimulating piece in the 1991 volume of *Proceedings of the Aristotelian Society*, by T. S. Champlin, called, appropriately enough, 'Tendencies.'[5]

Now so far I have been stating Radford's position, as he has himself often enough, as that sad music causes us to be sad, and that happy music causes us to be happy. And I have said that I am in something of a dilemma with regard to his claim because although the

---

[4] Colin Radford, 'Muddy Waters,' *Journal of Aesthetics and Art Criticism*, 248.
[5] T. S. Champlin, 'Tendencies,' *Proceedings of the Aristotelian Society*, NS 91 (1991).

analogy Radford draws between the power of depressing days to depress us, and the power of sad music to sadden us, seems very plausible, it cannot be correct to say that sad music saddens us, all of us, since it does not sadden me. But if one restates Radford's position as that sad music *tends* to make us sad, the dilemma immediately evaporates. For it is perfectly consistent to acknowledge that music does indeed *tend* to arouse in listeners the emotions it possesses as perceptual properties while insisting that it does not arouse these emotions in me, or others who experience music the way that I do. As Champlin observes, 'even in examples in which *all* A's have a tendency to be B's, tendencies to do something are essentially "patchy"'; and, further, '. . . "This A tends to be always a B" is, in spite of the "always," still essentially "patchy."'[6] Or, in other words, '"to tend to" . . . acts as a modifier, indicating that there is a shortfall in either frequency or extent in comparison with . . . unmodified claims . . .'[7] Thus, even if it is true that *all* expressive music has a *tendency* to arouse the expressive properties it possesses in listeners, it is also true that there are 'patches' of cases in which listeners are not so aroused; and even if it is true that the melancholy opening bars of Mozart's Quintet in G minor (K. 516) *always* tends to arouse melancholy in listeners, it is also true that there are 'patches' of cases in which listeners are not so aroused. Music that possesses expressive properties *tends* to arouse them in listeners; but the use of 'tends' to modify the arousal claim implies 'a shortfall in either frequency or extent'.

The kernel of truth that, from the start, I felt must lie in Radford's position now stands revealed. It is common sense, and does not require empirical evidence, that music expressive of emotions and moods must have some tendency to arouse those emotions or moods in listeners. It just stands to reason that it must if expressive qualities of other things—the dreariness of cloudy, wet days, for example, or the cheerfulness of sunny ones—have, in our ordinary experience, caused us to feel depressed or cheerful, which, indeed, they have. But, of course, acknowledging that truth leaves it entirely open as to how strong or weak the tendency in music is, as compared to the tendency in cloudy or sunny weather, and under what conditions the tendency might be systematically suppressed. These questions are crucial, and will occupy me now.

[6] T. S. Champlin, 'Tendencies,' *Proceedings of the Aristotelian Society*, NS 91 (1991), 128.
[7] Ibid. 132.

III

I suppose, given our divergent experiences of music, that I am far more skeptical than Radford is about the *strength* of music's tendency to arouse the emotions it is expressive of in auditors. Given my own experience, I am tempted to appropriate for my motto in this regard Aristotle's remark about the power of the living over the fortunes of the dead: the tendency of happy and sad music to make folks happy and sad is 'something too small and insignificant to make the unhappy happy or to deprive the happy of their bliss.'[8]

But let us see if we can get some sort of idea about why the tendency of music to make me and my ilk sad and happy is so much weaker, as I think it is, than the tendency of cloudy days to depress or sunny ones to cheer us. To begin with, I observe that the depressing effect of cloudy days, for example, is cumulative. If I have awakened thirty days running to sunny, cloudless, Caribbean skies, one day of cloudy, depressing weather is hardly going to depress me, even though it still possesses a tendency to do so. It takes a good deal of piling up before the tendency can have its way. And it is just that piling up that, under normal circumstances, music lacks. Not to put too fine a point on it, a depressing day lasts all day, and *still* cannot depress us in that period of time, whereas a melancholy composition lasts . . . well, for how long? The melancholy opening of Mozart's G-minor Quintet lasts for only 35 measures before it modulates into sunnier climes. So given that it may take a few days for depressing weather to depress me, I hardly find it surprising that listening to 30 measures of melancholy music should fail to make me melancholy, even though I acquiesce in the notion that it possesses a *tendency* to do so. Perhaps, of course, listening to melancholy music without surcease for seven days and seven nights might make me melancholy. However, such suggestions fall well outside the listening situations about which I theorize. And I have absolutely nothing to say about them, one way or the other, except to say that they are irrelevant.

A second thing to observe about how cloudy days depress us is that a dismal, cloudy day is a completely enveloping phenomenon of one's life. It pervades one's living space in a way that melancholy music, at least as I experience it, does not. A dismal day tends to

[8] Aristotle, *Nicomachean Ethics*, trans. Martin Ostwald (Indianapolis: Bobbs-Merrill, 1963), 27 (1101b).

work its way with us by, so to say, bombarding our circuits. It is inescapable. However, for me the expressive properties of music are quite another matter. They form, after all, only a part of the musical structure or surface to which they belong, even where they play an important role. And in a lot of very great music they play very little role at all. *The Art of the Fugue*, for example, displays an overall expressive character that might be described as somber, or serious, or even melancholy. But anyone who paid a great deal of attention to this expressive character, or looked to *The Art of the Fugue* for expressive 'interest' would, it seems to me, be missing just about everything important in the work, and pretty much assuring total boredom for the duration of its performance. Yet even in a work such as Brahms' First Symphony, where expressive properties are a very important musical aspect, they are hardly the whole ball of wax; and it would produce a very skewed, out-of-proportion hearing of the work if they were glommed onto, to the exclusion of the other very important structural, formal, harmonic, and contrapuntal aspects of its wonderfully rich and complex fabric. Thus, expressive musical properties, although they play a very important role, at times, in my listening experience, never dominate it to the exclusion of other musical aspects. So they never gain that ascendancy over my total being that dismal cloudy days do: they do not snow me under. And that is another part of the reason why their tendency to arouse is blunted in my listening circumstances, and under the control of my listening attitudes.

To sum up this part of the argument, then, I am in full agreement with Radford that the expressive properties of music have a *tendency* to arouse those same emotions in listeners. Indeed, I go further than Radford in this because, strictly speaking, Radford claims only that sad music makes him sad and happy music happy, explicitly denying that angry music makes him angry. But I see no reason not to take the analogy between the tendency of dreary weather to depress as giving some evidence, anyway, that anything with a perceivable expressive quality of emotion or mood *tends* to arouse that emotion or mood in the perceiver. And if Radford does not accept that conclusion I think he must explain why, since its denial, it seems to me, would be incompatible with his argument.

But I, and others, who share my listening habits and attitudes, find, as Radford does not, that music expressive of the garden-variety emotions fails to arouse those emotions. I do acknowledge

the unavoidable, commonsensical conclusion that, given the undeni-
able effect of such things as dismal weather on people's emotions and
moods, there must be at least *some* tendency for the expressive properties of music to arouse the corresponding emotions in listeners.
None the less there is, as I have pointed out, no contradiction here;
for my claim that music fails to arouse the emotions it is expressive
of in me and others of my kind is perfectly consistent with the further
claim that the expressive properties of music, even while they are failing to arouse the corresponding emotions and moods in me and my
kind, still have the tendency to do so.

Now this latter claim, that music still retains the tendency to
arouse the garden-variety emotions, even while systematically failing
to do so, may strike the reader as highly paradoxical. And it therefore may also seem that my concession to Radford is, after all, simply vacuous. For what of real substance am I admitting in admitting
that yes, music has a tendency to arouse the garden-variety emotions
in us while insisting that it *never* as a matter of fact does? The suspicion of paradox and vacuity is quite understandable, but, as I shall
argue in the next section, quite unfounded.

IV

Let us begin with the feeling that it is paradoxical for a tendency to
be deflected systematically and yet still exist. Champlin, in the aforementioned essay on tendencies, is well aware of this feeling, and
responds to it with a very simple, and convincing example, that not
only should lay this feeling to rest, but also cast some light on the specific case of music and the emotions. He writes:

I suggest the following explanation for the possibility of a tendency which is
suppressed but not eliminated to carry on existing throughout its period of
suppression. Suppose the zip on a new jacket tends to come undone when it
is being worn for the first time. As a temporary measure the owner of the
jacket inserts a safety pin to secure the zip and as a result of this temporary
repair the zip no longer tends to come undone. But if the owner of the jacket
takes it back to the supplier he will say, 'This jacket has a fault; the zip tends
to come undone' even when the safety pin holding the zip is securely in position on the jacket which he is still wearing, so that, as a description of what
is actually happening, the temporary repair is preventing the permanent
fault from manifesting itself. . . . The owner of the jacket is not contradicting

himself when he says of the zip which is being prevented from coming undone that it tends to come undone . . .[9]

So for me and my ilk there is a safety-pin on the zipper: whatever tendency expressive music may have to arouse in us the emotions it is expressive of is systematically suppressed. But as the above example is meant to show, contrived though it may be, there is nothing paradoxical in this, nothing paradoxical, that is, in claiming both that music has a tendency to arouse the emotions it is expressive of and that it continues to possess that tendency while consistently failing to arouse those emotions in a specific group of listeners under specific listening conditions.

Of course it is bound to be asked just what the safety-pin is that, in my case, suppresses the tendency of music to arouse the emotions. What is it and how does it work? I wish I knew the answers to these questions. I don't. But nor do Radford or I know how the tendency of music to arouse emotions works either. And since I, for one, because of my own musical experience, think this tendency of music to arouse the emotions it is expressive of is very weak anyway, I am not much bothered by my ignorance of the matter.

Probably the ambience of the sonic museum itself *tends* to suppress the arousal of the garden-variety emotions. But obviously that is just a tendency, and not a sufficient condition, since there are people, like Radford, who claim to have such emotions aroused in the concert hall.

Probably, too, listening attitudes play some important part in either suppressing or facilitating the tendency of music possessing expressive properties to arouse the corresponding emotions in listeners. But my own listening attitudes are a complicated set, as, I am sure, are Radford's and others'; and I am in no position to present any reasonable hypothesis, right now, as to how my attitudes suppress the arousal tendency, or how the attitudes of others support it.

In any case, whether or not we can know exactly why the tendency of expressive emotions to arouse emotions in listeners is systematically suppressed for significant groups of them, there is nothing paradoxical in the view that that is exactly what is happening. But is the view vacuous?

Suppose I were to make the claim that while agreeing with Radford wholeheartedly that expressive music has a *tendency* to

[9] Champlin, 'Tendencies', 130.

arouse the emotions it is expressive of, there never was a *bona fide* case of an expressive property in music actually arousing the corresponding emotion. That, indeed, does sound very much like admitting nothing at all. And yet even this claim would at least be an intelligible one. 'Can a tendency exist in an object in which it has *never* been actually manifested?' Champlin asks. He answers with this example: 'even a brand new car in the showroom, the very one we are about to buy, may have a tendency to pull to the left at speeds over thirty miles per hour even when it has so far never been driven at speeds of more then ten miles per hour.'[10]

Nevertheless, although I am very much of a skeptical cast of mind as to the strength of the tendency of expressive music to arouse emotions, I do not deny that there is indirect evidence for such a tendency, and nor do I deny that there are *bona fide* manifestations of it in actual cases of arousal. To begin with, we can have evidence of a tendency even though that tendency has never actually been manifested. Champlin's example of the brand new car with a tendency to pull to the left, that has never been driven fast enough to do so, provides such a possible case. For we might determine, prior to the car's ever having pulled to the left, that it has such a tendency, by taking it apart and discovering the structural defect responsible for the tendency. Likewise, I believe that we have evidence, *some* evidence, anyway, that music has a tendency to arouse emotions it is expressive of, even if there were no *bona fide* manifestations of it, in the fact that there are other cases of expressive properties arousing emotions and moods, such as the dreariness of cloudy days causing depression in London and its environs. Thus, even if someone were to assert that the expressive properties of music have a tendency to arouse the corresponding emotions in listeners, while denying that this tendency has ever manifested itself in the form of actually aroused emotions, he or she might still have evidential grounds for the first assertion, and the position would not be empty, in the old positivist sense of 'unverifiable.'

But as a matter of fact, in spite of my skeptical attitude, I am not denying that there are *bona fide* cases in which music expressive of an emotion has aroused that emotion in listeners. At least some of the first-person reports of such arousals I feel bound to accept at face value. Not *all* by any means: for I have frequently encountered

---

[10] Champlin, 'Tendencies', 122.

listeners not given to thinking extensively about these matters, reporting that sad music has made them sad, or happy music happy, but who, when encouraged to analyze their experiences more carefully, and the implications of how they have described them, have come to admit that they have not, in fact, been aroused to sadness or happiness, or the like, though they have indeed perceived those emotions in the music. And, on the other hand, there are sophisticated thinkers on these matters, such as Jerrold Levinson, who although they describe the emotions music makes them feel in ordinary, garden-variety terms, admit that these emotions are not *exactly* the 'real thing.' However, when someone of the sophistication of a Colin Radford reports that he is regularly made sad by sad music, happy by happy music, and *means what he says*, quite literally, I am obliged to accept that as true. I can find no reason not to; and it would be presumptuous of me to do otherwise than to admit that these are, indeed, *bona fide* cases of the tendency of expressive music to arouse emotions having its full effect.

But there is this further to say by way of a warning. It is frequently very difficult to discern, in specific cases, just what causal role the expressive properties of music are really playing. And an example of Radford's, of which he makes rather much, serves nicely to illustrate this point. It is supposed to be a devastating *reductio* of the view that the expressive properties of music lack the power to arouse the garden-variety emotions in listeners. Here is how it goes.

Consider that great piece of popular music, 'La Bamba' and the effect it has on its listeners. . . . It has a very strongly accentuated Latin American rhythm, it is 'brightly' orchestrated, and has a gay 'catchy' tune. Its effect is to make people move in time to the beat, they tend to sing along with the tune, to smile at each other, etc. This exuberant, gay music—I am using 'gay' in its old-fashioned sense—makes its listeners feel gay and exuberant. They are often unable to resist the effect of the music which is to make them get up, dance, sing, etc.[11]

Well, what musical curmudgeon could have the courage to deny, or the will to resist the emotive power of 'La Bamba'? Surely not I. I would be up there dancing and laughing with the rest. But this example, after all, is painted in pretty broad and garish strokes. There are a lot of things we want to know before we can draw any reasonable conclusion about the tendency of *expressive properties* to arouse

[11] Radford, 'Muddy Waters,' 248.

emotions within the confines of the sonic museum. We might like to know what exactly the *setting* is for this hoedown. We would like to know who the participants are and what their emotional (and physical!) state might have been prior to their encounter with 'La Bamba.' And, most important of all, we would like to be sure just what the causal story is here. What is the order of events, and *what* is causing *what*?

Let me tackle the last question first. Here is what I take Radford's causal story to be. A group of people listen to 'La Bamba.' It is exuberant and gay. Upon, or while listening, 'The exuberant, gay music . . . makes its listeners feel gay and exuberant.' And, having thus been made to feel gay and exuberant by those expressive properties of the music, they laugh, sing, and dance—unmistakable behavioral evidence or expression of their elevated mood, and clear proof of the power of expressive music to arouse emotions *by* its expressive properties.

But there is quite another causal story that might be told, consistent with the facts as Radford presents them, that does not demonstrate the arousal power of the expressive properties of 'La Bamba' at all. Interestingly enough, Radford seems sometimes to slip into it in his account. It is the *order* of events that is crucial; and it is not clear, in Radford's account, just what the order of events is.

So here is another causal story. A group of people listen to 'La Bamba.' 'It has a very strongly accentuated Latin American rhythm, it is "brightly" orchestrated, and has a gay, "catchy" tune. . . . They are often unable to resist the effect of the music to make them get up, dance, sing, etc.' They become, in the process of singing and dancing, pretty gay and exuberant themselves. Indeed, they get rather wild, clear behavioral evidence or expression of their elevated spirits, and incontrovertible proof of the cheering powers of communal singing and dancing.

In this scenario, what has happened is that the music has, as certain music will do, *in the proper circumstances*, motivated people to move, dance, and sing together to its accompaniment—as, indeed, it has been specifically designed to that end. And such behavior has, as it frequently will, *in the proper circumstances*, made these people exuberantly happy. Nor should there be much doubt about what it is in 'La Bamba' that has done most of the work, at least in making the audience move and then dance. It is, of course, the Latin beat, not the other expressive properties of the music, that compels people to move and to dance. One can convince oneself of this, I think, by recalling that a great deal of Latin music is in minor keys, and does not necessarily have particularly gay or cheerful characteristics; yet it will have the same tendency to make people move and dance to it. (The tango, which, of course, is Argentinian, is a particularly good example of this.) That of course is what this music is for: it is *dance* music. You do not even, in fact, need melody or harmony. You can get the same effect, under suitable conditions, just with bongos.

Now both of these causal stories can be described, broadly speaking, as showing that music can arouse emotions. But only the first, if it is the right one, shows that an expressive property of music, by merely being perceived, arouses the corresponding emotion in listeners. And it is only that claim that is at issue here. I never denied, nor do I deny now that the simple, unadorned statement is true that 'music arouses emotions.'

Which scenario *is* the right one? Well, I suspect the latter. However, the point of this exercise is not to convince the reader of that but just to suggest, to warn that it is frequently difficult, in specific instances, to tell just what it is in the music, and in collaboration with what other circumstances, that is doing the arousal, where arousal does take place. And that brings us to the question of circumstances.

'La Bamba' is a loaded example. We readily acquiesce in the effect on listeners Radford describes it as having because we have observed such occurrences ourselves, if not involving 'La Bamba,' then other instances of the genre. But let us remember *where* we have observed them: not in Lincoln Center for the Performing Arts or Wigmore Hall but in disco joints and Latin night spots. What part of 'La Bamba' 's effect is due, do you think, to its expressive musical properties, and what to the rest of what is going on in a disco or night club? Of course I cannot suggest, as a controlled experiment, a change of venue to Lincoln Center or Wigmore Hall. For the effect of 'La Bamba' in either of those two places of entertainment would hardly test the power of musical expressiveness either. Doubtless, a performance of 'La Bamba' slipped in between Beethoven's *Consecration of the House* and Mozart's D-minor Piano Concerto would produce surprise, outrage, amusement perhaps, but hardly gaiety and high spirits—and *that* would prove nothing at all.

Let me add one further point about 'La Bamba.' There is no musical composition in the Western art music tradition that is more gay and exuberant than the finale of Beethoven's Seventh Symphony, at least as I use such words, which is as aesthetic characterizations. Surely the Beethoven finale is orders of magnitude more gay and exuberant than 'La Bamba.' But if behavioral response to expressive properties is proportional to the intensity for the properties, then I would have to conclude that 'La Bamba' is more gay and exuberant than the Beethoven finale. This strikes me as a false conclusion, and suggests to me that the response Radford describes people as having to 'La Bamba' does not have much to do with the causal efficacy of its expressive properties of gaiety and exuberance. Let's face it: 'La Bamba' is a palpable red herring.

V

Where does this leave us? Well, for my part it leaves us with the conclusion that the expressive properties of music have a *tendency* to arouse, upon perception, the corresponding emotions, but that for a significant group of listeners, to which I belong, that tendency, although not extinguished, does not prevail. In a word, we are not aroused. But there is another group of listeners, to which Colin Radford belongs, who are aroused to melancholy by melancholy music, to happiness by happy music, and so on (although some in this group would claim to be aroused to a greater variety of emotions than does Radford, who only admits to sadness and happiness, as I understand him).

Where do we go from here? If it is just the case that some listeners experience music as I do, deeply moved by its beauty, but not moved to sadness by the sadness of the music, happiness by the happiness of the music, and so on, and some who experience it as Radford does, deeply moved to sadness by sad music, deeply moved to happiness by happy music, then the argument about whether or not music can or does arouse the garden-variety emotions is at an end. So be it.

Where we do *not* want to go, it seems to me, is now into a normative dispute as to which is the *better* way of responding to music. For one thing, it may not be in my power to listen to music Radford's way, or in Radford's power to listen to it my way. That is to say, we may have no choice in the matter, in which case it would be pointless for us to urge upon one another our own way of listening. Our urgings would be powerless to have their intended effects: here, as elsewhere ought implies can. And anyway, one suspects that such normative disputes, even if their conclusions could alter behavior, are, in the long run, going to be inconclusive. Doubtless, there are pay-offs in both ways of listening, at least in the eye of the beholder; and I doubt if a sermon on behalf of my own listening habits is going to be convincing to any but the already converted.

What does appear to me to be a fruitful program, is for each party to determine, for his or her respective musical experiences, what role the expressive properties of music play in the musical work. I can explain what I mean by quoting a passage from Radford in which, as I see it, he tries to do just that for his party. With regard to the last movement of Mozart's Sinfonie Concertante (K. 364), Radford writes:

does not the gaiety of this movement lift the spirits, actually making the listener feel gay and joyful? Is not this emotional response congruent with and elicited by the gaiety of the gay music, which music is the focus of one's attention? If this were not so, it is difficult to see why Mozart characteristically chose to end so many of his compositions with movements which, however beautiful or moving, are gay and thus tend not to leave listeners discomposed.[12]

The general point here seems to be that the role of expressive properties in musical composition is to be cashed out in terms of their arousing those emotions in listeners. Radford suggests that the only plausible reason why Mozart characteristically chose to end his compositions with light, cheerful finales—and this, by the way, is not true just of Mozart but of the classical period as a whole, including a great deal of early and middle Beethoven—is that he followed the good old vaudevillian aesthetic of 'Always leave 'em laughing.' What possible role, then, could there be for these expressive properties of Mozart finales for someone like me who doesn't laugh?

I have argued elsewhere that music analysis has neglected the 'syntactic' role expressive properties play in musical structure, and have suggested in that place specific syntactic roles for some expressive properties in certain kinds of sonata form.[13] That kind of syntactic role is my answer to the question of what other reason there might be for the preponderance of light-hearted finales in the classical period besides the 'Always leave 'em laughing' aesthetic. As I hear the mature classical style, these finales play a syntactic role in that style of achieving musical resolution and closure within the stylistic

[12] Ibid. 250.
[13] Peter Kivy, 'A New Music Criticism?' *The Monist*, 63 (1990), 260–7.

parameters peculiar to it. I cannot be more specific than that here for two reasons: there is not time, and, more importantly, I am still in the process of working out the bill of particulars for the musical syntax of expressive musical properties—it is part of an ongoing agenda. I can, however, add a trio of cases to the ones I have considered elsewhere, to ponder on and perhaps to amplify these few brief remarks.

A clear example of the kind of light-hearted classical finale Radford speaks of is to be found in the last movement of Mozart's great G-minor Quintet for strings. It is in G major, and light-hearted indeed—*so* light-hearted, in fact, that some listeners, myself included, find it a somewhat unsatisfactory conclusion.[14] The movement simply does not supply a completely successful, satisfying syntactic resolution to the tremendous musical tensions that Mozart has set up in the monumental and profoundly disturbing movements that come before, including the highly unusual (for that period) slow, minor introduction to the finale itself.

But it seems to me that for someone who reacts to the expressive properties of music the way Radford does, this finale *should* be musically satisfactory. For it is absolutely suffused with joy: and that supercharged joy certainly should be able to evoke joy in its listeners, if any musical joy can, thus fulfilling in spades the 'Always leave 'em laughing' aesthetic.

Perhaps Radford *does* find this movement a satisfactory conclusion to the work. If so it reveals something that should not be at all surprising, namely, that these two different ways of hearing and responding to music, Radford's and mine, are bound to result, somewhere down the line, in differing evaluations of certain works, or parts thereof.

Perhaps someone will object here that if my way of listening to music should result in my finding the finale to one of Mozart's— therefore the world's—greatest chamber works somewhat unsatisfactory in any respect, it merely proves the wrongheadedness of my listening habits. Without trying to answer this objection directly, let me just deflect it by providing a second case, where the shoe is on the other foot: a case in which I find a finale totally satisfying but in which I think a listener of Radford's stripe should find it not so.

Mozart's great Serenade in C Minor for winds (K. 388), which some of my readers may be more familiar with as arranged by the composer for string quintet (K. 406), has a very different kind of

---

[14] See e.g. Alfred Einstein, *Mozart: His Character, His Work*, trans. Arthur Mendel and Nathan Broder (London: Oxford University Press, 1945), 192.

finale from those of the Sinfonie Concertante and G-minor Quintet. It is a theme-and-variations, in C minor, and displays the same somber, anguished, searing expressive character as the first movement and the minuet. Only in the last 37 bars of this 354-bar movement (if the repeats are taken, as they certainly should be) is the somber, anguished, and searing character of the movement broken by a sudden modulation to the expressively bright tonic major.

My first point, with regard to this ending, is that I find it thoroughly satisfying, while I would think someone for whom the aesthetic payoff of expressive properties is in their power to arouse would not. My reason for saying that as an emotive stimulus, the coda to the last movement of K. 388 must fail, is that it is just too little too late. If the finale of the Sinfonie Concertante satisfies because it makes us cheerful and gay at the end, thus not 'discomposed,' as Radford would have it, the last movement of the C-minor Serenade must, expressed in that way, leave us much 'discomposed' indeed. For unless I grossly underestimate the emotive susceptibility of the normal human being, I do not see how someone having been bombarded with C-minor anguish for as long as a listening to K. 388 has been, and been aroused accordingly, can possibly be brought, in 37 measures of C major, from those depths of anguish to the state of exuberantly cheerful buoyancy that these final measures are expressive of. That seems to me a psychological impossibility; and thus I would think the ending of K. 388 must leave the emotive listener profoundly discomposed and dissatisfied with this Mozart ending, as I am somewhat dissatisfied by the ending of the G-minor Quintet.

But I find the close of K. 388 entirely satisfactory, because I hear it as a perfect 'syntactic' resolution; I hear it as what I would call an 'extended picardy third.' The picardy third, it will be known to some of my readers, is the major third used for the final chord of a composition in a minor mode. It is heard as giving a more decisive syntactic close than the minor, probably because from the point of view of music theory (*c.* 1550–1750) the major third was considered the more consonant interval. Furthermore, however, the picardy third is expressively more bright and cheerful than the minor. It not only is more consonant but is more emotively upbeat as well. And it is my view that that cheerful quality also contributes, syntactically, to the more decisive close that the picardy third gives, as opposed to the minor.

Nor do I think it can be plausibly claimed that the emotive brightness of the picardy third helps to provide a more decisive or restful close by making us feel happy upon hearing the final chord. For surely it seems beyond belief that even the most emotively susceptible listener will be made happy by the happiness of a single final chord, after having been made melancholy (say) by 300 bars of minor tonality and chromatic harmony preceding it. The picardy third illustrates, if anything does, what I have called here and elsewhere the syntactical role of the expressively cheerful in music, in making decisive closure; and it is this syntactical role that the expressive quality Mozart gives to the final 37 bars of K. 388 plays in my listening experience.

I can, I think, nail this point home, more completely, by contrasting the finale of K. 388 with yet another, again by Mozart, again in a minor key, and again in theme-and-variation form: the last movement of the D-minor String Quartet (K. 421). This finale, *Allegretto ma non troppo*, in 6/8 meter, has a melancholy and (to my ear) somewhat sinister quality to it, broken only once, in the penultimate variation, which is in the tonic major. The final variation returns to D minor, and we know we are pressing on to the close because Mozart increases the tempo to *più allegro*. In spite of the faster tempo the movement maintains its melancholy mien, and, indeed, the sinister quality, perhaps because of it, seems even more marked: like a witch's sabbath dance.

At measure 134 we begin to get unmistakable evidence, in the form of an obviously cadential figure, that the movement is winding down; and at measure 139 Mozart makes a cadence to a picardy third. A lesser composer would, undoubtedly, have ended here. But Mozart extends his close, over a pedal point in the cello, for 5 measures more, and completely *suppresses* the bright emotive tone of the extended picardy third, with a marvelous touch: a descending chromatic line beginning with a lowered seventh in the second violin.

FIG.2 W. A. Mozart String Quartet in D Minor (K. 421),
Fourth Movement.

Thus, while in the coda to the finale of K. 388 Mozart has *both* the syntactic force of the expressively bright major close, *and* the syntactic force of its more consonant harmonic character, in the final measures of K. 421 he intentionally suppresses the former while still maintaining the latter. The result, as might be predicted, is that the close of K. 421 is more restless, far less decisively final than the close of K. 388. But, let me hastily add, a more restless, less syntactically decisive conclusion by no means implies a less musically (or less aesthetically) successful one. Indeed, many, I imagine, will find the conclusion of K. 421 more subtle and more musically sophisticated than the rather straightforward, out front, and more conclusive one of the Serenade, and, a fortiori, than the bumptious finale of the G-minor Quintet.

VI

I have tried, with these examples, to spell out, all too briefly, what I mean by the syntactic function, in music, of its expressive properties. More I cannot do because, as I said previously, this is still a project in process, which brings me, therefore, to the only real conclusion I can make.

Argument, I think, has come to an end. It would be foolish to think I can convince Colin Radford that he is not made happy by happy music, or that he should not be, as it would be foolish for him to think he can convince me that happy music makes me happy, or that it should if it doesn't. That it has a *tendency* to do so I have already granted; and more than that, for myself, I cannot grant.

What is left, as a project of considerable interest and importance as I see it, is for Radford, and others who experience music as he does, to explore the ways in which the expressiveness of music functions aesthetically in their experience. What is left for me is the very same project against the background of my own musical experience. I think there is a lot left to be done, employment enough for all.

6

Experiencing the Musical Emotions

I want to discuss a problem that I have puzzled over from time to time for the past twenty years or more: that is, the nature of our experience of the emotions in music. Before I get to my problem, however, I thought I might take the time to give some historical background to it, for although these historical matters are well known within the small philosophical and musical communities in which I usually ply my trade, they might not be to the general reader. And acquaintance with them, although not essential to the understanding of my enterprise, will, nevertheless, be of great help.

Some History

If we want to be charitable towards our ignorance, we can say that the peculiarly intimate relationship music is supposed to have with the human emotions was already established philosophical doctrine in ancient Greece. I say charitable to our ignorance because we have little or no inkling of what Greek music sounded like. Whatever it was that the contemporaries of Plato and Aristotle did in the name of what our translators render as 'music,' we know nothing *of* it. And for us truly to understand what the two greatest philosophers of antiquity really were saying about music and the emotions would be tantamount to someone in 4000 AD trying to understand what I am saying in complete ignorance of the Western musical tradition from Pope Gregory to their own time. To understand the philosophy of music one must not only understand the philosophy but the *music*— the *sound* of the music—as well. And with regard to the sound of Plato's and Aristotle's 'music,' we are as the deaf.

For us the real history of speculation concerning music and the emotions begins at the end of the sixteenth century, with the writings of Vincenzo Galilei and the Florentine Camerata, which formed the theoretical basis for the first operas. It is already clear in these writings that there are two questions about what I will call musical 'expression': the question of what one means to say when describing music in emotive terms—sad, happy, angry, and so on, what I shall call the garden-variety emotions—and the question of what one is experiencing when one describes oneself as being deeply moved, emotionally aroused by music. I say that the two questions are already clear in these writings, but not, I hasten to add, necessarily clear to the writers themselves, who tended to blur and conflate them. They are clear to us, in hindsight; and the answer that, in hindsight, they can be perceived to be giving, is that music is sad or happy or whatever in virtue of arousing sadness or happiness in the listener, and emotively moving in virtue of the very same thing. In other words, to say that a passage of music is sad (for example) is to say that it has the dispositional property of making competent listeners sad, and to say that someone is deeply moved by a passage of sad music is to say that that person has been moved to sadness by it.

That basic view of musical expression endured pretty much unchanged through the end of the eighteenth century. What changed was the apparatus by which music was supposed to accomplish the emotive arousal. For the early theorists of music drama it was, not surprisingly, a form of empathy, for the seventeenth and eighteenth centuries it was, again not surprisingly, the mechanical paraphernalia of Descartes's highly influential *Passions of the Soul*. Towards the end of the eighteenth century, especially, but not entirely in Britain, Cartesian psychology gave way to the association of ideas, as systematized and disseminated by David Hartley in his *Observations on Man*, with empathy theories a perennial contender now and again.

The first major philosophical departure from this 200-year-old hegemony of arousal theories of musical expression was effected by Arthur Schopenhauer in *The World as Will and Idea*. It is no exaggeration to assert that Schopenhauer single-handedly put music on the philosophical map in a major way. He was the first philosopher of impressive stature fully to endorse absolute music as a fine art, and ranked it as the highest. But, for present purposes, his most significant accomplishment was to relocate musical expressiveness: what, that is to say, we ascribe to music when we call it sad, or happy, or whatever, so to speak, *in* the music, not as a disposition to produce an emotive effect in the listener but as a *bona fide* perceptual quality of the music itself. He famously said that music is an image of the metaphysical will: *Abbild des Willens selbst*.[1] As such, music, and, in particular, melody, 'relates the most secret history of the intellectually enlightened will, portrays every agitation, every effort, every movement of the will, everything which the faculty of reason summarizes under the wide and negative concept of feeling.' 'Hence,' Schopenhauer continues, 'it has always been said that music is the language of feeling and of passion . . .'[2]

It would be useful, perhaps, to pause for a moment over Schopenhauer's view of musical expression. It really does turn a historical corner.

As readers will know, Schopenhauer's entire philosophy of art is embedded in an imposing metaphysical scheme that can have little if any interest to the contemporary philosopher except as an important stage in intellectual history and, in particular, the history of the Romantic movement in Germany. But denuded of this metaphysical shroud there is a living core that has the firm outline of a contemporary analysis, as we shall see in a little while.

Schopenhauer clearly wanted to put expressiveness into music as a positive, perceived quality, not merely a disposition to produce what I call the garden-variety emotions: joy, anger, melancholy, love, fear, and so on. The most readily available feature at the time for serving this purpose was representation. And so Schopenhauer turned to that concept, I suggest, as the only one available to him to give to music emotive features as part of its perceived phenomenal surface and structure.

Furthermore, in locating the expressiveness of music in the music itself rather than in its propensity for arousing the garden-variety emotions in the listener, Schopenhauer was by no means denying that music has an emotional impact upon human beings, that it moves them deeply. He thought, indeed, that just because of its representational relation to the most fundamental concepts of will and emotion, of all of the fine arts it has the most profound emotional effect on us. As he puts this point: 'For this reason the effect of music is so very much more powerful and penetrating than is that of the other arts, for those others speak only of the shadow, but music of the essence.'[3]

---

[1] Arthur Schopenhauer, *Die Welt als Wille und Vorstellung, Sämtliche Werke* (Stuttgart: Suhrkamp, 1960), i. 359.

[2] Arthur Schopenhauer, *The World as Will and Representation*, trans. E. F. J. Payne (Indian Hills, Colo.: Falcon's Wing Press, 1958), i. 259.

[3] Ibid. 257.

To sum up, then, metaphysics aside, Schopenhauer was the first thinker of major stature to see clearly that musical expressiveness belongs *in* the *music*.[4] But in so doing he strongly affirmed, nevertheless, music's power to move the listener deeply. In other words Schopenhauer separated off, in his theory of musical expression, the question of music's expressiveness from that of music's emotional effect for the first time. He thereby set the stage for contemporary philosophical analysis, and for the position I am going to stake out in this chapter.

The next important event in our history was the publication, in 1854, of a small volume that has had an effect on the philosophy of music far out of proportion to its modest size. I refer to Eduard Hanslick's *Vom Musikalisch-Schönen*, called by its first English translator, Gustav Cohen, *The Beautiful in Music*, and, by its more recent one, Geoffrey Payzant, *On the Musically Beautiful*. This work went through ten editions during its author's lifetime and has had both a positive and a negative effect on subsequent thinking.

On the positive side, Hanslick's healthy skepticism with regard to the extravagant claims made for music's vaunted emotive powers, including Schopenhauer's, brought the subject of musical expression down to earth. Hanslick introduced plain-speaking, common sense, and good philosophical instincts to a subject that resembled more the Orphic mysteries than a branch of rational enquiry.

But on the negative side Hanslick, perhaps in overcompensation, denied to music even the most minimal power to embody the garden-variety emotions. He affirmed, correctly I think, that music does not arouse those emotions, at least as part of its legitimate aesthetic effect. But he argued too, that music could not be said to possess them as perceptual features either, which seems plainly false. Like Schopenhauer he envisioned only one possibility in this regard: that music might embody the garden-variety emotions by somehow representing them. And against this possibility he argued, famously, that since there is absolutely no consensus as to what emotive predicate, in any given instance, characterizes a musical passage, music

---

[4] I say that Schopenhauer was the first *major* thinker to see clearly the distinction between musical expressiveness and musical arousal. But, in my view, he was not the first *thinker* to do so. That honor, I have argued previously, belongs to the eighteenth-century composer and prolific writer on musical subjects, Johann Mattheson. On this see Peter Kivy, 'Mattheson as Philosopher of Art,' *The Musical Quarterly*, 70 (1984), repr. in Peter Kivy, *The Fine Art of Repetition: Essays in the Philosophy of Music* (Cambridge: Cambridge University Press, 1993).

cannot sensibly be said to represent any emotion at all. 'Can we call it the representation of a specific feeling when nobody knows what feeling was actually represented?' Hanslick asks rhetorically.[5] The answer he expects is 'No.'

Hanslick's argument, if good, is good against *any* theory of emotive expressiveness in music. But it is not a good argument because the main premiss on which it is based is palpably false. There *is* substantial agreement at least within broad boundaries as to what garden-variety emotions various passages of expressive music are expressive of, as anyone can demonstrate to himself by playing well-chosen passages to competent listeners and asking for their responses. So obvious is this fact that I will say no more about it.

For the rest of the nineteenth century, and a good part of the twentieth, philosophical speculation with regard to music remained in the doldrums. England produced, in 1880, one masterpiece, Edmund Gurney's *The Power of Sound*, unjustly neglected because of its turgid prose and unwieldy dimensions. The rest is silence until, in 1941, Susanne K. Langer revived, single-handedly, the philosophy of music in her book, *Philosophy in a New Key*. It is remarkable that this book should have had the effect it did, given that only one of the ten chapters had to do with music. But the title of the book was, after all, a musical one, suggesting that music was at the heart of the enterprise. In any case, it is what Langer said about music in that book that had the profoundest effect, and has caused it to be remembered.

It was Susanne Langer who first singled out Schopenhauer as a pioneer in the theory of musical expression, writing of him that 'his novel contribution to the present issue was certainly his treatment of music as an impersonal, negotiable, real semantic, a symbolism with a content of ideas, instead of an overt sign of somebody's emotional condition.'[6] Her major point was that Schopenhauer, like herself, located musical expressiveness in the music, as a perceived aspect of it, rather than representing it as, in her words, 'a stimulus to evoke emotions . . .' Her own view was that music embodies emotions as symbol. 'Music,' she wrote, 'is not the cause or the cure of feelings, but their *logical expression* . . .'[7]

---

[5] Eduard Hanslick, *On the Musically Beautiful: A Contribution Towards the Revision of the Aesthetics of Music*, trans. Geoffrey Payzant (Indianapolis: Hackett, 1986), 14.

[6] Susanne K. Langer, *Philosophy in a New Key: A Study in the Symbolism of Reason, Rite and Art*, 2nd edn. (New York: Mentor Books, 1979), 186–7.

[7] Ibid. 185.

Langer's notion that music is, as she called it, an 'unconsummated symbol' of the emotive life, in virtue of an isomorphism to it, has not fared well in the philosophical community, and did not, right from the start, although it found a good deal of sympathy in musical circles. For myself, her denial that music could embody the specific emotions that we identify there without trouble, as a matter of course, is fatal to her project, and I will say no more about it except to say again that Langer reintroduced music to the Anglo-American philosophical world as a significant object of scrutiny, and preserved Schopenhauer's insight that musical expressiveness resides in the music, not in the listener. For that she has my praise and thanks.

One more event of recent history requires mention before I can bring these remarks to the cutting edge, and that was the publication, in 1956, of Leonard Meyer's *Emotion and Meaning in Music*. It requires mention not merely because of its importance to the present enterprise but for its significance in my own intellectual life. As I have said on other occasions, *Emotion and Meaning in Music* taught me that one could write philosophically about music without writing nonsense; and although Meyer neither is nor aspires to be a philosopher, his book had deep philosophical import.

Of the many points of philosophical interest in *Emotion and Meaning in Music*, none is more germane to my problem than Meyer's insistence on the division between arousal and embodiment of emotions in music. On this, Meyer wrote, in 1956:

a clear distinction must be maintained between the emotions felt by the . . . listener or critic—the emotional response itself—and the emotional states denoted by different aspects of the musical stimulus. . . . And it may well be that when a listener reports that he felt this or that emotion, he is describing the emotions he believes the passage is supposed to indicate, not anything which he himself has experienced.[8]

The clear distinction Meyer urges us to preserve, between emotion felt, and emotion in the music, 'depicted,' as he says, is, of course, the selfsame distinction that I suggested was already implicit in the writings of the Camerata in the late sixteenth century, and finally made explicit by Schopenhauer in 1819. Meyer reaffirms it with particular emphasis and conviction. Furthermore, his suggestion that listeners may well mistake one for the other, the emotion depicted for the

---

[8] Leonard B. Meyer, *Emotion and Meaning in Music* (Chicago: University of Chicago Press, 1956), 8.

emotion felt, is an intriguing one, and I shall take it up again when I come to the view I wish to develop here. For although I do not subscribe to it in letter, in spirit it anticipates what I aim to propose.

As Things Now Stand

I took up the problem of musical expression in the late 1970s and published a book on it in 1980 called *The Corded Shell*. In that book I tried to give an explanation for how music is expressive of the garden-variety emotions. I had the advantage, which my predecessors did not, of advances in analytic philosophy that provided more options than merely representation or symbolic content as alternatives to a dispositional account of musical expressiveness. More and more, philosophers of art were coming to realize that it made good sense—good metaphysical sense—to think of emotive properties in music as perceptual properties pure and simple; or rather, pure, if not simple. The view was summed up, in a classic essay, and with characteristic puckishness, by the Wittegensteinian philosopher, O. K. Bouwsma, when he quipped that: 'For the sadness is to the music rather like the redness to the apple, than it is like the burp to the cider.'[9] Or perhaps like the sadness to the St Bernard's face, an analogy I found much use for in my book.[10]

In any case, a consensus developed, in which I shared, that the expressive properties of music, the garden variety emotions, were heard properties of music, its *expressiveness*, not dispositions to arouse emotions in listeners. My own view of how music did embody such expressive properties was rejected by some, accepted, at least partially, by others. But the central thesis of *The Corded Shell*, that expressiveness is in the music, the redness to the apple, not the burp to the cider, was accepted by almost the entire community of British and American philosophers interested in the question.

However, part of the argument of *The Corded Shell* consisted in a vigorous rejection of the view that music could, in any *aesthetically*

---

[9] O. K. Bouwsma, 'The Expression Theory of Art,' in O. K. Bouwsma, *Philosophical Essays* (Lincoln, Nebr.: University of Nebraska Press, 1969), 49.

[10] The view that affective qualities are part of the perceptual world was given an elaborate statement much earlier in Charles Hartshorne's remarkable book, *The Philosophy and Psychology of Sensation*, where he wrote, for example: 'Thus, the "gaiety" of yellow (the peculiar highly specific gaiety) is the yellowness of the yellow' (*The Philosophy and Psychology of Sensation* (1934), reissued by Kennikat Press (Port Washington, NY: 1967)), 7.

relevant way, arouse the garden-variety emotions it was expressive of, or any others for that matter; in other words I denied that sad music makes people sad, happy music makes them happy, and so on. This aspect of my view was roundly criticized, and, much to my surprise I was put down as someone who must listen to and participate in music in a purely cerebral way, completely uninvolved, emotionally, in what I listened to and performed. I was amused as well as surprised by this because anyone who is acquainted with me personally, as a listener or musician, knows that quite the opposite is true. I am an emoter from way back. But I was also shocked because I realized that *if* the view expressed in *The Corded Shell* implied that listening to music is not or should not be an emotionally moving experience, it must be a mistaken view.

At this point it became clear that the question of musical expression was becoming a tripartite one. There was consensus that music was expressive of the garden-variety emotions in virtue of possessing them as heard properties. But three further questions remained on which there was, and still is, substantial disagreement. The first question is how, by what process, music is able to embody the garden-variety emotions. The second question is what role these expressive properties play in the musical structure to which they belong. And the third is, given that the garden-variety emotions are, as expressive properties, in the music, not the listener, what is one saying when one says one is deeply moved by the music?

In my own case, I ceased to be interested in the first question, although it has remained a frequently written about one. I thought, and still do think that, given the general consensus about the metaphysical status of music's expressive properties, the really interesting and compelling projects are to spell out what exactly these properties are doing, aesthetically, in the musical composition, and, given their status as perceptual properties, not dispositional ones to make people sad, happy, angry, and the like, how music can still be said to be a deeply moving, emotionally involving experience. It is the third of those questions that I want to address and, I hope, make some progress with.

In the next section I will present my own view of *how music moves*, as it was formulated in 1987, and, later, reiterated in 1990.[11] And I

---

[11] See Peter Kivy, 'How Music Moves', in Philip Alperson (ed.), *What is Music?: An Introduction to the Philosophy of Music* (New York: Haven, 1987), later reprinted, with revisions, in Peter Kivy, *Music Alone: Philosophical Reflections on the Purely Musical Experience* (Ithaca: Cornell University Press, 1990).

will present, as well, the view that has been developed, partly in opposition to mine, by my good friends and most valued critics, Stephen Davies and Jerrold Levinson. In the final section I shall develop my own views further, with the intention of showing the two opposing positions, mine and theirs, closer together than they might heretofore have been thought to be. On, then, to the apparent philosophical stand-off.

Oppositions

I should begin by laying my cards on the table. When I argued against the notion that music moves us by making us sad when it is sad, happy when it is happy, and when I provided my own account of how music moves us emotionally, I subscribed—and still do—to a philosophical analysis of the garden-variety emotions, that is sometimes called the 'cognitive' analysis or theory. According to this analysis when I am sad (say), my sadness takes what philosophers have called, after Brentano, an intentional object. I am sad *about* something or other: sad about the death of a loved one, or not passing an examination, or whatever. It normally does not make sense to say that I am just sad, but not about anything at all, although that is not to deny that there might be bizarre or unusual cases of that kind.

Second, the cognitive analysis has it that there must be a relevant belief or set of beliefs in place for it to make sense to say of someone, in the ordinary cases, that he or she is said. If she is sad about the death of her father, she must, of course, believe that he has died, and that will doubtless involve other beliefs. Of course her beliefs might be false, and her father still alive, in which case, the intentional object of her sadness, his death, is a non-existent intentional object. But no matter: the intentional object of a child's fear might be ghosts and goblins.

Third, there is frequently a feeling of some identifiable kind when one is in a particular emotional state, although this need not necessarily be the case nor need the feeling be of the same quality in each instance of someone's being sad, or angry, or afraid. Thus, people characteristically describe fear as involving a sinking feeling in the pit of the stomach, or a constricted feeling in the chest. But I have been afraid, for a long time, that a friend of mine is so depressed over his divorce that he might attempt suicide; and I can identify no particular subjective state at all, anything like a sinking feeling in my stomach, or a constricted feeling in my chest when, now and then, I become aware of this fear, or express it to someone.

Fourth, the intentional objects of our emotions have a good deal to do with how we feel when we are in one emotional state or another. If I love my new Lorée violet wood oboe, and I love my neighbor's poodle, and I love the woman I live with, it is, needless to say, *love* that I am experiencing in each case. But if one asks me what it *feels* like to love an oboe, or love a dog, or love a woman, I doubt if I am going to get very far by talking about visceral sensations. I think the best I can do is to say that it is *love*, and to say what it *is* I love, that is to say, what the intentional object of that love is. To love an oboe is to love a musical instrument, to love a poodle is to love a very responsive pet, to love the woman with whom one lives is (frequently) to love a sexual partner. *That* is what the feeling of love is in each of these cases, and, unless one is a poet, that is probably all that *can* be said.

I shall return to the role of intentional objects in differentiating the feeling component of the emotions in a while; it is very important to my argument. For now, though, I will simply say that one here has the bare bones of the analysis of the emotions that I take for granted in my account of how music moves us. But before I continue with that, one further preliminary remark is necessary.

The question I am raising is how we are emotionally aroused by what the nineteenth century called absolute music, and what I like to call 'music alone': that is to say, music without text or title or programme; or, in other words, pure instrumental music. It is important to remember this because when the resources of language are added to the musical work, the terms of the argument are radically changed. I have no quarrel, for example, with someone who says that when he attends a performance of *La traviata*, he experiences real and intense sorrow over the death of Violetta, or that when he hears the great aria of reconciliation that Friar Laurence sings in the finale of Berlioz's 'dramatic symphony,' *Romeo and Juliet*, he experiences that feeling of true love that the good friar is attempting to instill in the hearts of Capulets and Montagues. This is not to say that there is no philosophical problem in just how real emotions of sorrow and love can be aroused by the fates of fictional characters. There is; it has been written about extensively in the last twenty years or so, and I will return to it briefly further on. But the presence of language, with all its potential for conveying concepts, and the presence of fully delineated characters such Violetta and Afredo, Romeo and Juliet and Friar Laurence provide materials for arousal of the garden-variety emotions far exceeding anything that can be reasonably postulated in absolute music. And that is why absolute music poses a problem far beyond that of opera, oratorio, song, and programme music to those who wish to claim that it arouses the garden-variety emotions, or even to someone like myself who seeks *another* way to understand the power of music alone to move us emotionally.

My problem is this. In the normal case, when I am angry at my Uncle Charlie, say, there is an intentional object of my anger: my uncle. There are also things that I believe about Uncle Charlie that make my anger understandable: I believe that he behaves badly to Aunt Bella, that he cheats at pinochle, and that he engages in shady business deals. In other words, all the pieces have to be in place that are required by the conceptual analysis or theory of the emotions to which I subscribe. If an emotion is to be aroused, that is to say, there must be an Uncle Charlie kind of explanation in place for it.

My problem with the claim that absolute music is moving in virtue of arousing the garden-variety emotions is that I can find none of the materials for an Uncle Charlie explanation present in that kind of music, except in the aesthetically irrelevant cases such as being made sad by a piece of music because it has sad 'associations' for you—the 'our song' phenomenon. (It was Hanslick's problem too, and his most penetrating insight.) So the requirement that I set for myself when trying to come up with a plausible way in which to understand how absolute music moves us emotionally is that it fulfil all the conditions of an Uncle Charlie explanation, as laid out just now. Here is what I came up with.

Well, if I am emotionally moved by music, the first thing I suppose I must look for is an intentional object of my emotion. And what could be more plausible than to say that if the music is stirring an emotion in me, it is the *music* that is the intentional object of my emotion? After all, it is Uncle Charlie's shenanigans that are moving me to anger, which, obviously, makes *Uncle Charlie* the intentional object of my anger.

What is it in the music, then, that is moving me, and what is it moving me *to*? Here I can turn only to my own experience of music. And what that experience suggests to me is that I am deeply moved, emotionally stimulated to a very high degree by the beauty of music; by, in other words, how wonderful the music is. The beauty of great music, then, is the intentional object of my emotion.

But what *is* this deep emotion, this emotionally intense feeling that is stirred in me by beautiful music? It is not fear or hope, hate or happiness. So what is *it*? What is its *name*?

If I say, which is true, that it is a nameless emotion, my response is likely to be disappointing or upsetting: disappointing because I am admitting that I cannot solve the problem I set out to solve; upsetting if one thinks I am reverting to talk about some occult, ineffable aesthetic emotion that used to be the stock-in-trade of those who gave a bad name to aesthetics, both among philosophers *and* artists.

But to say that the emotional excitement stimulated in me by the music is a nameless emotion is not to mark it out as in any way mysterious or ineffable. Lots of perfectly ordinary emotions have just that nameless character. If I am moved by a sunset, or the face of a child, or a kind and generous action, not done to me but to someone else, those emotions have no names: they are not sadness or fear, anger or gratitude: their names are their descriptions. I can do no better in identifying them than to say: 'the feeling one gets in watching the sun go down, seeing the face of a child, hearing about a benevolent act to a perfect stranger'; three different intentional objects, three different emotions—but not three different names. In a perfectly benign sense these emotions are nameless, but hardly ineffable or occult. And one is hardly admitting either ignorance or defeat in recognizing the obvious: that many emotions are differentiated neither by name, nor by some special subjective qualia—merely by the objects that arouse them.

And that brings us back again to the emotion I am moved to by the beauty of music. Is it one emotion all the time? After all, it has the same intentional object all the time: the beauty of music. But that doesn't seem right. And it isn't. I do not experience the same emotional response to Bach as to Mozart, to Brahms as to Beethoven. Neither do I experience the same emotion when I am moved by the quiet opening of the slow movement of Mozart's 'Jupiter' Symphony as the one when I am moved by the blazing coda of the finale.

Not to worry, though. The intentional object of these various emotions is, under one description, the same object, the beauty of the music. But of course, under different descriptions there are many different intentional objects. And that makes all the difference in how we characterize the emotions, just as in the case of the sunset, the child's face, and the benevolent act. When our intentional object of musical appreciation is the muted, simple, aria-like opening of the slow movement of the 'Jupiter,' the intentional object of the emotion we are moved to is quite different from the one that moves us in the coda to the finale, where Mozart, in that tremendous feat of contrapuntal virtuosity, puts the four themes of the movement together in the climactic fugato passage. And, needless to say, when my intentional object is some similar feat in a fugue by Bach, it is, by virtue of everything that makes Bach's one style, Mozart's another, a very different intentional object, even though in both cases it bears the same name: 'quadruple counterpoint.'

It may be objected to the view I am defending here that the emotion I claim music arouses is not the sort of thing that can take an intentional object, as I claim it does. One is moved *by* the beauty of music, it might be claimed, the way one is exhilarated by a cold shower or a parachute jump. One is not moved *about* the music, or the shower, or the parachute jump.

Traditionally, the distinction in this regard is between emotions and feelings or sensations. The former take intentional objects, the latter two do not. So is the subjective state I am talking about, which the beauty of music occasions, an emotion, or a feeling, or sensation? If the former, then the beauty could be its intentional object, if the latter it could not be.

But I think it would be a mistake to let the question turn on whether or not the subjective state *is* an emotion. For if I should decide in the affirmative, which is indeed my view, it would, of course, appear to be begging the question in my favor. Rather, we should approach it from the other end. What kind of an experience *is* the experience of musical beauty? When we can answer that question, we can then go on to answer the question of whether that experience is going to arouse a subjective state that *does* take an intentional object, or one that does not.

Unfortunately, I cannot go deeply into these matters here, although some of my views in this regard are sprinkled around throughout the essays in this volume. I have, as a matter of fact, spent some considerable part of my career as a philosopher trying to convince people that music is *not* like a cold shower or a parachute jump, which give you a quick rush of exhilaration, but a thing of the mind, which excites through one's perceiving that musical events of beauty or high musical excellence are taking place. To put it briefly, because that is the only way it can be put in a chapter of this length, the musical emotion that the music I take to be beautiful or excellent in some other musical way arouses in me is an enthusiasm, an intense musical excitement *about* what I am hearing. Nor, as far as I can see, is there anything either philosophically wrong or ungrammatical about that statement. A pain cannot be 'about' what causes it. But excitement or enthusiasm can be, and in the musical cases it *is*. So if the question of whether the subjective state I have been talking about is an emotion or not turns on whether it can take an intentional object, the answer seems to be that it *is* an emotion, because it *can* take an intentional object.

Until someone comes along to show me that what I am talking about is *not* an emotion, I will go on talking about it as an emotion. The term 'emotion,' as has frequently been pointed out, is pretty fuzzy around the edges: certainly fuzzy enough to encompass musical 'enthusiasm' and 'excitement.'

To sum up, then, what moves us in music is the myriad of ways in which music can be beautiful—or, to avoid putting too much weight on the concept of beauty, the myriad of ways music can be supremely successful, *musically*. And the beliefs listeners hold, that make it plausible to say that they are being emotionally stirred *by* music, are beliefs *that* the music is wonderful, beautiful, supremely successful in all the ways that it can be.

But you should not think that I am saying a person's beliefs about music must be informed by music-theoretic concepts or knowledge of style at the musicological level. A person need not believe that he is listening to quadruple counterpoint to be moved by the coda of Mozart's great fugal finale. He need not know what counterpoint is, or a fugue. He does have to have some beliefs about what he is listening to, and that what he is listening to is beautiful, or wonderful, or marvelous. I have spelled this out in greater detail elsewhere.[12] I will amplify my view somewhat in the final section, but for now I will leave it alone, in its present sketchy state, and go on to examine the rival view—the one which, in the end, I hope to make some accommodation with.

The view that opposes my own is succinctly put by Stephen Davies in his recent book, *Musical Meaning and Expression*. He writes that 'sad music might lead some listeners to feel sad, even if music's

---

[12] See Kivy, *Music Alone*, chs. 5 and 6.

expressiveness is not to be explained by its power to awaken that response.'[13] Jerrold Levison had already put forward such a view,[14] and he has now reiterated it in more detailed form, averring that 'Musical expressiveness should be seen to belong unequivocally to the music—to be a property or aspect thereof—and not to the listener . . .' while insisting, nevertheless, that 'when perceived or registered by a listener, evocation of feeling or affect . . . naturally, if not inevitably, ensues . . .'[15]

I take it, then, that Davies, Levison, and I agree that music is expressive of the garden-variety emotions in virtue of the emotive qualities we recognize in it. We disagree in that Davies and Levinson think music is moving, emotionally, in virtue of the expressive qualities arousing corresponding emotions in us, whereas I believe it is moving in quite a different way, already described.

There are two aspects of the views of Davies and Levinson that interest me. One is the explanation they offer—and here they do not agree with one another—of how the expressive properties of music arouse emotions. The second—and here it is not clear whether they agree or not—is how the experience of these aroused emotions is described: that is to say, what it is like, what it feels like, to be made sad by sad music, happy by happy music, and so forth.

The first question is a very involved one, and would require a chapter devoted to it alone. However, it is the second question, anyway, that I am concerned with here. Nevertheless, I do want to say a few words about the question of how, on Davies' and Levinson's views, the expressive qualities of music are supposed to arouse emotions in listeners, as preliminary to the description they give of how the aroused emotions are to be characterized.

It might be appropriate to describe Davies' theory as the 'contagion' theory of emotive arousal, Levinson's as a version, at least, of some kind of empathy theory. Very briefly, what Davies suggests is that if we saturate our environments, so to speak, with objects expressive of sadness or happiness, the only two emotions, by the way, that Davies thinks music can arouse, we will end up feeling

[13] Stephen Davies, *Musical Meaning and Expression* (Ithaca: Cornell University Press, 1994), 279.

[14] Jerrold Levinson, 'Music and Negative Emotion,' in Levinson, *Music, Art, and Metaphysics: Essays in Philosophical Aesthetics* (Ithaca: Cornell University Press, 1990), 306–35.

[15] Jerrold Levinson, 'Musical Expressiveness,' in Levinson, *The Pleasures of Aesthetics: Philosophical Essays* (Ithaca: Cornell University Press, 1996), 91–2.

these emotions ourselves. He uses the example of the frowning tragic and smiling comic masks, and he writes: 'A person surrounding herself with masks of the tragic type (or working in a factory in which they are made, say) might find the atmosphere depressing and catch the sad mood; a person surrounding herself with masks of the comic type might be inclined to feel more cheerful than otherwise would be the case.'[16]

Levinson, on the other hand, suggests that we are moved to the garden-variety emotions in music by hearing them in the music as the expression of some imagined persona, somewhat in the way we are made sad by, as it is sometimes put, identifying with a fictional character in a novel or a play who is feeling and expressing her sadness. As Levinson puts his view in one place:

Since a listener is standardly made sad by apprehending and then identifying with sadness in the music, naturally the thought of that emotion is present to the mind concurrent with whatever is felt. In the second place, identifying with the music involves initially the cognitive act of imagining that the music is either *itself* a sad individual or else the *audible expression* of somebody's sadness. In the third place, such identification involves subsequently a cognitive act of imagining that one, too, is sad—that it is *one's own* sadness the music expresses—and thus, however amorphously, that one has something to be sad about.[17]

In his latest statement of his view, Levinson suggests that 'different mechanisms may be in effect in different cases [of arousal], or with different modes of listening.' He suggests three such. But among them remains, most prominently, the one in which the listener identifies with a musical persona, as he now puts it, 'consciously recognizing and identifying a passage's E-ness, and then reacting to that, empathetically, sympathetically, or antipathetically.'[18]

I find neither of these mechanism for the arousal of the garden-variety emotions by music at all plausible, although Davies' possesses, I think, a kernel of truth which, in the event, tends to mislead. The kernel of truth, to take Davies's view first, is this. It might well be that the comic mask has a *tendency* to make folks happy, the tragic mask a *tendency* to make them sad. It might very well be that music expressive of happiness *tends* to make folks happy, music expressive of sadness to make them sad. And it might very well be

[16] Davies, *Musical Meaning and Expression*, 303–4.
[17] Levinson, 'Music and Negative Emotion,' 321–2.
[18] Levinson, 'Musical Expressiveness', 114.

that my car has a tendency to swerve to the left. The question is under what conditions do these *tendencies* become *effective*?[19]

My car does have a tendency to swerve to the left. But the tendency only makes itself manifest at speeds over 100 miles per hour; and as I never drive even close to such speed it is a tendency I may safely ignore, even though it does indeed exist. Likewise, the tendency of the tragic mask to make one sad may be real enough. But recall Davies' example: 'A person *surrounding* herself with masks of the tragic type (or *working in a factory in which they are made*, say) might find the atmosphere depressing and catch the sad mood . . .' (my italics). If *that is* what it takes to effectuate the tragic mask's tendency to make one sad, then one can each safely ignore it and hang the mask in his or her parlor without fear of melancholia, all the while recognizing that the tragic mask *has* that *tendency*.

Now what of sad music? Well I dare say it may have a tendency to make folks sad, as Davies avers. And I thoroughly concur that the tragic mask is, in this regard, a good analogy; but so also, then, is the analogy with the *conditions* under which the tendency of the tragic mask to sadden us can be rendered operative. I am prepared to admit that if I am exposed, eight hours a day, five days a week, to unremittingly sad music. I may well be driven to melancholy (if not to madness). I presume that would be the musical counterpart to working in a tragic mask factory. Why, however, should the philosopher of art be the least bit impressed by this melancholy conclusion? As a philosopher of art I am concerned with the experience of music under the conditions which customarily prevail when normal people listen to it for purposes of aesthetic gratification. I am glad I do not work in a tragic mask factory (although working in a philosophy department presents its own psychological hazards). And I am certainly glad I have not been locked in a room by a mad psychologist and made to listen to unremittingly sad music eight hours a day, five days a week, in an attempt to prove that the stuff has a *tendency* to make folks sad. Of course it might, and under these bizarre conditions the tendency may very well become effective. But in the circumstances in which

---

[19] I base my analysis of the concept of 'tendencies' on that of T. S. Champlin, in 'Tendencies'. All the ground I cover here, in arguing against Davies, was covered in 1993, in arguing against a similar view of Colin Radford's. See Peter Kivy, 'Auditor's Emotions: Contention, Concession and Compromise,' repr. in this volume as Ch. 5. My article came out in time for Davies to mention in *Musical Meaning and Expression*, but 'too recent to be discussed here' (282 n.). I therefore have no way of knowing what response he may have.

you and I listen to music, that tendency is, I am happy to say, ineffectual, at least in my experience.

Moving on, now, to Levinson's mechanism for arousal, let me begin by suggesting why it is at least initially attractive. Most people, both among theorists and the laity, agree that works of fictional art arouse the life emotions as part of their intended literary effect. Furthermore, most agree that one of the principal ways this is accomplished is by identification and empathy with the characters inhabiting the worlds of these works. That this explanation might be extended to works of absolute music as well satisfies our natural desire for explanatory unity and parsimony. All things being equal, one explanation for two phenomena is much to be preferred to two. Thus, the attempt of Levinson and others to explain how music moves us emotionally by averring that it does so in virtue of arousing the garden-variety emotions, and explaining this arousal in listeners through identification and empathy with some postulated or imagined musical persona joins two seemingly disparate art forms, literary fiction and absolute music, in a single theory, at least as regards this one aesthetic phenomenon, satisfying at once the theoretic criteria of unity and parsimony. That's the good news.

The bad news is that the explanation is problematic at both ends, the musical end most particularly. At the fictional end, it is far from clear, indeed a much-visited paradox, how it can make sense for us to feel real life emotions in response to the trials and tribulations of made-up, non-existent persons. It is perfectly obvious why and how I come to identify with, and feel sympathy with or for a person whom I know, and who I am told has suffered some misfortune or other. And if I come to learn that I was misinformed, that that person did not suffer that misfortune after all, it is perfectly clear why and how my feeling of sympathy would evaporate. When the appropriate beliefs are in place, I feel the emotion; when they are gone, the emotion goes with them. But the appropriate beliefs, apparently, are *never* there when we are feeling sympathy with or sorry for a fictional character. For we do not believe *anyone* has really suffered a misfortune, as we do not believe the person in question exists at all. To quote the man who, so far as I know, was the first to state this paradox: 'What's Hecuba to him or he to Hecuba,/That he should weep for her?'

There have been a number of resolutions suggested for what has come to be known in the literature as the paradox of 'feeling for fiction.' This is not the place to rehearse them. Suffice it to say that even if one could find direct and convincing analogues to fictional characters in absolute music, using such analogues to explain the purported power of absolute music to arouse the garden-variety emotions in listeners would hardly be unproblematic: the paradox of feeling for fiction would have to be dealt with in the musical cases as well as in the literary ones. It comes with the territory.

The paradox of feeling for fiction has not, however, succeeded in dislodging from very many people the belief that they feel real sorrow, real joy, real anger, real fear over the fates of fictional characters. So if we really could find believable counterparts to the fictional characters of literature in absolute music some palpable progress would have been made in convincing skeptics like me that absolute music, by identification and empathy, really does arouse the garden-variety emotions.

Well, if there are really, in absolute music, counterparts to Anna Karenina and Hamlet, Hans Castorp and Willie Loman for us to identify with, there is something very peculiar about them. They all have the same name: Persona. Notice that the purveyors of this literary approach to music alone cannot even get themselves to call this musical wraith a *person*, or even tell us its sex. So Latin is resorted to—the traditional language of philosophical abstractions—and we are asked to identify not with Anna Karenina or Hamlet, Hans Castorp or Willie Loman, but with, as Levinson describes him or her or it, 'an indefinite agent, the music's persona.'[20] One is being asked to identify with an 'indefinite agent.' One might just as well try to form a personal attachment to Spinoza's God, or cozy up to a barber's pole.

Now of course we all know why the musical Persona cannot be Anna Karenina. Tolstoy had all the resources of language with which to form the warm, living, three-dimensional character with whom we identify, and all those resources to paint us the picture of her misfortunes. Music alone cannot provide that. The analyst who tries to tease a persona and her misfortunes out of a symphony or a string quartet is between Scylla and Charybdis. If she stays within the bounds of sanity, she gets an abstraction that nobody can identify or emphasize with. And if she tries to get Anna Karenina or Hamlet out of Opus 131, she stretches our credulity well beyond the breaking

---

[20] Levinson, 'Musical Expressiveness', 107.

point. Whatever the plausibility of the standard explanation for the emotions aroused by fictional characters, it will not survive the passage to absolute music. That is why Levinson's mechanism for how music moves us emotionally must fail.

However, I have not discussed Davies' and Levinson's explanations for how music might arouse emotions in listeners merely for the purpose of refuting them. For each of these explanations has implications for how the emotions supposed to be aroused are characterized by the two. And it is the characterization of these emotions, theirs and mine, with which I want to conclude, and which is, indeed, the main point of the chapter.

Accommodations

What is a musically aroused emotion like? Well, one thing is very clear. The behavioral manifestations of the garden-variety emotions are absent. So that if you are made happy by happy music, apparently you don't do the things that happy people are incited to do by this emotion, if you are made sad you don't do the things that sad people are incited to do. You remain seated, listening to the symphony, and you seem about the same in both cases.

Stephen Davies thinks it is one of the virtues of *his* account of how music arouses the emotions that it implies just such an absence of behavioral response. In the non-musical cases, 'If I feel sad because I believe the situation to be unfortunate and regrettable, I will try if I can to alter the situation so that it is no longer unfortunate and regrettable.'[21] But in the musical case, 'Not only does the [emotive] response lack many beliefs which, standardly, would lead to action, it also lacks the beliefs that give intensity to those feelings.'[22] After all, the intentional object of musical sadness is not an unfortunate and regrettable situation; it is merely, on Davies's view, the expressive quality of sadness the music possesses. Thus we do, according to Davies, experience real sadness in the presence of sad music, real happiness in the presence of happy music, but in a weakened, behaviorally ineffectual form. In the musical situation, as Davies points out, 'our feelings lack the intentional elements on which their strength commonly depends.'[23]

Levinson goes even further than Davies in distinguishing the emotions aroused by music from those aroused in the world of action and

---

[21] Davies, *Musical Meaning and Expression*, 305–6.
[22] Ibid. 307.   [23] Ibid.

affairs. With many of the same general reasons that Davies adduces, Levinson explains why emotions aroused by music do not motivate the behavioral responses one ordinarily associates with them. As he puts it, the 'weakening of the cognitive component in emotional response to music generally results in inhibition of most characteristic behaviors and in the significant lessening of behavioral tendencies.' But his conclusion as to the status of musical emotions, as compared to their real-life counterparts, is even further in the direction of *difference*. He writes that 'the standard emotional response to a musical work—e.g. what I have called a sadness-reaction—is not in truth a case of *full-fledged emotion*.'[24]

Thus it is fair to say that both Davies and Levinson, when the chips are down, want to back away from the baldfaced assertion that sad music makes one sad, *sans phrase*. For Davies the emotion that music arouses is sadness, but only in a weakened form, impotent to effectuate any of the behavioral responses ordinarily associated with that emotion. Whatever it *is*, it is not sadness in exactly the ordinary sense, a conclusion Levinson draws even more strongly, averring, in his latest description, that musical emotions 'do not amount to the full experiential component of standard emotions . . .' but merely 'are ingredients in, and suggestive of such states, even if not by themselves uniquely indicative of any.'[25] In short, emotions aroused by musical expressiveness are, on Davies's view, anemic emotions and, on Levison's, emotion-like, quasi-emotions. And the question I now want to broach is how close this brings them to being the kind of emotions that I claim music arouses.

Let me say straightaway that the emotions aroused by music, on my view, are neither anemic emotions nor quasi-emotions, both of which I find highly dubious: they are full-blooded, down and dirty emotions. They require no apologies. But that being said, it would appear that my musical emotions are far removed from Davies' or Levinson's. Furthermore, my musical emotions are *not* the garden-variety emotions but, so to speak, various kinds of excitement over music; whereas although neither Davies's nor Levinson's emotions are quite, in the literal sense, fully-fledged garden-variety emotions, they are intimately connected to them descriptively, being, for Davies, pallid sadness and happiness, and,

[24] Levinson, 'Music and Negative Emotion,' 313–14.
[25] Levinson, 'Musical Expressiveness,' 113.

for Levinson, sadness-like, happiness-like, and so forth. So, it would seem that in two absolutely crucial respects my musical emotions are completely different. However, I shall try to show that, in the latter respect, there is a closer affinity than might be expected: that, in other words, although my musical emotions are not the garden-variety emotions, there are, in specific instances, important connections between them.

Recall that the intentional object of the musical emotion is always, on my view, some excellence in the music. Recall, too, that on my view, as on Davies's and Levinson's, the character of emotion felt is, in some large measure though not entirely, determined by the intentional object of the emotion. That being the case, let us now look more closely at what the intentional object of the musical emotion is, according to me. In particular, let us look at cases where the intentional object involves an expressive property of music, as many times it will.

Suppose, then, that I am listening intently to the second movement of Beethoven's Seventh Symphony. I find myself, as I frequently do, deeply moved by its somber, stately melancholy.

But what am I really moved *by*? Certainly not *merely* somber melancholy. Lots of music that is somber and melancholy moves me not one whit, because lots of music that is somber and stately and melancholy is not very good music. And to move me by its somber, stately melancholy music must be *beautifully* somber and stately and melancholy: it must embody somber stately melancholy in a musically wonderful, a musically beautiful way. The intentional object of the emotion I am talking about, that the second movement of Beethoven's Seventh Symphony inspires in me, is musically beautiful melancholy, musically beautiful in that special way that only Beethoven's music can be. *That* is the intentional object.

What, one may now want to ask, does it feel like to be deeply moved by how beautifully melancholy the second movement of Beethoven's Seventh Symphony is? And what do we call that emotion?

To both of these questions we must give substantially the same answer: the character and the name of the emotion are given by its intentional object and nothing more, except perhaps to add that it is a feeling of excitement, of enthusiasm, and not some other feeling, say of depression or boredom. The feeling of musical excitement one gets in contemplating the beautiful melancholy of this music of

Beethoven's is very different from the feeling of musical excitement
one gets in contemplating the beautiful way in which Bach sneaks in
the final return of the subject of the A-flat Fugue in the *Well-
Tempered Clavier*, Book II, into the tenor voice, so that its fall to the
major third makes the final cadence. But how else can we characterize this difference than by simply saying what the intentional object
of my musical excitement is in the first instance, and in the second?
And what else could it be called than 'the excitement that *that*
particular intentional object evokes'? In short, the intentional objects
of musical emotions, like the intentional objects of many other
emotions, are major determiners of what these emotions are.
Furthermore, when we remind ourselves that the intentional objects
are often expressive properties of the music, we are in a position, I
think, to make an important breakthrough in the apparent stand-off
over what the nature is of the musically moving experience.

To see this, let me return to the suggestion of Leonard Meyer's,
quoted earlier: 'it may well be that when a listener reports that he felt
this or that emotion, he is describing the emotion he believes the passage is supposed to indicate, not anything which he himself has experienced.' Let us call this the 'error theory' of musical arousal,
because, as Meyer seems to be suggesting, the listener may be *mis-
taking* the emotion perceived for an emotion aroused—a sort of mir-
ror image of the so-called 'pathetic fallacy.'

In its extreme form, the error theory would have it that the listener
thinks she is feeling sadness, or happiness, or whatever, when listening to the music, when, really, she is feeling no emotion at all, but
perceiving the emotion in the music, which she mistakenly thinks she
is feeling. This theory may contain a kernel of truth. However, as it
stands, it appears too implausible, because, for one thing, there is no
reasonable explanation for *why* such a mistake should be made.

Let me suggest, then, a modified form of the error theory that does
provide an explanation for the error. Assume that I am correct in my
view of how music moves us emotionally. If that is so, then when
someone is moved (say) by how beautifully sad a musical passage is,
the intentional object of her emotion is (in part) the musically beautiful sadness. She perceives the sadness in the music—she is not herself sad. But she *is* in an elevated state of emotional excitement over
the musically beautiful sadness. What more natural than for her
to misdescribe the emotional excitement as sadness, since sadness is
its intentional object? The error theory, then, is true to this extent:

sometimes, when one is deeply moved emotionally by a passage of expressive music, one will mistake the emotion that is aroused for the emotion that the music is expressive of, and that is the intentional object of the emotion.

Let me return, now, the the views of Davies and Levinson. How far apart really are we in regard to the way the emotions stirred in us by music should be described? Levinson and I seem very close indeed. He describes the emotions that music arouses as emotion-like; but, as one might put it, *specifically* emotion-like. That is to say, in response to the sadness of music one's emotion is sadness-like, in response to the happiness of music, happiness-like, and so on. But it is never, as Levinson puts it, 'a case of *full-fledged emotion*.'

But although I believe that in every case it is a case of 'full-fledged emotion,' it seems a fair description of my position to say that in all the cases in which the musical emotion has, as its intentional object, the expressive beauty of music, the emotion is, in a very obvious sense, emotion-like as well. It is a real emotion that is not the emotion of its intentional object. Its intentional object is the sadness of the music, or the happiness of the music. *It* however is not sadness or happiness. But often sadness *does* have sadness as its intentional object (when I am sad about someone else's sadness), and often happiness *does* have happiness as its intentional object (when I am happy about someone else's happiness). So in those cases where the musical emotion, on my view, has, as its intentional object, musical sadness, or musical happiness, and so forth, it is sadness-like, or happiness-like, or whatever, because like some real cases of sadness and happiness, it has those emotions, at least as expressive properties of the music, as its intentional objects. Thus, both on Levinson's view and on mine, when an expressive property of music moves us emotionally, the emotion is 'emotion-like.' Not a great deal separates us in this regard.

On the other hand, it may seem that, with regard to this issue, Davies and I are irreconcilable. And perhaps we are. But let me at least suggest some possible common ground. Staking it out would require a crucial redescription of Davies's musical emotions. Whether it would preserve the spirit of his proposal I will let the reader be the judge.

According to Davies, sad music makes us sad, happy music happy—but they are sadness and happiness of greatly diminished strength: they are weakened emotions. They must be weakened, that we know, because they do not have the power to make us *behave* the way those emotions would do in ordinary circumstances. And the cause of their weakness, on Davies's view, is that the beliefs and intentional objects that customarily form the causal background for our garden-variety emotions are not present in the musical cases.

At this point the skeptical (myself included) may feel obliged to ask whether a sadness or happiness that cannot motivate, and lacks the beliefs and intentional objects of the normal cases can *really* be sadness or happiness at all? Is a poison that has been rendered completely ineffectual, *qua* poison, still properly called a poison? In the case of Davies's musical emotions, would it not be more appropriate to take a leaf from Levinson's book and call them sadness-like, happiness-like, rather than sadness and happiness properly so called? I am inclined to think so. Indeed, if you read Davies's and Levinson's descriptions of the musical emotions, *as felt*, there is not much to distinguish them. If Levinson's are quasi-emotions, so too, so far as I can tell, are Davies's.

What, then, is there to choose between my description of how music moves, and the descriptions of Davies and Levinson? There are, let me suggest, at least three prima-facie advantages of my account.

First, Davies and Levinson are both troubled by what Levinson calls the 'negative emotions', whereas I am not. There are, I am sure we would all agree, emotions that in life are unpleasant to experience and to be avoided when possible—sadness, for an example. And if the emotion aroused by sad music is enough like sadness to be unpleasant too, as both Davies and Levinson believe to be the case, then it is puzzling why people should listen to sad music, thus willingly to cause themselves to have an unpleasant experience they usually shun.

Both Davies and Levinson, therefore, are obliged to provide elaborate explanations for why listeners seek to experience what they know will be unpleasant. But on my view there is no reason to believe that the emotion aroused by sad music should be an unpleasant one. For it is the emotion of enthusiasm over beauty, over how beautifully sad the music is; and I see no reason at all to believe that the experience of such an emotion should be anything but positively pleasurable. It is, after all, *beauty* that is its intentional object.

Second, both Levinson and Davies, it appears to me, have a problem with music that is moving emotionally, but has no identifiable expressive properties at all, or none aesthetically relevant, which would be the case, in my experience, with a great many musical compositions. For if to be emotionally moved by music is to be moved to the garden-variety emotions by music that possesses them as expressive perceptual properties, then it would be impossible for music to be moving emotionally, if it did not possess such properties, which is patently false. So one then must find another account of how non-expressive music is emotionally moving, which seems to me to result in an overly complicated account in violation of Occam's razor.

On my account, however, there is one explanation of why all music is moving, that *is* moving, whether or not it possesses expressive properties. All other things being equal, that seems to me to speak decisively in its favor.

Finally, it would seem that music can be expressive without being emotionally moving at all. Music can be very sad, or very cheerful while leaving the listener quite apathetic, completely unmoved emotionally. That happens, in my experience, when the music is sad, or happy, or whatever, but not very good. Mediocre music—that is to say, music the listener takes to be mediocre—does not move at all, even when it is expressive. On my account there is a very simple reason for that. Music moves us in virtue of its beauty, and mediocre music, whether expressive or not, is, by definition, not beautiful or, if you prefer, not wonderful music.

But on the accounts of both Davies and Levinson, the mechanism for arousal is in place when the music is expressive of sadness, or happiness, or whatever, whether or not it is good, which is to say beautiful, wonderful music. On Davies's view, expressiveness by itself is contagious, whether or not it is embodied in a great work of art, or no work of art at all, witness the tragic mask. And on Levinson's view, all that is needed for music to arouse an emotion is empathy with a musical persona imagined to be expressing that emotion. There is, so far as I can see, no particular reason why the persona need express the emotion eloquently or well. If it is someone's sadness that makes me sad, it is their *sadness* that makes me sad, whether they express it beautifully or not, or however else I learn of their condition. Thus it seems to me to be a consequence of both Davies's and Levinson's views that bad or mediocre music will be emotionally moving, just so long as it is expressive of the garden-variety emotions. That is, in my experience anyway, just plainly false.

Conclusion

I have argued in the preceeding pages that the way music moves us emotionally is by its sheer musical beauty. But I have tried to make an accommodation with those who think it moves us by making us sad by its sadness, happy by its happiness, by pointing out that, at least in the case of Davies and Levinson, it is a highly qualified 'sadness' and 'happiness' that they are talking about, not the emotions in their full embodiment. That being the case, it is not so far from their claim to mine, since I too acknowledge that the expressive properties of music move us in a way specific to them. Sad music emotionally moves me, *qua sad* music, by its musically beautiful sadness, happy music moves me, *qua happy* music, by its musically beautiful happiness. Davies and Levinson and I seem to be converging on some sort of single way of putting the matter: that music sometimes moves us emotionally by its expressive properties, and the emotions it moves us to in those cases are not, *literally*, sadness, happiness, and the like. I don't know how much closer we can get without coming to agreement. Wouldn't that be a surprising outcome for three philosophers?

The relation of music to the emotions has fascinated philosophers almost from the very beginning of philosophy itself. I will conclude simply with the thought that perhaps too much time and effort has been spent all along on the emotions in the listener, not enough on the emotions in the music. Narcissus-like, we listen to music and hear only ourselves. How about hearing the *music* for a change? Isn't that the point of it all?

The Arousal Theory of Musical Expression: Rethinking the Unthinkable

I

When I began writing about what is now called 'the philosophy of music' in the late 1970s, the first order of business, it seemed to me, was to refute for good and all the 'arousal theory' of musical expression: that is to say, the theory that when, in the ordinary instances, one calls a passage of music sad, or happy, fearful, angry, or depressing, it is in virtue of its arousing in that person, regularly, if not always, sadness or happiness, fear, anger, or depression. The expressive properties of music, on this view, then, are dispositional properties: dispositions of the music to arouse the garden-variety emotions in qualified listeners to that kind of music.

This analysis of musical expressiveness was almost universally subscribed to at the time, and had been since at least the beginning of the seventeenth century. There were, of course, a few dissenters. These were of two kinds. There were those who, following Eduard Hanslick and the so-called formalists, simply denied that it ever made sense at all to describe music in emotive terms, and hence no analysis was needed of what expressive properties were (they weren't). And there were a daring few, such as Carroll Pratt, Charles Hartshorne, Susanne Langer, and O. K. Bouwsma, who, through various ontological, semantic, or analytic strategies, tried to get the emotions out of the listener and into the music.

It is extremely important to emphasize, at the outset of the discussion to follow, that the arousal theory of musical expressiveness, as it was held at the time of which I speak, really meant what it said. Music—and we are considering here exclusively pure instrumental music, *sans* text, title, program, or dramatic setting—was supposed, according to the arousal theorists, to arouse the real article. When they said a passage was expressive of sadness in virtue of arousing that emotion, it was *that emotion* they meant, not proto-sadness, or pseudo-sadness, or something sadness-like, but full-blooded sadness; the thing you felt when misfortune struck. It was this arousal theory of musical expressiveness, and not some other arousal theory, that we called *the* arousal theory of musical expressiveness. And it was this theory that my colleagues and I thought madly implausible, and necessary to refute before any real progress could be made in understanding musical expressiveness in particular, or the musical experience in general. (This is not a trivial point, as shall become apparent soon enough.)

I think we did our work pretty well. For since the publication of the late Alan Tormey's *The Concept of Expression* (1971), and my *The Corded Shell* (1980), a general consensus has developed among analytic philosophers that *the* arousal theory of musical expressiveness is, indeed, hopelessly wrong-headed, and that the expressive properties of music are not dispositions to arouse the garden-variety emotions, but perceived properties of the music. One, in other words, perceived sadness, happiness, anger, depression *in* the music, as one did turbulence, or tranquility, or 'a flowing quality,' or any other of its, so to say, 'phenomenological' properties.

This is not to say that there was consensus across the board, with regard to music and the emotions. Far from it. On three important issues there were differing opinions. There was disagreement, to start with, about what the 'machinery' (if that is the right word) was by which music possessed its perceived expressive properties. There was disagreement about what function those properties performed in the musical structure. There was disagreement about what emotional response the listener had to music, and what role expressive properties might play in it, given that music was not expressive in virtue of arousing the emotions it was expressive of: i.e. the garden-variety emotions.

The Corded Shell dealt extensively with the first question. The account I gave has been roundly criticized by some, partially accepted by others. As for myself, I have lost interest in the business altogether. That is not to say that I think it unimportant to understand how it is that music possesses expressive properties as heard properties. It is just that I think we have become transfixed by the problem to the exclusion of the other two. So in recent years my attitude has been, and remains, given the general consensus that expressive properties of music are perceived properties of the music, not dispositions to arouse the garden-variety emotions in listeners, to leave the question of how the emotions get into the music—let it be a 'black box,' if you will—and get on with the (to me) far more intriguing 'musical' questions of how expressive properties function in formal structure, and how listeners are emotionally moved by the music they hear.

Until very recently I could say with some confidence that there indeed was a general consensus with regard to the expressive properties of music: they were perceived properties, phenomenological properties, if you will, *in* the music itself, not dispositions therein to arouse the garden-variety emotions in the qualified listener. But there now appears to be some breaking of the ranks. To be specific, Derek Matravers, in his recent monograph, *Art and Emotion*, has presented both criticism of the cognitive approach to musical expressiveness (which is what my position is sometimes called) and an account of his own which he takes to be a version of the arousal theory. It is the purpose of the present essay to answer the criticism and critically examine Matravers' theory.

There are two aspects of Matravers' animadversions on musical expressiveness I want to deal with here. First, Matravers attempts to answer the criticism I gave of the arousal theory in *The Corded Shell*. In the next section I will attempt a response to that answer. But in so doing I wish also to make some positive steps towards clarifying and amplifying my refutation of the arousal theory, because, although I do not think Matravers' answer to it is good, I do think that he has put his finger on some ways in which it is unclear, and some ways in which it is incomplete.

Second, Matravers has a positive account of his own of what he calls the arousal theory of musical expression, and which he defends with vigor and ingenuity. In the third section of this chapter I will try to show that his theory has serious problems, and also that there is some serious confusion in his calling it an 'arousal' theory at all.

It may seem, from these introductory remarks, that this paper is going to be of a completely negative kind. Such is not my intention at all. Were there not something to be learned from Matravers' thoughts on musical expression, I would hardly be bothering to give them critical scrutiny. But good philosophy always pushes a subject forward for me, whether or not I agree with it. I do not agree with Matravers. That he has done good philosophy, however, I do not doubt for a moment. And so I have some good hope that if I criticize it rather than leave it alone, I will, in the long run, be producing a positive rather than a negative result.

II

Matravers marks out four of my previous arguments against the arousal theory with which to take issue. I shall discuss these objections, and Matravers' proposed answers to them, one by one, as they occur in his book.

1. *The behavior argument.* In *The Corded Shell*, and elsewhere, I have argued that there is no behavioral evidence for the arousal theory of musical expressiveness. The garden-variety emotions typically have their pay-off as appropriate behavior, either in the form of action or, at least, of expression. But no such behavior seems to be elicited by music expressive of the garden-variety emotions. And if behavioral manifestations are *consistently*, without exception, lacking, it seems unlikely that the garden-variety emotions are being consistently, without exception, aroused by music expressive of them, as the arousal theory would have it.

In pressing this objection I must admit to having employed some rhetorical flourishes at which Matravers has taken aim. In so doing he has not, I think, successfully answered my objection. But he has revealed to me two weaknesses, as it was then stated: it was, to begin with, *overstated*, painted with far too broad a brush; and it failed to take account of the parallel case of fiction, where the same argument might be used to show, contrary to my own belief, that fictional works do not arouse the garden-variety emotions. Both these points need clearing up.

Here is now Matravers replies to what I am calling 'the behavior argument'.

Recall the sort of manifestations [of emotions] Kivy is looking for. 'When I am angry, I strike out; when I am melancholy my head droops and my appetite wanes.' Kivy's target is an absurdly strong version of the arousal theory in which the postulated feeling is strong enough to overwhelm any thought of restraint. It may be true that the feeling associated with anger does characteristically cause one to 'strike out,' but it does not invariably do so. If the person experiencing the feeling is in a situation in which action would be inappropriate, the action can be suppressed. Clearly, a concert hall is an inappropriate venue for such an action. . . . It is altogether unsurprising that an audience should not act so as to mar their experience of the concert, hence the absence of such action is no guide to their psychological state.[1]

It must be noted first of all that Matravers does not use the term 'emotion' at all in this answer to my criticism, but, rather, the word 'feeling.' This is not an accident, and must be explained before we go any further.

'Feeling,' for Matravers, is a term of art. I will state his definition of it fully further on. For now all we need know is that 'The characteristic state aroused by an expressive work of art . . . is a feeling and not an emotion: that is, it does not have a cognitive component.'[2]

Now the theory that I was at pains to refute, in *The Corded Shell*, and which I called the arousal theory, was the theory that music is expressive of the garden-variety emotions in virtue of arousing those emotions in the qualified listener. Any *other* theory that involves the arousal of anything other than the garden-variety emotions is not *the* arousal theory (as I shall henceforth call it) at which my objections were raised. Thus, it cannot be called a failure of my argument against *the* arousal theory, as understood in that book, that it fails to engage some other theory, what is now called an arousal theory, unless it is *the* arousal theory as then understood.

Indeed, it is fair to point out that Matravers pretty well admits the effectiveness of the behavior argument against *the* arousal theory when he writes: 'Kivy's first argument is simple, and he states it with persuasive force,' and adds: 'Kivy does indeed have a point.'[3]

But Matravers too has a point, an important one that deserves serious consideration. The point is that I certainly did overstate my case. Matravers is right that the appropriate behavioral manifestations of emotions (or feelings) being absent from the concert hall is not, in itself, evidence that the emotions in question are not being felt. Surely, if we did feel these emotions, that is, the garden-variety emotions, we would, as Matravers correctly observes, repress them, as we would in other situations where their manifestations, as action or expression, would be socially unacceptable.

Furthermore, what I did not see, when I offered this rather overstated argument in *The Corded Shell*, was that it proved too much.

[1] Derek Matravers, *Art and Emotion* (Oxford: Oxford University Press, 1998), 154–5.
[2] Ibid. 147–8.   [3] Ibid. 147.

For we do not see manifestations of the garden-variety emotions, either, in the theatre or the living room, when we see *King Lear*, or read *Crime and Punishment*. Yet I believe that although absolute music doesn't arouse the garden-variety emotions, works of fiction do.

Matravers locates my problem in my supposed failure to recognize 'feelings come by degrees, and the degree of feeling generally provoked by expressive art is sometimes comparable to that generally provoked by reading the newspaper and at other times extraordinarily acute.' He concludes that 'most of the time such feelings are insufficiently strong for external manifestations.'[4]

He is quite wrong, I think, in his diagnosis of my problem. If I have one (I probably have many) it has nothing to do with that. But his bringing up of the subject, and, in particular, his example of reading a newspaper, is most instructive. I shall, therefore, in trying to answer him, compare the following cases: attending a performance of *King Lear*, reading an account, in the *New York Times*, of ethnic cleansing in Kosovo, and attending a performance of a *Very Sad Symphony*.

One preliminary point before going on with this. As noted previously, Matravers holds that expressive artworks arouse feelings, not emotions. Surprisingly, he retains the word 'feeling' when he speaks of our reactions to reading the newspaper: surprisingly, I think, because it seems obvious that newspaper reports, because we take them not to be fiction but fact, are eminently capable, on anyone's view, of arousing full-blooded, motivating emotions in us. That being the case, and given my insistence that my arguments against *the* arousal theory are arguments against expressiveness being cashed out in dispositions to arouse full-blooded, garden-variety emotions, I will simply read 'emotion' for 'feeling' here.

Imagine, now, some of the behavioral responses people might exhibit to reading a newspaper account of ethnic cleansing in Kosovo. I am assuming a group of readers who will, uniformly, react with anger at the perpetrators and pity for the victims, and assuming, as well, they are reading it in a public place, a commuter train, for example, where the same constraints on overt emotive expression would be in place as in the concert hall or theatre.

Imagine our commuter, now, boiling with anger, consumed by pity, arriving at her place of business. What can we expect her to do?

<hr />

[4] Matravers, *Art and Emotion*, 155.

Here are some of the things I can think of. She says to a coworker: 'Did you read that article on Kosovo in this morning's *Times*? Are you as angry as I am at those bastards?' She slams the paper down on her desk. She calls up the Red Cross to see if there is anything she can do to help. She has an animated discussion with her boss about what President Clinton can do. She sits at her desk seething (or crying) for about twenty minutes before she can put it behind her and get to work. Or she shows absolutely no reaction at all. (That is always a possibility.)

Suppose the last named? The news story seems not to have motivated her to anything at all. But is that necessarily so? Not at all. For emotions are not, after all, always manifested in overt behavior, as Gilbert Ryle and others have forcefully argued. They are also cashed out in dispositions to behave in appropriate ways, under various circumstances. So our angry commuter may express herself in words, when asked if she read the story, or kick the cat if it gets in the way, or be rude to the plumber, and so on. But let me suggest that someone who showed no overt anger behavior at all, nor any disposition to behave angrily when in the appropriate circumstances, where there would be no reason to suppress it, is someone I would be very reluctant to call 'angry.'

Without running through all of this again in detail with regard to attending a performance of *King Lear*, and the aftermath thereof, let me simply say outright that I think pretty much the same applies to the emotions being aroused by that great tragedy. This is not to deny that there are serious philosophical problems about how a fictional work such as *Lear* arouses the garden-variety emotions since, unlike a newspaper story, we do not take the events and characters therein for fact. But most believe that because of the events depicted in *Lear* and its ilk, and our perception and understanding of them, we are indeed moved to real, full-blooded emotions. Furthermore, it seems reasonable to believe that people really are motivated by those emotions to behavior and expression, though not *in* the theatre, any more than in public when reading the newspaper. After all, many fictional works were intended by their authors to alter attitudes and change or motivate behavior. And, of course, the arousal of emotions is one very powerful way of doing that.

When people leave the theatre after a performance of *King Lear* they talk about what they have experienced: not merely about the beauties of Shakespeare's poetry, the quality of the acting, the success (or lack thereof) of the production. They talk about the moral and other issues raised by the king and his daughters and what they do. To be sure, they are also deeply moved to pity and anger and other of the garden-variety emotions. And will they not, too, *behave* in response to those emotions, when circumstances make it appropriate? I think it reasonable to believe that someone who has seen, understood, been emotionally moved by *King Lear*, cannot but be motivated to behave in ways appropriate to that understanding, and those emotional states. Would it not be quite sensible, not by any means odd, for someone to say, after seeing the play for the first time, 'You know, I don't think I can be quite the same, anymore, with regard to my parental or filial relationships'? We don't all have kingdoms to give away, or parents who have. But we do get the point. We all have charge accounts and most of us will grow old.

In short, even though we should not expect people to gnash their teeth and angrily shake their fists at Goneral and Regan at the Old Vic, there is a wide repertory of behavioral expressions of emotion aroused by *King Lear*, and dispositions to behave, that we have some reason to expect will outlive our direct experience of the play, and manifest themselves in our lives outside the theatre. Furthermore, I suggest that someone who claimed to feel anger and pity in response to *King Lear* but showed and claimed no motivation at all to do *anything* in his or her life reflective of them should at least be suspected of having no such emotions. There is, one has a right to suspect, an emotional screw loose in that spectator.

But how do your intuitions go in the case of listeners to *The Very Sad Symphony*? They emerge from the concert very deeply moved, emotionally, by what they have heard. (As an opponent of the arousal theory of musical expressiveness, I need not, and do not deny that we are, at times, moved emotionally by the music we hear.[5]) What do they talk about? What do they do?

I suppose the answers to these questions might depend, to some degree, on what musical circles one moves in. But I, and the people I go to concerts with, would find it weird to encounter someone who, after hearing a performance of *The Very Sad Symphony*, wanted to talk about the nature of sadness, how *The Very Sad Symphony* had

[5] See Peter Kivy, 'How Music Moves,' in Philip Alperson (ed.), *What is Music? An Introduction to the Philosophy of Music*, and revised in Peter Kivy, *Music Alone: Philosophical Reflections on the Purely Musical Experiences* (Ithaca: Cornell University Press, 1990), ch. 8.

motivated him to change his behavior in some way or other with regard to that emotion. What my friends and I talk about—and, I hasten to add, the lay people as well as the professional and amateur musicians—are all the familiar aspects of performance that make up the stock-in-trade of informal 'music talk,' as well as aspects of the works themselves that have been performed. Indeed, it is hard to imagine talking about the one without to some extent talking about the other. What we do not talk about are the garden-variety emotions we were moved to by the music, nor does our behavior alter, so far as I have been able to discern. Granted, we do not express our sadness during the performance of *The Very Sad Symphony* any more than we do at a performance of *King Lear*, or while reading about ethnic cleansing in Kosovo on the 8.10 from Stamford. But, nevertheless, there is a big difference between the case of *The Very Sad Symphony* and the other two. In the aftermath of the latter two, we expect behavior to reflect, at some point or other, if the garden-variety emotions are aroused, that the emotions have been aroused. In the case of *The Very Sad Symphony*, I don't think most people either expect or observe any such thing. I don't; and that is why, if I wanted to arouse people's anger, to spur them to action, I would write a news story or a play, not a symphony.

To be sure, the behavior of concertgoers during musical performances is a red herring for which I take some of the blame. But although the behavior argument against *the* arousal theory, as laid out in *The Corded Shell*, may be flawed, in spirit it holds good. When viewed on a broader landscape, the behavior of listeners to music does not appear consistent with *the* arousal theory: the theory that music is expressive of the garden-variety emotions in virtue of arousing them.

2. *The argument to negative emotions.* The second argument of mine, against *the* arousal theory of musical expressiveness that Matravers takes issue with taps into a problem in the philosophy of art as old as philosophy itself: the problem of the tragic emotions. Briefly stated, it is that, were music expressive of the garden-variety emotions really so in virtue of arousing them, then people would not choose to listen to music expressive of those garden-variety emotions that are unpleasant to experience, fear, anger, sadness, and the like. But listeners have no aversion to such music, therefore it seems implausible to think that such negative emotions are aroused by the music that is expressive of them. Of course this argument is not good

against music expressive of the pleasant, positive emotions such as love, say, or joy. But it would be odd to think that there is one explanation for negative emotions in music, another for the positive; so an argument casting doubt on *the* arousal theory of the negative emotions I take to be good, obliquely, against *the* arousal theory of positive emotions as well.

In response to this frequently raised objection Matravers points out, quite rightly, that just because an experience has an unpleasant component it does not follow that the experience, overall, is unpleasant. The arousal theory 'leaves it open as to whether or not there may be (as indeed there are) other aspects of the experience which, taken altogether, explain our enjoying the experience as a whole.'[6] Matravers claims that I deny this. But that is just false. I never denied it, and indeed, the passage he quotes from me in this regard *clearly* does not deny it. The question I posed was not why people should choose to experience unpleasant music but why people should choose to experience music that arouses unpleasant emotions. The question cannot be answered by pointing out that the overall experience might be pleasant because one need not choose music which arouses unpleasant emotions *at all*. Even though I don't like artichokes, I might have a dinner in which they are the only thing I don't like, and the whole dinner pleasing overall. What would be perplexing is if I could choose, rather, a dinner without *anything* I didn't like, and yet persisted in choosing the one with the artichokes. And that is exactly the position we are in in the case of expressive music. We can have music that does not arouse painful emotions at all, so why should we choose music that does, never mind that it may, for all of that, be pleasant overall?

Matravers points out, correctly, in my opinion, that 'It would be a mistake, however, to rest the defence of the arousal theory on the claim that we enjoy expressive art in spite of, rather than because of, the feelings it arouses.'[7] But having made this correct observation, Matravers follows it up with some very bad arguments, as well as an example which appears not to be consistent with it.

He begins by saying of my argument: 'The argument relies on the assumption that voluntarily submitting to unpleasant feelings is, if not straightforwardly absurd, something which requires justification.'[8] I think this assumption is true; Matravers does not. Let us see what he comes up with in opposition to it.

---

[6] Matravers, *Art and Emotion*, 157.   [7] Ibid.   [8] Ibid.

Matravers objects, for one thing: 'The claim that pleasure is the overarching justification for all our voluntary activities has been repeatedly and successfully criticized . . .'9 That is quite true. But why Matravers thinks anything I have said implies a denial of its truth I cannot imagine. The point simply is that in the case of listening to music—the only case my argument is about—the motivation for listening is the desire for musical enjoyment. And *if* music expressive of the negative emotions aroused the negative emotions, *then* it would be inexplicable why someone would choose to listen to music expressive of the negative emotions, all other things being equal. One would expect there to be a systematic avoidance of that music, if music not expressive of the negative emotions were available that was just as good, just as interesting, etc. There is no evidence of such a systematic avoidance; and that, so I argue, is evidence against the arousal theory of negative emotions and, obliquely, against *the* arousal theory of musical expressiveness *tout court*.

Matravers says that '. . . Kivy's argument has no force for the simple reason that all except the spiritually desolate *do* have reason to explore the negative feelings and emotions'. He adduces, as evidence for this assertion, the well-known case of fiction that arouses the negative emotions. 'Certainly, some representational art arouses some negative feelings in us: the final scene of *King Lear* should cause feelings of utter desolation in the audience. This could not be so on Kivy's argument, because if it were, people would not go to see the tragedy, while plainly they do.'10

It might be remarked, straightaway, that Matravers has overstated his case somewhat, I think. We *do* tend to have what psychologists used to call an 'approach-avoidance conflict' with regard to such searing, harrowing fictional works as *King Lear* or *Medea* just because there are repellent qualities in them that arouse extreme, excruciating negative emotions. There *is* a systematic avoidance of these works. We have to steel ourselves for them. And sometimes we say, 'I am just not up for that kind of excruciating experience tonight. Let's go and see *As You Like It* instead.' Of course we *do* see them on occasion. But there *is* resistance to overcome for just the reason one would expect: such works arouse very painful negative emotions in us that no one really wants to undergo.

---

9 Ibid. 158.   10 Ibid.

Furthermore, let me suggest that there are no approach-avoidance conflicts with regard to musical works expressive of the painful emotions because of *that*. Brahms' C-minor Symphony is one of the most popular works in the concert repertory, as are Mozart's G-minor Symphony (K. 550), and many more melancholy Romantic works expressive of the dark emotions. There is, indeed, an aversion to overcome with regard to some very great musical works. It is, I would argue, with regard to 'difficult' music. I have to be 'up' for Bach's *Art of Fugue*—but scarcely because it is emotionally dark-hued; rather, of course, because it requires intense concentration, over a considerable period of time, to follow Bach's intricate, complicated, and profound contrapuntal 'logic'. It requires, in other words, hard work on the listener's part.

Thus, I want to argue, there is an approach-avoidance conflict observable with regard to the negative emotions in fictional works but not in absolute music. And that is exactly what one would expect if fictional works did arouse the negative garden-variety emotions and absolute music did not—which is precisely my view.

But all this aside, Matravers' criticism here is, in one respect, well taken. I do plead guilty to not having considered the case of representational fiction and its arousal of the emotions in *The Corded Shell*, although I did, subsequently, deal with that question elsewhere. But, in any case, my views bear repeating and expanding in this place.

The crucial point to bear in mind, here, is that music is *not*, on my view, a representational art. And this was assumed in *The Corded Shell*, when the argument in question was presented. Clearly, the representational arts—and I, as Matravers, am thinking primarily of literary fiction—provide materials for our understanding of why we want to experience them even though (or perhaps *because*) they arouse painful emotions in us.

Now, as Matravers very well knows, the problem of the negative emotions in fiction is itself a very thorny one which he has himself discussed with great insight. In particular, it has been of considerable puzzlement, from Aristotle to Hume to the present, why we desire to experience the so-called 'tragic emotions' and whether they remain painful in tragic representations, or are somehow made pleasurable.

I cannot discuss the question of the negative emotions in fiction now. I will simply follow Matravers' lead in his criticism of me, and assume that, as he puts it, our reason for experiencing the tragic, and other highly unpleasant emotions in fiction is 'to *explore* the negative feelings and emotions' (my italics). 'Explore' I take to have epistemic connotations, and thus to imply that the major redeeming pay-off of fiction's painful emotions is knowledge of them.

There are two ways of dealing with the pay-off and its price in pain: the 'in spite of' way and the 'integrated' way. One might argue that, like going to the dentist, going to a tragedy entails pain, but to a satisfying end, overall, the gaining of knowledge. Or, one might insist that the arousing of painful emotions is part of an integrated package, and somehow part of the tragic pay-off in the experiencing; which is to say, part of the knowledge gained somehow lies in part in the painful experience itself.

Fortunately, we do not have to decide between the two for present purposes. All I need to point out is that whatever sense it makes to talk about *King Lear* or *Crime and Punishment* 'exploring' the negative emotions, no one has ever (to my satisfaction at least) made sense out of it as a characterization of what goes on in music expressive of the negative emotions. Precisely because music is not a representational art, and, more importantly still, not a linguistic art, it lacks the materials to 'explore', in an epistemic sense (or any other sense I can think of), the negative emotions, or, for that matter, anything else, except *music* itself. (The *Art of Fugue* does indeed 'explore' in a fairly robust sense of that word the possibilities of fugal composition in the High Baroque.)

One thing that is very peculiar about Matravers' argument here is that there seems to be a volte-face towards the end. At the outset he claims that I have got things wrong because I have falsely assumed that 'voluntarily submitting to unpleasant feelings is . . . something which requires justification.'[11] And at the end he seems to be claiming that I have got things wrong because I have not realized that 'all except the spiritually desolate *do* have reason to explore the negative feelings and emotions.'[12] If 'submitting to unpleasant feelings' is coextensive with 'to explore the negative feelings and emotions,' then, apparently, I am being criticized for mistakenly demanding a justification for doing this, when none is required, and being too obtuse to discern what the real justification is (which was previously asserted to be unnecessary).

But let me conclude by saying, simply, straight out, that I cling tenaciously to my heresy. It is absolutely the case that voluntarily

---

[11] Matravers, *Art and Emotion*, 157.   [12] Ibid. 158.

submitting to unpleasant feelings requires justification, as does voluntarily submitting to pain of any kind. I cannot think of an instance in which this is not so. It is certainly not the case that I need always *give* a justification, as, in many instances, the reason why someone voluntarily chooses pain or painful emotions is well known and obvious. I don't have to explain the pain every time I go to the dentist or justify the nervous anxiety I endure before every lecture I give. However, that there *be* no justification available on demand suggests pathology. People who voluntarily choose pain or the painful for no reason at all are called masochists.

Music—absolute music—is different from the linguistic, fictional arts. They provide, within themselves, the justification for our desiring to experience them, painful emotions notwithstanding. Music—absolute music—provides no such justification. That is why *if* music expressive of the painful emotions were expressive by arousing them, we would shun it. We would shun it because music expressive of the pleasurable emotions would provide the same musical satisfaction without the pain. And someone who did not shun it, but voluntarily experienced it, would be a musical masochist. The argument to negative emotions may have been presented, in *The Corded Shell*, in an over simplified form. But, suitably amplified, it remains, I claim, a good argument against *the* arousal theory of musical expressiveness.

3. *The full-blooded emotion argument.* Here I can be brief. I have maintained, according to Matravers, the implausibility of 'holding that music arouses a full-blooded emotion, including a cognitive content.' He answers: 'Kivy rightly holds that, as music is not representational, to maintain this would be problematic. However, as I claim that music arouses feelings rather than emotions this criticism does not apply.'[13]

As I have pointed out before, there is a kind of *ignoratio* here that infects Matravers' whole account of musical expressiveness. He concurs with my argument that, because of its lack of representational content, music cannot arouse real, full-blooded emotions, with *their* cognitive content. I thank him for that.

But he then goes on to reply that, not to worry, this does not count as an argument against the arousal theory of musical expressiveness, because, on Matravers' version of that theory, music arouses 'feelings,' not 'full-blooded emotions,' and the present argument is not good against the arousal of *those*. But as my argument was directed

[13] Matravers, *Art and Emotion*, 159.

only at *the* arousal theory of musical expressiveness—the theory that is to say that music is expressive of the garden-variety emotions in virtue of arousing them in the full-blooded state—his reply simply misses its target.

4. *The Uncle Charlie argument.* In the aftermath of *The Corded Shell*, with its insistence that music does not, in any aesthetically or artistically significant way, arouse the garden-variety emotions, the belief arose that I must believe the musical experience to be a coldly intellectual one, in which the listener has no emotional involvement. It seemed to many as if music was, for me, the proverbial entomologist's 'bug on a pin.' The reason for this conclusion was, no doubt, that the traditional account of how music moves us just is *the* arousal theory of musical expressiveness—the very theory I was attacking—that music is expressive of the garden-variety emotions in virtue of having dispositions to arouse them. On the traditional account, music is deeply moving to listeners just because it moves them to the garden-variety emotions, as the arousal theory of musical expressiveness says it does. And since no one was able to think of any *other* way music could be emotionally moving, to deny that it moved in this way was, *ipso facto*, to deny that it moved at all.

It therefore behooved me, as I did believe music to be a deeply moving experience, to explain how I thought it moves us emotionally, given that I didn't think it moved us by arousing the garden-variety emotions. In order to do that I laid out two conditions I thought (and still do think) must be in place for such an explanation to work. The first is that in the usual cases, when I am in thrall to one of the garden-variety emotions, the emotion takes an 'intentional object': I am afraid of *the tiger*, I am in love with *Joan*, I am angry at *Uncle Charlie*. I am not, under normal circumstances, just afraid, in love, angry, *sans phrase*.

Second, what causes my fear or love or anger is an appropriate belief, or set of beliefs *about* the intentional object of my emotion. I am afraid of the tiger because I believe tigers are dangerous, and the cage is unlocked. I am in love with Joan because I believe she is beautiful, sexy, intelligent, fun to be with; I am angry at Uncle Charlie because he mistreats Aunt Bella, cheats at cards, and does shady business deals. And were my beliefs about these objects of my emotions to change, so that the emotions would no longer be appropriate, then, under the usual circumstances, my emotions would dissipate or change.

These two conditions together form the core of what is known as the cognitive theory of the emotions, to which I (more or less) subscribe, and I have, in previous writings, presented them as constituting what I called 'Uncle Charlie arguments.' Furthermore, I insisted that since Uncle Charlie arguments must be in place for us to ascribe the garden-variety emotions to people, and they are unavailable in the case of absolute music, absolute music cannot arouse the garden-variety emotions, hence *the* arousal theory of musical expressiveness must be false.

Matravers launches a somewhat predictable two-pronged attack on my argument. His first point, not surprisingly, is that since my objection depends in part upon the fact that full-blooded emotions have a cognitive aspect—beliefs and intentional objects—it is impotent against his version of the arousal theory, which does not involve the arousal of emotions at all. Thus Matravers writes that 'as I claim that music arouses feelings rather than emotions this criticism does not apply.'[14]

Equally unsurprising is my response. As often as Matravers tries to blunt criticism of *the* arousal theory—the theory that music is expressive of the garden-variety emotions in virtue of arousing them—by substituting feelings for emotions, it must be repeated that the criticism was fashioned for *the* arousal theory as stated, and that that, as we shall see, is no trivial matter: it is not nit-picking. What appears to be the quite innocent and plausible move of defending *an* arousal theory that substitutes something less troublesome than full-blooded emotions for the subjective state aroused, proves, in the end, to be something other than what it appears to be. (But more of that anon.)

The second prong of Matravers attack is aimed at the cognitive theory of emotions itself, and, in particular, what I called Uncle Charlie arguments. The general drift is that on my view the regular presence of Uncle Charlie arguments in ordinary cases where the garden-variety emotions are aroused, and the regular absence in musical cases counts fairly decisively against the notion that music arouses the garden-variety emotions, as *the* arousal theory requires. But to the contrary, according to Matravers, Uncle Charlie arguments are not generally present in ordinary cases of the garden-variety emotions being aroused; so their absence in music is no

---

[14] Matravers, *Art and Emotion*, 159.

argument against music's being capable of arousing the garden-variety emotions, as *the* arousal theory requires.

Matravers concentrates on the causal aspect of my Uncle Charlie arguments. He begins: 'Although usual, it is (contrary to Kivy's claim) by no means necessary that we know *why* we feel the emotions we do. We might be wrong about the cause—it is the drink and not my friend which is making me feel sorry for myself—or I might not have any beliefs about what the cause is—I simply hate someone without knowing why.'[15]

To start with, I agree with Matravers that it is 'normal' for people to know what causes their emotions, not absolutely necessary. That is why here, and elsewhere, I have been careful to qualify my claim by saying 'in the central cases,' and other words to that effect. Of course there are the odd cases; and if they are odd enough then psychotherapy is indicated. What the argument is is that in the *usual* cases people know what is causing their emotions: it is the beliefs they have about the objects of these emotions. That is why we can alter their emotions by altering their beliefs. (How else?) Thus it is quite false to say, as Matravers does, that 'contrary to Kivy's claim' it is 'by no means necessary that we know *why* we feel the emotions we do.' It is quite consistent with Kivy's claim, as it is consistent with it where Matravers admits that it is 'usual' for us to know '*why* we feel the emotions we do.'

Matravers says that we can sometimes be mistaken about what is causing this or that emotion. Of course we can be. But surely we usually know what is causing our emotions, as Matravers himself admits. And the example of being mistaken that Matravers offers completely misfires.

In this example Matravers suggests that I think it is my friend who is causing me to feel sorry for myself but really it is the alcohol. The example, as it stands, tells us nothing, because there is not enough detail to the story. So I will have to fill it in myself in the hope of catching Matravers' meaning (and his mistake).

Let us say that things are going really well for my friend, professionally, and really badly for me. I have a few jars, get a little tight, and start feeling sorry for myself. Well, of course, I know perfectly well what is causing me to feel sorry for myself: it is my friend, in particular, my friend's success. But, you say, had I not had a snootful I would

---

[15] Ibid. 160.

not be feeling sorry for myself. Yes: that's right. Under the influence, beliefs about certain circumstances, people, and events may well arouse emotions in me that they would not were I sober. Nevertheless, the Uncle Charlie argument is there, and it is a *good* argument; I am not mistaken about either the object of my emotion or its cause. The object of my pity is myself, and I know that. The cause of my self-pity is my beliefs about my friend and myself, and I know that. And when I sleep it off, my beliefs will not make me feel sorry for myself. Rather, they will rouse me to jealousy of my friend, and stir me to action. Matravers has simply confused the 'conditions' that must be in place for A to cause B with the cause of B (which is A). If I tell the insurance man that it wasn't my smoking in bed that caused the fire but the presence of oxygen, I am not going to score a point in his book.

At one point Matravers wonders whether by the cause of an emotion, in an Uncle Charlie argument, I mean, rather, its *justification*. 'Perhaps what Kivy means is that if we do not know why we are feeling an emotion we cannot justify it. To justify an emotion is to show that it is an appropriate response to some cause, which is something we cannot do if the cause is not known.'[16] My reply is that in the central cases what causes the emotion is, indeed, at the same time its justification, when adduced. I am angry at Uncle Charlie because I believe he lies and cheats, and my anger is justified by these beliefs, if indeed they are true. I see no problem here for Uncle Charlieism.

Matravers opines that I may have been making a point not about whether music arouses the garden-variety emotions but about whether we are *justified* in being aroused to them by musical works. For example, he thinks I might be arguing that 'the second movement of the *Eroica* is not an appropriate cause of sadness in the way that death is an appropriate cause of sadness'.[17] That was not the point I was making; but it is worth taking a look at.

In order to ask whether or not someone is justified in being aroused to a certain emotion by a certain object, person, or event, it must first, of course, be the case that that person, object, or event,

---

[16] Matravers, *Art and Emotion*, 159. In a footnote to this passage Matravers makes the rather strange response that 'this seems an implausibly strong claim. We ought sometimes to trust our emotions, even if we do not know why we have them.' Matravers seems to be confusing here the justification for *having* an emotion with the justification for *trusting* one. Indeed I may be justified in trusting or acting on an unjustified emotion, just as I may be justified in trusting or acting on an unjustified belief.

[17] Ibid.

along with the appropriate beliefs, has indeed aroused that emotion. And since I am arguing that music cannot arouse the garden-variety emotions in aesthetically appropriate ways that track the expressive properties, the question of justification does not come up at all in that context.

But I never denied, nor did Hanslick, that arch-denier, that music can arouse the garden-variety emotions in various artistically irrelevant ways. And whether one is justified in feeling some particular emotion in those cases, as in any others, depends upon the intentional objects of the emotions, and upon the relevant beliefs.

The second movement of the *Eroica* makes an excellent case in point. It may remind me of funerals, or even some particular funeral, and the thought of the funerals or funeral may make me sad. That seems to be an altogether justified emotion in the circumstances. Thought of funerals, ordinarily, should make one sad. On the other hand, if the second movement of the *Eroica* reminds me of snails (because of its slow pace), and I become frightened because I believe snails are dangerous, then my fear is not justified, even though totally explainable, because my belief about snails is false.

Furthermore, there is a hint in what Matravers says in this regard that he is taking 'justified' as synonymous with 'appropriate', and this is a mistake. For on my view, anyway, the person who is made sad by funereal thoughts in listening to the second movement of the *Eroica* is perfectly justified in feeling sad; but the feeling of sadness is not appropriate, aesthetically or artistically, whichever way you like to put it, and I think, best suppressed if possible. In any case, I think justification is a red herring and appropriateness an appropriate consideration in the way just stated.

A final point: counterexamples to the belief/intentional object condition on the garden-variety emotions are frequently cited in the literature. I do not deny that there are counterexamples; but they are the proverbial exceptions that prove the rule and irrelevant to the argument.

Suppose someone who lives on the eastern seaboard of the United States is afraid every time she sees a snake. It is pointed out to her time and again that there are no venomous or otherwise dangerous snakes in the region. Nevertheless, even though she has come to believe this, she cannot get over her fear of the things. Such instances are common enough. But even though they are not unusual, they are, of course, anomalous. They are judged as such against a background of normal cases where the garden-variety emotions come and go, answering to our beliefs, in a perfectly rational manner. If that were not the way of it, life would be nasty, brutish, and short. It would be hard to credit natural selection with such an arrangement.

But, the arousal theorist might argue, there are cases where, in ordinary circumstances, no Uncle Charlie argument is in evidence, as with the lady's fear of snakes; so why cannot this *always* be the case with music?

I think the answer to this question is plain, although not absolutely conclusive to the fanatic. One wants to be able to make the distinction between rational and irrational, justified and unjustified emotions *anywhere* emotions may be claimed to be felt. If someone, in the absence of an Uncle Charlie argument, feels frightened of snakes, we say that she has an irrational, unjustified fear of snakes. And if someone claims music is expressive of the garden-variety emotions in just that way, that is, without an Uncle Charlie argument, then one is bound to say that *systematically*, we are always responding irrationally to music, when we find it expressive of the garden-variety emotions. The expressiveness of music is *always* the result of an irrational, unjustified emotive response to the music. I find that impossible to swallow, although of course it is a logically possible position to take. To me it is a last desperate fanatical position: a counsel of despair.[18] If it is not an irrational position, it is close to it.

I have now defended as best I can my past objections to *the* arousal theory of musical expressiveness: the theory that music is expressive of the garden-variety emotions in virtue of possessing dispositions to arouse them in listeners. All the while I have repeatedly pressed home the point that my objections were not aimed at the notion that music arouses other conscious states in us, including what can properly be called 'emotions,' 'feelings,' and the like. Thus the response to my objections, that I have too narrowly defined what an arousal theory of musical expressiveness might be, completely misses the point. *Everyone* who writes about music has some arousal theory, if you are

---

[18] Nevertheless, there are always some takers for *any* philosophical position, no matter how outlandish. If I understand him correctly, this is indeed something like the position Colin Radford takes with regard both to emotions in fictions and emotions in music. On the former, see his 'How Can We Be Moved by the Fate of Anna Karenina?' *Proceedings of the Aristotelian Society, Supplementary Volume*, 49 (1975); on the latter, 'Emotions and Music: A Reply to the Cognitivists,' *Journal of Aesthetics and Art Criticism*, 47 (1989), and 'Muddy Waters', *Journal of Aesthetics and Art Criticism*, 49 (1991).

liberal enough about what is aroused. But to see the significance of this we must now, at last, look at Matravers' 'arousal theory' itself: the theory he thinks rescues the arousal theory of musical expressiveness from criticism such as mine.

III

Let me begin by pointing out that what I have been calling *the* arousal theory of musical expressiveness—the theory that music is expressive of the garden-variety emotions in virtue of the dispositions to arouse them in listeners—has one distinct advantage over any other that I know. It makes crystal clear *how* music possesses expressive qualities. If you understand why the news from Kosovo is sad news, even though news cannot feel sad, if you understand why the birth of a baby is a joyful event, even though events cannot experience joy, then, if *the* arousal theory of musical expressiveness is right, 'The music is sad' and 'The music is joyful' are no more puzzling than 'The news is sad' or 'The event is joyful.' We sometimes, not necessarily always, name things after what they have the dispositions to arouse or do, and so if music's expressive properties are dispositional properties, the mystery of musical expressiveness—how music has emotive properties that are centrally properties of sentient beings—is instantly solved: it is a case of naming the object for its disposition.

What I want to suggest, as a consequence of these observations, is that there are two ways of looking at arousal theories of musical expressiveness: either there is only *one*, or *every* theory of musical expressiveness is an arousal theory. The former seems to me the more informative way of representing things, but in the end it is merely a matter of 'notation.'

The arousal theory of musical expressiveness is the only theory, so far as I know, that makes the sadness, happiness, etc. of music simply a direct result of the arousal. All the rest, including my own early effort, are more or less elaborate explanations of how music comes to be perceived as possessing such emotions; and they all involve postulating the arousal of *something*: some conscious state or other. If you wish to construe arousal theory widely enough, as Matravers seems to want to do, then every theory is an arousal theory, including the one I proposed in *The Corded Shell*.

To see just how drastic a result his way of looking at things has, let me point out that in ch. 10 of his book, Matravers compares *his* arousal theory of musical expressiveness to one of the standard analyses of color properties! Indeed, he claims that his theory was 'deliberately modelled on the familiar "basic equation" for colour (in this case red)', to wit: 'x is red iff [i.e. if and only if] for any observer p: if p were perceptually normal and were to encounter x in perceptually normal conditions, p would experience x as red.'[19]

To see how strange this attempt to model an arousal theory of musical expressiveness on the standard dispositional account of colors, let us remind ourselves of what the *original* terms of the dispute were, when I framed them in *The Corded Shell*. There I opposed the cognitive theory of musical expressiveness to *the* arousal theory. *The* arousal theory has it that the music is sad in virtue of arousing, or having the disposition to arouse sadness in the listener. The cognitive theory (which I defended) has it that the music in some way possesses sadness as a perceptual property of the music, *much in the way an apple possesses redness.* (The analogy with redness was drawn from O. K. Bouwsma.)

Suppose, now, that someone should produce (*per impossibile*) an analysis of the expressive properties in music point for point analogous to the standard analysis of colors. (*Per impossibile* because, for one thing, colors are 'simple' properties, expressive properties of music 'complex' ones.) I would take *that* to be a triumph for the cognitive theory, not *the* arousal theory, or any other arousal theory. But Matravers seems to be implying that that would be a vindication of arousal theory. Not *the* arousal, of course, but some arousal theory. On Matravers' view it would be *an* arousal theory because the standard account of color perception is an arousal theory (according to him): colored objects have the colors they do in virtue, in part, of arousing appropriate color sensations in perceivers. (Indeed, color perception, however, is customarily adduced by aestheticians as a paradigm instance of the perception of 'objective' properties and presumed to be the very antithesis of arousal theories of aesthetic properties, the expressive ones included.)

But to claim to have rehabilitated arousal theory in one's account of expressiveness in music by showing how one's theory is modelled on color perception is surely perverse. Every account of expressiveness in

[19] Matravers, *Art and Emotion*, 188.

music is an arousal theory in that sense (unless one believes that expressive properties are *primary* qualities). Every account has as part of its machinery a physical stimulus, sound, that arouses some state or states in a conscious, sentient listener, which state, one way or another, causes the listener to perceive 'in' the music its expressive properties. Thus, Matravers' theory is not, it seems to me, reasonably viewed either as a rehabilitation of *the* arousal theory of musical expressiveness (which is obvious enough), or even a rehabilitation of it 'in spirit.' It is merely yet another theory of how expressive properties get 'into' the music, and should be evaluated as such.

It is time now to say exactly what Matravers' theory of musical expressiveness is. It is stated in the traditional philosopher's formula of necessary and sufficient conditions. 'A work of art x expresses an emotion e if, for a qualified observer p experiencing x in normal conditions, x arouses in p a feeling which would be an aspect of the appropriate reaction to the expression of e by a person, or to a representation the content of which was the expression of e by a person.'[20]

There are a number of problems with this definition (if that is what it is). Principal of these seem to me to be the nature of the 'feeling' which Matravers postulates (if that is what he is doing, and more of that anon); and the notion of what emotion felt is 'appropriate' to what emotion expressed.

Let us begin by taking a look at the 'feeling' that lies at the heart of Matravers' arousal theory. In contrasting his view with mine, what I have been calling *the* arousal theory of musical expressiveness, Matravers writes: 'Amongst the mental states caused by perceiving such and such a work [an expressive work], it would be appropriate if there were a state (or incipient state) whose nature were in some way bound up with the emotion.'[21]

What is this 'state'? Well it appears to be what the cognitivist theory of emotions calls the 'feeling component' of the emotions. On the cognitivist account, an emotion has an intentional object (I am afraid of the *tiger* in my garden), it involves a belief or beliefs (I *believe* there is a tiger in my garden, and I *believe* tigers are dangerous), and I 'feel' a certain way (the way fear feels, as opposed, say, to hope or joy).

Now I presume all cognitivists believe emotions do have a feeling component. What they certainly do not believe is that it is the same

---

[20] Matravers, *Art and Emotion*, 146.   [21] Ibid. 146–7.

in all cases of a given emotion. The adrenalin rush and the rest that accompany my fear of the tiger in my garden is certainly not the feeling component of my persistent, gnawing fear that I am suffering from incipient stomach cancer.

Matravers is well aware of this as a potential problem, and discusses it. I am neither clear on, nor convinced by what he says.

What I take to be Matravers' answer to the objection that a given emotion, say sadness, has no common 'feel' in all of its instances, is as follows, and needs to be quoted at some length. It is a gloss of a point of Malcolm Budd's. Matravers writes:

> The main point here is that the list of *kinds* of emotion that music can express is 'embarrassingly short'. A brief and unsystematic review of music criticism (on the programme note level, these being intended to capture the experience of music) supports this view. Certain emotions occur with much greater frequency than others. Among the most popular we find such terms as: melancholy, gay, gloomy, joyful and calm. Thus the problem for the arousal theory is not as might have been supposed. If there are only a small number of kinds of expressive judgement, there need be only a small number of kinds of feeling aroused by music. This, it seems to me, is very probably true.[22]

Now if the above *is* a response to the present objection, it is a palpable *non sequitur*. Recall the objection. Matravers claims that I am caused to believe a work of music is sad in virtue of its having aroused in me the feeling component of an emotion that would be the appropriate response to someone's expressing the emotion I come to believe the music is expressive of. So, the story goes, the music arouses in me the feeling component of sadness (not, mind you, sadness itself); the arousal of this feeling causes me to believe the music is sad; sadness is an appropriate response to someone's expressing sadness.

The objection is: there *is* no common feeling component to sadness. The subjective feel of sadness varies with the circumstances: the beliefs and intentional objects involved in any given experience of sadness. So if the theory Matravers is touting requires that there be a common 'feel' to all cases of music expressive of sadness etc., it cannot be right. There does not seem to be any such common feel.

But not to worry, Matravers seems to be saying: there is only a very small repertory of musical emotions. So there could be, in the musical case, a small repertory of common 'feels.'

---

[22] Matravers, *Art and Emotion*, 153.

That response, however, completely misses the point. The objection is not that the variety of 'feels' is due to the variety of emotions. It is that there is a variety of 'feels' to the *same* emotion. Even if there were only two musical emotions, sadness and happiness, there still would be, if non-musical experience is any guide (and what other guide is there?), a large variety of 'feels' to each of these two emotions. Sadness does not 'feel' the same every time we experience it in our extra-musical lives. Why should we think there is a common 'feel' every time we experience sad music? Why should we think the sadness of a particular movement of Mahler's feels the same as the sadness of a particular movement of Bach's or Mozart's?

Now Matravers might reply here that his theory in no way requires all cases of perceiving the sadness of music to arouse the same feeling, in the sense of a feeling with the same phenomenological, experiential quality. All his definition says is that it be the feeling component of sadness. And since, in non-musical cases, this feeling component is experientially different in different instances, why cannot that be so in the musical cases as well?

To begin with, if some piece of music arouses one feeling in me, that piece of music another, even though both might, in extra-musical contexts be feeling components of different kinds of sadness, why should both of them, and many others as well, cause me to believe the music is sad? The fact is that 'raw feels' of different emotions are often the same. The 'excitement' of fear and the 'excitement' of joy might well involve the same visceral sensations: the same gut feelings. What differentiates them is the attendant beliefs and intentional objects. If the 'feels' are more or less the same, why should one cause me to believe the music is sad, another the music is happy? I suppose one can reply, 'They just *do*, that's all.' But why should I believe that?

In any event, that is not the direction Matravers seems to want to go. For he is at pains to show that the feeling aroused by music, which causes us to believe it is sad, does have the same introspective quality each time. 'The phenomenological profile of melancholy differs from that of joy and, I suspect, differs from that of sadness and gloom as well.'[23]

Indeed, the analogy Matravers wants to draw between his arousal theory of musical expressiveness and color perception pretty much requires this move. We assume, in color perception, that all things perceived as red arouse the same sensation, and that the arousal of this sensation causes us to see things as red. Likewise, we assume that all things perceived as blue arouse the same sensation, different, of course, from the sensation of red, and the arousal of *this* sensation causes us to see things as blue. That is part of what makes the standard causal theory of color perception seem plausible to us.

If the analogy Matravers wishes to draw, between color perception and the perception of music's expressive qualities, is to reap any benefits for the latter, it must trade on this aspect of the former: in other words, it must preserve, in the analogy, the correspondence of feelings in the latter to color sensations in the former. Sensations of redness are different from sensations of blueness: hence sensations of redness cause us to believe objects are red, sensations of blueness cause us to believe objects are blue. But all sensations of redness are the same to each other, all sensations of blueness the same to each other, else the causal regularity that makes the whole scheme plausible would break down. And by parity of reasoning, all feelings that are feeling components of sadness must be the same (subjectively) to each other, all 'feelings' that are feeling components of joy must be the same (subjectively) to each other, else the causal regularity that makes this whole scheme plausible would break down.

But there is evidence that the feeling components of various instances of sadness are *not* always the same to each other. And there is also evidence that the feeling components of different emotions are sometimes more or less the same to each other. The evidence comes from our everyday experiences of the emotions, and it counts *against* the thesis that the feeling components aroused by different pieces of sad music are always the same (subjectively) to each other, if, indeed, sad music arouses them (which I doubt, since I know of no mechanism that would enable it to do so). It also counts against the thesis that music expressive of the different emotions always arouses different feeling components (if, indeed, they are aroused at all, which, I repeat, I doubt). In this respect the analogy between color perception and the perception of expressive qualities breaks down, and, along with it, the causal regularity of the expressive scheme that Matravers is advancing.

What also counts against Matravers' thesis, and I turn to that now, is the notion of the 'appropriate response' to the expression of an emotion by a person, which notion is essential to his project. In this Matravers inherits a problem that goes all the way back to the very first account of our emotional reactions to art works, to wit, Plato's, in the *Republic*. So I shall call it 'Plato's problem.'

Plato is the original propounder of what is sometimes called the 'identification' theory of audience emotion. According to this theory, we, as audience to fiction, 'identify' with the characters in stories, and feel the emotions they feel. And as is well known, the theory cannot be right, because, among other things, it produces the 'wrong' audience emotions. In fiction, *as in life*, the appropriate and forthcoming emotional response to someone's expression of an emotion is *not*, usually, that same emotion, but a different one, appropriate to the occasion. If a villain, in fiction or in life, expresses joy, I will react, appropriately enough, with sadness or anger, but not joy; and if he should express sadness, likely as not my reaction will be joy. If, in fiction or in life, someone should express anger, anger *might* be the appropriate reaction to it, but so also might fear be, if the angry person is dangerous: fear for myself or for some third party. In sum, the appropriate and expected emotional reaction to someone's expressing an emotion will not necessarily, or even usually, be that same emotion but one of a variety of many different emotions, depending upon who is expressing it and under what circumstances and at whom.

According to Matravers, a work of music expresses a certain emotion if it arouses in the listener the feeling component of an emotion that would be the appropriate response to that expressed emotion, if it were expressed by a person. That at least is how I interpret what he is saying. Does Matravers fall foul of Plato's problem? One way or another, I think that he does.

Let me instance some cases in point. The first movement of Mozart's Fortieth Symphony, the second movement of Beethoven's Seventh Symphony, and the first movement of Brahms's First Symphony—the opening anyway—are deeply melancholy. That being the case, they are supposed to arouse, according to Matravers' theory, the feeling component of an emotion that would be the appropriate response to a person who is expressing deep melancholy. In contrast, the Gavotte of Bach's Third Suite for Orchestra, the last movement of Beethoven's Seventh Symphony, and the second scherzo of Brahms's First Orchestral Serenade are expressive of exuberant joy. That being the case, they are supposed to arouse, according to Matravers' theory, the feeling component of an emotion that would be the appropriate emotional response to a person who is expressing exuberant joy.

But the question is: What would be the appropriate emotive response to the expression of deep melancholy, in the first three cases, the exuberant joy in the second three? The answer is: *there is no answer*.

If I were to say: 'A man is dancing for joy. What is the appropriate emotional reaction to that?' One would reply: 'Who is the man? What is he joyful about?' Is it Adolf Hitler, rejoicing over the capitulation of Paris? The appropriate reaction to that, on any patriotic Frenchman's part, is anger, revulsion, fear, deep melancholy: certainly not joy. Is it my rival for a job we were both keen on getting, rejoicing that he was hired and not me? The appropriate emotional reaction on my part, not being a saint, is a sharp pang of jealousy and regret: certainly not joy. Need I go on with this, and go over the cases in which melancholy is being expressed? Surely the lesson is clear. The appropriate emotional reaction to the expression of an emotion by a person is, more likely than not, *not* that same emotion, but a different one.

What, now, of the musical cases? Clearly, Matravers expects us to think it obvious that in all three cases of melancholy music, the appropriate emotional response to a person expressing that emotion is melancholy, and hence that the feeling component of melancholy is what the music arouses in all those cases. Likewise, he expects us to think it obvious that in all three cases of exuberantly joyful music, the appropriate emotive response to a person expressing that emotion is exuberant joy, and hence that the feeling component of exuberant joy is what the music, in all three cases, arouses.

But why should we acquiesce in this? Why should we accept the conclusion that in all three cases of melancholy music cited, the appropriate reaction to a person expressing this emotion is the same emotion, melancholy, when that is only infrequently the case in life? Why should we accept the conclusion that in all three cases of exuberantly joyful music cited the appropriate emotional reaction to a person expressing this emotion is the same emotion, exuberant joy, when that is only infrequently the case in life? The answer is, we *shouldn't*. Plato's problem, clearly, is Matravers' problem as well.

Furthermore, we shouldn't even accept the question. It has no rational answer. To ask what *the* appropriate emotional reaction to a person's expressing a given emotion is makes no sense outside of a context, as we have seen. And the musical cases give us no context at all. To the question what *an* appropriate emotional response to a person's expressing a given emotion is, the answer is, any emotion at all, including the same emotion, since there are circumstances in which *any* emotion, you name it, is appropriate as a response to any other emotion, you name it. Again, Plato's problem is Matravers' problem.

Return, for a moment, to Matravers' 'definition.' It says that music expressive of an emotion arouses in the listener the feeling component of an emotion that is the proper response to someone's expressing that emotion. Suppose the feeling component that is aroused is the feeling component of joy. Does it follow that the music is joyful? Why should it? Joy is the proper emotional reaction to many emotions other than joy. It is frequently the proper emotional reaction to sadness. Why shouldn't the feeling component of joy that the music arouses cause us to believe the music is sad? But would anyone find it in the least bit plausible that the arousing of the feeling component of joy by a piece of music should cause someone to believe the music is sad?

Take our three examples of sad music: the Mozart, the Beethoven, the Brahms. What feeling component does each of these three movements arouse? Don't say, 'The feeling component of sadness; after all, the music is sad.' That would be arguing in a circle. The music is sad in virtue of arousing the feeling component of sadness, presumably. And it just begs the question in favor of Matravers' theory to assume or stipulate that the feeling component aroused by the music *must* be the feeling component of sadness because the music is sad.

I suppose a more reasonable response to the question of what feeling component is aroused by sad music would be an appeal to introspection. The problem is that the introspective reports of writers on this subject seem to pretty much correspond with their own particular theories. Many people in the past have insisted that sad music makes them sad. Jerrold Levinson says it makes him 'quasi-sad.' I suppose Matravers thinks it arouses in him the (or a?) feeling component of sadness. And I find none of the above in my musical experience. I experience unalloyed joy when I listen to sad music that is great music, utter boredom when it is sad music that is bad music.

With regard to the examples of sad and joyful music, Matravers seems to me to have two choices, both equally unpalatable. He can say that some sad music arouses one appropriate feeling component, some another, that some joyful music arouses one appropriate feeling component, some another, as in life. But then he will be hard pressed to make it the least bit plausible as to why we should call all the music that arouses these *diverse* appropriate feeling contents, sad and joyful, respectively. (Why should I call a piece of music that arouses the feeling component of anger or jealousy 'joyful,' or a piece that arouses the feeling component of joy 'sad'? Yet jealousy and anger are appropriate emotional responses to the expression of joy, joy an appropriate emotive response to the expression of sadness.)

Contrariwise, Matravers may claim that all sad music arouses the (or a) feeling component of sadness, all joyful music the (or a) feeling component of joy, thus making his causal thesis at least prima facie plausible. But he must then dispel the implausibility of the thesis that, in musical cases, the appropriate response to an emotion is *always* that same emotion, whereas in life it is not: indeed seldom is. The removal of one implausibility simply substitutes another in its place.

In concluding this discussion, it is only fair to point out that Matravers is not totally unaware of what I have been calling Plato's problem, and he devotes some brief remarks to it. But judging from them, I suspect that he does not fully realize its real force.

Matravers considers, to begin with, the possible objection that since an appropriate reaction to an expression of grief might be grief or might be pity, his theory would not track the right expressive property. He replies that 'This objection obviously does not touch the version of the arousal theory I am putting forward, in which the appropriate reaction to expressive music is just the feeling component of that emotion in the central case.'[24] And he goes on to conclude that whether the feeling component aroused is of grief *or* of pity, the conclusion will be that the music is expressive of grief. 'Given the links established in the central case, both the feeling aspect of pity and the feeling aspect of sadness will cause the belief that the music expresses grief.'[25]

But the problem with this response lies in Matravers' notion of 'the links established in the central case . . .'[26] What *is* the central case? Obviously Matravers thinks it is the case of grief arousing pity. So the reasoning would be something like this. Granted there are a lot of different emotions one might be moved to, appropriately, by an

---

[24] Matravers, *Art and Emotion*, 162.   [25] Ibid. 162–3.   [26] Ibid. 162.

expression of grief, by far the most frequently (and appropriately?) felt is pity. So the links between grief and pity are so strongly forged that, inevitably, if in music we are aroused to the feeling component of pity, we will ascribe grief to the music.

The problem is that the grief–pity links are just not dominant, as Matravers' view requires. (If they were, I guess there would be far less cruelty and indifference to suffering in the world.) The grief–joy links are certainly present. How frequently we rejoice in the misfortunes of others! That is not a bizarre, neurotic reaction: it is a perfectly natural one, given our motives of self-interest, our jealousies, our hatreds. The links between the expression of grief and the experiencing of joy *are* a 'central case.'

Matravers details his answer to what I have been calling Plato's problem more fully by adducing a distinction between two ways of hearing an expressive work: hearing it from 'within' and hearing it from 'without'.[27] Thus, when we listen (say) to Beethoven's *Eroica* Symphony, we can hear it as an expression of grief, identify with the persona expressing it, and experience the feeling component of grief; that is internal hearing. Or, 'we can react to it with the feeling component of pity—that would be to experience it from without'.[28] Matravers adds: 'But if we react with the feeling component of pity, that fact no more entails that the work itself expresses pity than our reaction to a sad person entails that they too are feeling pity.'[29]

Let me first remark that in real life, it is just as common, just as likely, just as appropriate, that when I observe someone expressing grief, I will feel joy, as that I will experience grief or pity (for reasons previously stated). Does Matravers want to argue that someone listening to the *Eroica* 'from without' would be just as likely to experience the feeling component of joy as the feeling component of grief or pity? He would have to if he is to maintain the analogy with 'real life' consistently.

Putting that aside, however, the whole 'mechanics' here seem out of kilter. In real life, *first* I perceive that someone is expressing grief, *then* I react with grief, or pity, or joy, or whatever, depending upon the circumstances and my relation to the person expressing the emotion. But I thought that in the musical case, according to Matravers' theory, *first* I experience the feeling component, *then*, and on the basis of that, I hear the emotion in the music. So if I experience the

[27] Ibid. 162.   [28] Ibid. 164.   [29] Ibid.

feeling component of pity when listening to the *Eroica*, I should, on
Matravers' theory, hear pity in the music and ascribe pity to it.

Matravers, furthermore, cannot have it the other way round, so
far as I can see. For if he says that *first* we recognize grief in the
Eroica, *then* experience the feeling component of pity, as, in real life
we recognize that someone is expressing grief, and then experience
pity, he no longer has *his* arousal theory, if an arousal theory at all.
(What theory he then would have is another question entirely.) So if
what I have just been discussing is an attempt by Matravers to defend
himself against what I have been calling Plato's problem, I cannot see
that he has succeeded in his attempt.

But I have gone on too long and must press on to my conclusion.

IV

I have argued in the preceding pages that there is, in fact, only *one*
arousal theory of musical expressiveness, properly so called. All the
rest of what might be widely construed as arousal theories are other
explanations of how music possesses expressive properties, which
rely, at some point, on the arousal of *some* conscious state or other
in the listener. But thus widely construed, *every* theory is an arousal
theory, including the very cognitive theory Matravers opposes and I
affirm.

Nevertheless, there are, after all, arousal theories and arousal theories, even in this wide sense; and perhaps some more than others
deserve to be called 'arousal theories' in more than the minimal sense
of involving the arousal of *some* state or other of consciousness.
What might those be?

One could, I imagine, rank order arousal theories as being more or
less distant from *the* arousal theory, depending upon how far or close
the conscious states involved in them are from the ones we call by the
names of the garden-variety emotions. In such a ranking, Matravers'
theory would be close rather than far, since the conscious state
involved is thought to be at least part of an emotional state, which is
to say, its feeling component.

Clearly, Matravers thinks that it is both a plus for his theory that
it does not say music arouses emotions, as well as a plus that the
conscious state it says expressive music arouses is *close* to emotions
on our scale, being an emotion-part. He is certainly right about the

former but not, I think, the latter. I would be the last to demur from Matravers' claim that music does *not* arouse the garden-variety emotions. In saying that he is, again, perfectly correct in thinking that he has avoided my criticisms of what I have been calling *the* arousal theory of musical expressiveness. To be sure he has: his theory is not *the* arousal theory.

However, as I have tried to show, it is definitely *not* a plus for Matravers' theory that it stays *close* to *the* arousal theory in construing what music arouses as an emotion-part. For even as an emotion-part, not an emotion, it suffers from many of the problems of *the* arousal theory, most particularly, what I have called Plato's problem.

To me Matravers' theory of musical expressiveness is not a forward but a backward step. Philosophy has a very predictable dialectic. No philosophical theory ever seems to die; but nor does it fade away, like old soldiers and scientific theories are said to do. Rather it goes into a state of hibernation; and when its time comes again it is reawakened. I had hoped the theory in question would have had a longer sleep, so that we could experience how good things are without it. Perhaps it is not yet fully awake—perhaps it is merely a somnambulist we can put back to bed for yet a while longer, so that we can get on with other business. That is what I hope. If it must walk again, let it be on someone else's watch.

PART III

More about Music

8

Absolute Music and the New Musicology

Introduction

In 1980, in my book *The Corded Shell*, I wrote,

Description of music is in a way unique. When it is understandable to the nonmusician, it is cried down as nonsense by the contemporary musician. And when the musician or musical scholar turn their hands to it these days, likely as not the nonmusician finds it as mysterious as the Cabala, and about as interesting as a treatise on sewage disposal.[1]

And I completed my thought with what certainly seems to me now the very modest suggestion, that 'We *can* have intellectually respectable description of music that is not remote from the humanistic understanding to which music itself has traditionally appealed. We *can*, in particular, have intellectually respectable description in the familiar emotive mode . . .'[2] Five years later, Joseph Kerman wrote, in a book well known to many readers, 'As a kind of formalistic criticism, analysis does not address all or even many of the problems that must be faced if music is to be studied in its integrity.'[3]

Both these passages were, I suppose, expressions of the same musical *Zeitgeist*; and both have been, in their way, prophetic. For the last ten to fifteen years have seen a profound change in the way professional, technically trained musicologists and music analysts talk about what I shall call here, 'absolute music'. And I understand this to be one aspect of what is currently being called 'the new musicology'. It is the aspect I am primarily concerned with and to which the title of this chapter refers.

[1] Peter Kivy, *The Corded Shell: Reflections on Musical Expression* (Princeton: Princeton University Press, 1980), 3.
[2] Ibid. 10–11.
[3] Joseph Kerman, *Contemplating Music: Challenges to Musicology* (Cambridge, Mass.: Harvard University Press, 1985), 115.

I cannot, of course, speak for Joseph Kerman. But speaking for myself, the profound change in how we can respectably speak about absolute music, which both Kerman and I called for in the early 1980s, has become a change that I do not find congenial or, sometimes, even respectable. However, I have not come to make an argument. Rather, I bring to this chapter a mind at least temporarily unmade-up rather than frozen in intransigency. It is in that spirit that I want to present my remarks concerning what I call the 'problem of absolute music', and how that problem stands between me and the new musicology. I confess that I do not thoroughly understand even what is at issue; and before I understand that I can scarcely argue for what I think I believe.

But this I *do* believe. Of the problems that currently concern those, like me, who describe ourselves as 'philosophers of art', none is more difficult, more important, or less understood than the problem of absolute music. I hope this chapter will help to advance our understanding of that problem. A solution, now, is too much to hope for.

The Problem

Now, obviously, we cannot discuss what I am calling *the* problem of absolute music without first knowing what we take the appellation 'absolute music' to denote. And that in itself is a job-and-a-half. I do not want to get bogged down in it. So let me begin by offering, not a definition, whatever that might mean, but a vague characterization, a rough-and-ready one of what a piece of absolute music might be.

I want to distinguish between what I shall call 'content interpretation,' and 'structure interpretation.' I shall not characterize them further, but merely present an example of each, and rely on shared intuitions and common sense to grasp the fairly obvious point. Here then first, an example of content interpretation: 'Stevenson suggests [in *Dr Jekyll and Mr Hyde*] that evil is potentially more powerful than good, and if we allow it to come into the open we are in effect allowing it to conquer. But in order to understand evil and oppose it we must examine it.'[4] And now, here, an example of structure interpretation:

---

[4] Jenni Calder, in her Introduction to Robert Louis Stevenson, *Dr. Jekyll and Mr. Hyde, and Other Stories* (Harmondsworth: Penguin Books, 1979), 10.

I intend the phrase 'weakly transitional' precisely, for it exactly captures the balance Milton achieves [in *L'Allegro*] by deploying his connections. If there were no transitions, the freedom of the poem's experience would become a burden, since a reader would first notice it and then worry about it; and if the transitions were fairly directing, a reader would be obliged to follow the directions they gave. Milton has it both ways, just as he does with the syntax that is not so much ambiguous as it is loose.[5]

I can now state without further ado what a piece of absolute music would be. It would be a piece of music for which only structural interpretations are appropriate. And the *problem* of absolute music, briefly stated, is the problem of why and how such music is enjoyable and important for us, given that it lacks just those things that content interpretation deals with, and which seem to play so prominent a role in our enjoyment and appreciation, and which seem so vital to the value that the fine arts hold for us. Denuded of the things that content interpretation reveals, which is left but an empty structural shell? Yet that empty, structural shell is just what a piece of absolute music must be, if it is defined as music for which only structural interpretation is appropriate. That is the problem.

The Solution

Now at this point, one might well be thinking, it would be useful not merely to have a characterization of what a piece of absolute music might be—namely a piece of music for which only a structure interpretation can be appropriate—but some examples of the beast. So here are three, Bach's *Art of Fugue*, Haydn's Symphony No. 83, and the Fourth Symphony of Tchaikovsky's, chosen, on purpose, from the three modern periods that constitute our mainstream concert repertory: the High Baroque, the Classical Period, and the Age of Romanticism. If these three are not absolute music as defined, then what is? It is music of *this* kind that poses, for philosophy, the problem of absolute music.

However, I have played a trick on myself. For, by some strange coincidence, all three of these musical works have been given content interpretations in recent years. And so they are *not*, apparently, on my own characterization of what absolute music is, examples of it.

[5] Stanley Fish, *Is There a Text in this Class?: The Authority of Interpretive Communities* (Cambridge, Mass.: Harvard University Press, 1980), 118.

Here are those interpretations, in brief.

First, Hans Eggebrecht's partial interpretation of the *Art of Fugue*:

Because Bach connected the pitches B-A-C-H to this emphatic cadential process, I cannot believe that he only intended to say: 'I composed this.' Rather, appending the double discant clausula to the B-A-C-H motto seems to say, 'I am identified with the Tonic and it is my desire to reach it.' Interpreted more broadly, this statement could read: 'Like you I am human. I am in need of salvation; I am certain in the hope of salvation, and have been saved by grace.'[6]

Second, David P. Schroeder's partial interpretation of Haydn's Symphony No. 83:

In the conclusion of the first movement of No. 83, Haydn can be seen to be demonstrating a very fundamental yet difficult truth: opposition is inevitable, and the highest form of unity is not the one which eliminates conflict. On the contrary, it is one in which opposing forces can coexist. The best minds of Haydn's age aspired to tolerance, not dogmatism. It is precisely this message that can be heard in many of Haydn's late symphonies.[7]

And, finally, Susan McClary's partial interpretation of Tchaikovsky's Fourth Symphony. In the Fourth Symphony, McClary believes, Tchaikovsky

is, in effect, deconstructing the powerful narrative paradigm of adventure and conquest that had underwritten the symphony since its beginnings.

For what we have [in Tchaikovsky's Fourth] is a narrative in which the protagonist seems victimized by patriarchal expectations and by sensual feminine entrapment: both forces actively block the possibility of his self-development.[8]

So, here we have three content interpretations by what I shall call the new musicologists (although that is perhaps a misnomer applied to Eggebrecht), that seem completely to explode my three examples of what I take to be paradigmatic instances of absolute music. For if these three compositions are all susceptible to content interpretation, they are not, by my own characterization of absolute music, examples of absolute music.

---

[6] Hans Heinrich Eggebrecht, *J. S. Bach's 'The Art of Fugue': The Work and Its Interpretation*, trans. Jeffrey L. Prater (Ames, Ia.: Iowa State University Press, 1993), 8.

[7] David P. Schroeder, *Haydn and the Enlightenment: The Late Symphonies and their Audience* (Oxford: Clarendon Press, 1990), 88.

[8] Susan McClary, 'Sexual Politics in Classical Music,' *Feminine Endings: Music, Gender, and Sexuality* (Minneapolis: University of Minnesota Press, 1991), 76–7.

Well, not to worry, the old musicologist might reply. You have simply picked bad examples. (What can one expect from a philosopher?) Take, rather, *The Well-tempered Clavier*, Mozart's Symphony No. 41, and Brahms's Third.

But I think it abundantly clear that this gambit will be totally ineffective. For there seems to be absolutely no reason to doubt that the same techniques that produced these content interpretations of the *Art of Fugue*, Haydn's Symphony No. 83, and Tchaikovsky's Fourth, can generate similar interpretations of *any* piece of instrumental music, from the sixteenth century to the day before yesterday. (Indeed, McClary has already produced a sexual interpretation of Brahms's Third Symphony.) So there is *no* example I could choose that would qualify, under my definition, as absolute music. That being the case, there is *no problem* of absolute music. For if, as I have formulated it, the problem of absolute music is the problem of explaining what we enjoy, appreciate, and value in music that contains none of the things content interpretations reveal, then absolute music is the null class: an empty set, literally *nothing at all*. And so there is nothing to explain. The new musicology has solved the problem of absolute music by simply demonstrating, by example, that there is no such animal.

Probing the Solution

Well at this point, since my problem has just dissolved before our very eyes, I suppose I should pack up my bags and take my show on the road. But no. There are two more acts to go, and I intend to stay for the curtain.

Of course, the old musicologist has not shot his bolt yet. He will, doubtless, argue that there are techniques abroad for generating content interpretations of absolute music. There have been all along, witness A. B. Marx *et al.* But what the old musicologist will claim is that they are not valid, correct, true, plausible interpretations (or whatever your favorite evaluative term is for them). So the definition of absolute music can now be rephrased as music for which there is no *correct* content interpretation, only a structural one.

Now it is no good for the old musicologist simply to claim that the three interpretations I have adduced of the three works in question are incorrect, for one reason or another. What he must claim is that *no* such interpretation is correct. It must be a general claim about *all* content interpretations whatever.

But how can that claim be made out? It is, after all, a pretty broad, arrogant claim. Who dares say what *cannot* be done in the future, in this line of work, even if it cannot be done today?

In order, then, for the old musicologist to fix the new musicologist's wagon, he must somehow show that the *kind* of content interpretation being offered is just not possible for the works under consideration, whether the content be religious, philosophical, sexual—whatever.

Here, however, we are liable to get hung up on the word 'kind.' There must be many different kinds of interpretational procedures that might be applied to instrumental music to the end of generating content interpretations, and I cannot hope to canvass them all in so short a discussion. So I will confine myself to three (what might be called) 'models' of content interpretation, and explore the issues raised by each. I shall call them the linguistic model, the representational model, and the anything goes model. Needless to say this is hardly an exhaustive list.

I can get right to the heart of the linguistic model and its problems by quoting from what I take to be one of the masterpieces of the philosophical literature. The reader will recognize it immediately without further help from me.

'[A]nd that shows that there are three hundred and sixty-four days when you might get un-birthday presents—'

'Certainly,' said Alice.

'And only *one* for birthday presents you know. There's glory for you!'

'I don't know what you mean by "glory," ' Alice said.

Humpty Dumpty smiled contemptuously. 'Of course you don't—till I tell you. I meant "there's a nice knock-down argument for you." '

'But "glory" doesn't mean "a nice knock-down argument," ' Alice objected.

'When *I* use a word,' Humpty Dumpty said, in rather a scornful tone, 'it means just what I choose it to mean—neither more nor less.'

'The question is,' said Alice, 'whether you can make words mean so many different things.'

'The question is,' said Humpty Dumpty, 'which is to be master— that's all.'[9]

Now the old musicologist might think that he can get a quick victory by merely appealing to the Humpty Dumpty syndrome. Just as

---

[9] Lewis Carroll, *Alice's Adventures in Wonderland, Through the Looking Glass and the Hunting of the Snark*, ed. Alexander Woolcott (New York: The Modern Library, n.d.), 246–7.

words *cannot* mean whatever we say they mean, so too with instrumental music. The new musicologists, so he will say, are just a bunch
of Humpty Dumptys, putting interpretations on music that the
music simply will not bear. The rules and conventions for generating
the kinds of interpretations the new musicologists put on the instrumental repertory are non-existent, just as are the rules and conventions for generating the interpretation Humpty Dumpty puts on the
word 'glory,' to wit, 'there's a nice knock-down argument'. And
without such rules and conventions, the interpretation cannot fly.

There are various possible answers, worth considering, that the new
musicologist might offer to the charge of Humpty Dumptyism, and I
cannot consider them all here, nor any in the detail it deserves. But I
will take a look at two, the second of which will segue nicely into the
second interpretative model, what I called the representational model.

One, somewhat radical direction the new musicologist's answer
might take is simply to reject the linguistic intuition underlying the
debate between Alice and Humpty Dumpty, that 'glory' cannot
mean 'there's a nice knock-down argument.' After all, it is not
simply the word 'glory' that Humpty and Alice are arguing about: it
is the word 'glory' *in a text*. And, on Stanley Fish's view of text-
interpretation, to take but one contemporary example, 'while there
are always mechanisms for ruling out readings, their source is not the
text but the presently recognized interpretative strategies for producing the text. It follows, then, that no reading, no matter how outlandish it might appear, is inherently an impossible one.'[10] For the
mechanisms that produce interpretations evolve: they are not time-
less logical rules. And although there *were* mechanisms in Alice's and
Humpty's world for ruling out the latter's interpretation of 'glory' in
that text, it does not mean that at some future time there might not
be a critical mechanism for enfranchising it.

And that's just the point, the new musicologist might triumphantly
retort to the charge of Humpty Dumptyism. *We* have, through our
interpretations, *created* the critical mechanisms that make such 'outlandish' interpretations outlandish no longer. Of course a sexual
interpretation of Tchaikovsky's Fourth Symphony, or Brahms's
Third would not have been possible in 1956. But they are possible
now because the rules have changed. By our *practice*, the new musicologist asserts, *we* have changed them.

---

[10] Fish, *Is There a Text in This Class?*, 347.

Of course Stanley Fish's view of interpretation, in particular that texts are *created* by critics, is a highly contentious one. Many people reject it and its implications, as do I. But for those of the brave new musicologists who want to defend it as a foundation for their interpretations of the instrumental repertory, it is still on offer.

But for those of the new musicologists who cannot accept Fish's theory, and those like it, musicologists who still retain Alice's intuition that words—for which read 'texts'—cannot mean what we want them to mean, even in Fish's sense, there is another, quite obvious ploy. It is to reject out of hand the linguistic model of content interpretation for music. We are not interpreting texts, they will reply, so the whole debate between Alice and Humpty talks right past us. Music does not *tell*, it *shows*. We hear things in music the way we see things in pictures. And that brings us to the second model of content interpretation for music, the representational model.

Pictorial representation—and that is the mode of representation I will be talking about now—has been under close philosophical scrutiny for the past twenty-five or thirty years, since, that is to say, the publication of Ernst Gombrich's *Art and Illusion* and Nelson Goodman's *Languages of Art*. There are, as might be expected, competing theories, and there is no time here to even begin to enumerate them. I shall simply adduce as an example, one fairly simple to state and intuitively appealing account, Richard Wollheim's, and see what it can do for the new musicologist.

Very briefly, on Wollheim's view, we have a natural psychological propensity for what he calls 'seeing-in': it is a propensity to 'see' things 'in' visual configurations, in visual patterns, whether these are 'natural,' like clouds, driftwood, or stains on a wall, or whether they are artefactual, like drawings and oil paintings. Thus we can see a face or figure in this cloud, or that stain on the wall, and we can see a face or a figure in this painting by Titian or that drawing by Rembrandt. But there is a crucial difference between seeing things in natural objects and seeing them in pictorial representations. To quote Wollheim: 'With clouds, rocks, sand, it is no more correct to see one thing in them than another. With paintings this changes. With Titian it is correct to see Venus in a particular stretch of canvas, and incorrect to see anyone or anything else there.'[11]

---

[11] Richard Wollheim, 'Pictures and Language,' *The Mind and its Depths* (Cambridge, Mass.: Harvard University Press, 1993), 188.

'And where does this standard of correctness come from?' Wollheim asks. His not altogether surprising reply is that: 'The criterion comes from the intentions, the fulfilled intentions of the artist . . . in so far as these guided the artist's hand and are retrievable from the work.'[12]

In sum, then, pictorial representations are, for Wollheim, artefactual visual patterns in which we can see those things that the artist who made them intended us to see. Musical representations, by parity of reasoning, will be artefactual audible patterns in which we can *hear* things that the composers who made them intended us to hear.

Now if the new musicologist should accept Wollheim's analysis of pictorial representation as a model for content interpretation in instrumental music, then it can easily be perceived that the intentional criterion of correctness is going to give the old musicologist a vulnerable point to assault. And this would be so, of course, for any other intention-based analysis. For it seems clear that whether composers could possibly have intended folks to hear in their works many of the things the new musicologists hear in them is a *very* contentious point. And on a Wollheimlike view, if we were not intended to hear those things, then it is incorrect to do so: *they are just not there*.

But why should not the new musicologist simply reject the appeal to intention as a 'fallacy'? After all, the New Criticism did a long while ago, and it is a very fashionable stance in literary criticism today as well, the 'death of the author' being one of the more popular slogans in recent years. Indeed, among literary critics the rejection of authorial intention as a critical criterion is far more widespread than its acceptance, even though its acceptance, among analytic philosophers of art, is on the upturn. The new musicologists tend to look about, in current critical theory, for anything that will allow them to widen the possibilities for content interpretation of music— that at least is my impression. So why should they not immediately cleave to the far from unpopular rejection of authorial intention, while embracing a representational model of content interpretation (or a literary one, for that matter)?

Yet musicologists, new *and* old, have tended, rather, to hold on firmly to composer-intention as an article of their faith. Why this is so is worth some thought.

---

[12] Ibid. 189.

My own view is that the so-called historically authentic performance movement, without a doubt the most publicly visible of academic musicology's contributions to contemporary musical culture, motivates musicologists' continued reliance on authorial intention. For adherence to the *performance* intentions of composers is the foundation stone of the enterprise—the most frequently adduced standard by which to measure historical authenticity in performance. And it would be a strange position indeed to take, that would enfranchise the performance intentions of composers as an inviolable standard of correct performance, while discarding *compositional* intentions as a standard of correct content interpretation.

Indeed, it is arguable that adherence to composers' performance intentions is a logical consequence of adherence to composers' compositional intentions. For, presumably, the reason for performing the music the way the composer intended is to the end of correctly conveying his *compositional* intentions. As Stephen Davies has quite explicitly put it, 'a concern with authenticity [of performance] takes its point ultimately from the authority of authorship, from a concern to present accurately (to an audience) what the composer "had to say." '[13]

Nor can there be any doubt that all three of the authors I have tapped for examples of content interpretation adhere to the composer's intentions as a criterion of correctness, at least negatively: which is to say, lack of intention ruling out proffered content interpretation. For all three present elaborate arguments and historical evidence to try to convince us that Bach, Haydn, and Tchaikovsky, could have intended, or very probably did intend us to hear in their music what these interpreters say *they* hear in it. Intentionality seems alive and flourishing in the world of the new musicology.

But suppose the new musicologist is willing to proclaim the death of the author and say 'Be damned!' to what the composer *intended* us to hear in his music. What we *do* hear is all that counts. In that case, representation would collapse into cloud gazing, on Wollheim's view, and, Wollheim says: 'With clouds . . . it is no more correct to see one thing in them than another.' And, we might add, with symphonies and sonatas as well. For now:

> Heaven knows,
> Anything goes.

---

[13] Stephen Davies, 'Transcription, Authenticity and Performance,' *British Journal of Aesthetics*, 28 (1988), 223.

The Problem (Again)

I have sketched, in my preceding remarks, three different ways of seeing the now prevalent tendency to put content interpretations on
what the purveyors of such interpretations might describe as
'absolute music *so-called*.' And I have tried to indicate, for discussion, some of the issues involved therein.

But you will recall, what seems to be the case is that if any one of
these ways of generating content interpretations of absolute music
'so-called' is valid, then what I touted in the beginning of this chapter as *the* 'big deal,' heavy problem of 'absolute music' evaporates
into thin air. No absolute music, no problem.

Actually this was not meant to be the main point of this chapter,
which I have only just now really reached. It will be a relief to know,
I am sure, that though it *is* my main point, and, I think, a very important one for the philosophy of music, it will not take very long to
make.

To make my point, let me introduce you to three folk called Hugh,
Lew, and Sue. Hugh likes to listen to recitations of German poetry,
and has a very large collection of recordings to feed his habit. The
odd thing is that Hugh does not understand a word of German. And
when you ask him why he does what he does, he replies: 'I like to hear
the pattern, sonority, and structure of the sounds.'

Lew is more interested in the visual arts, particularly Renaissance
painting, frequents fine arts museums, and has an impressive collection of slides. But he suffers from a very rare case of perceptual depri-
vation (indeed I don't know another such in the literature) called
'representation-blindness.' He can, for example, see the Sistine
Ceiling as an elaborate colored pattern, and can gaze at it for hours
in rapture; but he cannot see it as a picture of human beings. And so
with the rest of the paintings he loves. He sees them all merely as
lovely abstract designs.

Sue's preoccupation I am sure you have already surmised. I might
have called her Hanslick, or Schenker, or Kivy, for that matter. I will
come back to her in a moment.

Now if it were to be suggested that the aesthetic experience of
Hugh or Lew ought to be a problem of even marginal interest for the
philosophy of art, I think the suggestion would, quite rightly, be
rejected out of hand. Hugh's predilection for the mere *sound* of

German poetry is not pathological; but it is not an experience of German *poetry*, in a perfectly clear sense that I need dilate upon no further. And it is the experience of German *poetry*, or poetry in general, not its sound as perceived by someone who does not understand the language in which it is written, that the philosopher of art seeks to understand.

Lew, on the other hand, if such an affliction as his really exists, is clearly a case not for the philosopher but for Oliver Sachs. For to mistake the Sistine Ceiling for an abstract pattern is no less pathological than to mistake your wife for a hat. And, as a philosopher of art, I need say no more about it.

Of course one might choose, for one reason or another, in closely studying poetry, to concentrate temporarily on the mere sound structure of the words, or, likewise, temporarily fasten on the pure design qualities of a representational painting. But someone who regularly, exclusively, only attended to the sounds of words in poetry, not their meaning, or the patterns of pictures, not their content, if such stances are even possible, could hardly be considered an aesthetic appreciator of poetry or of painting.

Sue, however, is quite another matter. Is she to be dismissed as an amusing anomaly, like Hugh, or a pathological case, like Lew, just because she listens to Beethoven in the manner of Schenker rather than of A. B. Marx? That would be hard to credit.

To enjoy immensely the sound of German poetry, even though one knows not a word of German, is an amusing conceit. To enjoy the Sistine Ceiling as a pattern of lines and colors, without being able to see in it God and Adam and the rest is a pathological condition. But to enjoy the *Art of Fugue*, or Haydn's Symphony No. 83, or Tchaikovsky's Fourth, as pure, albeit expressive structures—what of that? Is it bizarre behavior like Hugh's, or dysfunctional, like Lew's? Can the answer to that question be anything but a resounding 'No!'?

Listening to music as pure sonic structure, in complete ignorance of any content interpretation of what one is listening to, is a fact of musical life. Large numbers of people listen to music in this way. Many of my readers are employed, at least in part, to teach undergraduates how to listen to what is called absolute music. And many, though not of course all, teach this contentless mode of listening. I was taught it; I didn't invent it for myself. Listening to music as pure sonic structure, without perceiving narrative or other content in it, is, in other words, part of Western musical culture, whether you like that way of listening or not. If it were not, the new musicologists could hardly present themselves, as they frequently do, as departing from this 'tradition.'

Thus, *the* problem of absolute music survives *any* kind of content interpretation. It can simply be restated as the problem of what those people who *do* appreciate music in the complete absence of content interpretation appreciate in it: what do *they* enjoy, value, even venerate? These people cannot be dismissed as a lunatic fringe, as the likes of Hugh and Lew might be, nor can their experience of the great instrumental repertory be dismissed as weird or pathological vapors. They are a firmly entrenched interest group, if I may so put it; and their aesthetic appreciation must be taken seriously. It cries out for philosophical understanding.

The new musicology may have introduced or reintroduced other respectable ways of listening to instrumental music than that of the so-called musical formalist. That remains to be seen. But the philosophical problem of absolute music still remains with us, just because contentless listening to musical artworks, unlike contentless reading of poems, or contentless viewing of paintings, provides a rich and completely satisfying aesthetic experience to a large, sophisticated (and unsophisticated) audiences.

Indeed, the problem of absolute music would endure even if the new musicologists should convert the whole world to content interpretation of absolute music, and contentless listening die out altogether. Even in that unlikely event, the problem of absolute music would remain to plague us, as the problem of what in the world we were doing in those Neanderthal days.

So, one way or the other, the puzzle of absolute music remains to be philosophically solved. Whether or not the 'formalist' way of listening to so-called 'absolute music' is the only acceptable, fruitful way of listening, it is certainly *one* acceptable, fruitful way of listening. And as such, it requires an accounting.

9

Movements and 'Movements'

The pun of my title will tell you a good deal about what the topic of this chapter will be. Sonatas, symphonies, concertos, string quartets are composed of 'movements.' That is the word we use to describe the individual, self-contained parts of which they are constituted. We do *not* use that word usually to describe the separate, self-contained parts of an opera, oratorio, song cycle, cantata, in short, the various forms of classical music with text. The word 'movement' seems to be reserved for what the nineteenth century came to call 'absolute music': pure instrumental music without text or title.

The topic of this chapter, then, is, literally, movements: social movements and absolute music. Why have I chosen this topic? A little common sense strongly suggest that I shouldn't have: that it is a topic of no real importance, if it is a topic at all. The organizers of a recent meeting on music and social movements tell us that 'Social Movements are collective efforts by relatively powerless, disadvantaged or threatened groups to protect or advance their shared interests, values and identities. Social movements,' they continue, 'are usually analyzed in terms of their "political" aims and impacts—as struggles to affect distributions of power and material goods to change policy and law, to win political voice.'

What possible role could *music* play, one might skeptically ask, in the facilitating of such practical, politically driven enterprises as *social movements*? Well, as the organizers are quick to point out, 'Music has, of course, many social uses. The anthem, the march, the hymn and the lullaby are all utilitarian musical forms created within, and serving functions for, such major social institutions as the nation, the church, the school and the family. Movements, throughout history, have made use of such traditional and familiar genres—adapting anthems, hymns, ballads, marches and other song forms—and created new ones as well.'

So there is the answer to the skeptic's question. What is so unbelievable, after all, about the claim that anthems unite us in our social movements, marches propel us into battle, political and revolutionary songs send us ideological messages and thereby incite us to action?

All well and good, the skeptic may reply, but the kinds of music just named have a text, or, at least, in the case of marches, and such things, a clearly defined function in the social scheme that one can well imagine enabling them to be a real motivating force in a social movement. Hanns Eisler's songs of the Spanish Civil War propagate a political doctrine. The music, of course, helps (and we shall talk about that later on)—but the words without the music carry the message too. The music without the words? Readers can answer that question for themselves. Did a string quartet ever send men to the barricades, or a symphony start a war?

Of course one might fairly ask, in a cynical vein, whether any work of art ever really had a palpable influence on a social movement. Abraham Lincoln is supposed to have said, when introduced to Harriet Beecher Stowe, 'So this is the little lady who made this big war?' But against this charming anecdote there is the Marxist *Realpolitik*, evinced by Stalin when, during the Second World War, he was confronted with a request from the Vatican. He asked, archly: 'And how many divisions is the Pope supplying?' I heard a well-known Marxist philosopher say once that he was doubtful there was one case in history where an artist really had a palpable effect on a social or political movement. Now I am not saying he was right. All I am suggesting is that even where works of art have out-front, unambiguous, readily discernible political or social messages, it is not simply received opinion, or altogether obvious that they can or have strongly influenced social revolutions. All the more reason, therefore, to be skeptical about whether sonatas and symphonies can or have.

Now it is clear that the people I have been quoting from must have been aware of the, at best, tenuous connection between absolute music and social movements, in particular, the difficulty in establishing that the former can or has influenced the latter. For when they *do* mention absolute music, there is a shift, not signaled to the reader, *from* the question of music's influence on social movements *to* the question of social movements' influence on music. They write: 'Alongside the utilitarian appropriation of music, movements historically have inspired creativity in less "functional" musical genres, such as the symphony, the opera, the Broadway musical.'

I am not quite sure why opera and musical should have been lumped together with symphony. Operas and musicals both include examples of social and political comment: *The Marriage of Figaro*, *Fidelio*, *The Masked Ball* among the former, *Lost in the Stars* and *Finnigan's Rainbow* in the latter category. But they are, perhaps, the exceptions rather than the rule. In any case, we can all agree that symphonies do not seem particularly promising examples of musical works that can or have had any palpable effect on social movements, as defined here; and that goes for concertos, string quartets, and the rest of the pure instrumental forms as well. So it is quite understandable that, in mentioning this so to speak 'non-utilitarian' musical form, the organizers of the aforementioned conference should have naturally slid from the less plausible relation of the music's influencing the social movement to the social movement's influencing the music.

However, it is not all that easy, as a matter of fact, even to show how social or intellectual movements *do* influence absolute music. Further on I shall go into that question a bit more deeply. But for now I merely wish to put on the table, for future discussion, the suggestion that, as opposed (say) to literature or representational painting, it is notoriously difficult to draw convincing lines of influence from social and intellectual movements to the parameters of absolute music contemporaneous with them.

The point I do wish to make right now, however, is that given the at least tenuous connection between social movements and absolute music—highly implausible going in the direction of music to social movement, highly speculative, at best, going in the direction of social movement to music—there seems to be little justification for making it a topic of discussion at all.

Furthermore, if one just considers the 'numbers,' so to speak, the study of the relation, in either direction, between absolute music and social movements is not only implausible but of pretty minimal importance or interest to boot. For, first of all, the number of people in the world today for whom absolute music holds any real attraction at all is so small, compared with the vast number who enjoy music of other kinds, that finding out *anything* about it is bound to be rather trivial, from the sociological point of view. And, second, viewed historically, the period in which absolute music has flourished in the West, let alone in the history of the world's musics, is so brief that, again, from a sociological viewpoint, it is something of little significance, if the numbers count as a criterion. In short, I think music theorists, musicologists, and philosophers tend to forget how really insular and temporally localized the interest in absolute music is, and how out of proportion, perhaps, the attention given to it in the theoretical and philosophical literature, which is not to underestimate its intrinsic interest to philosophers and theorists. Another good reason, therefore, *not* to pay it any attention.

What justification, then, can I possibly give for making the relation, if indeed there even is one, between absolute music and social movements my topic here? Well, I suppose there is always the mountain climber's well-known: 'Because it is there.' But, frankly, I do not think that is even an adequate reason for climbing mountains, let alone pursuing lines of philosophical enquiry. Nor, indeed, do I think it is really why mountains are climbed. No one before the eighteenth century would have dreamed of climbing a mountain except to get to the other side, if there weren't an easier way to do that. Mountains began to be climbed for climbing's sake when they became something more than merely inconvenient geographical impediments to terrestrial navigation: when, that is to say, they became, for us, aesthetic objects and moral challenges. And the last time I read in the news something being done 'because it is there,' it was an attempt to row a boat across the Atlantic Ocean for the first time. Nothing could be sillier, and the party in question got pretty much what he deserved (and you can pretty much guess what that was). 'Because it is there' is a necessary condition for doing anything, and a sufficient reason for doing nothing.

Let me begin my justification for discussing the relation of absolute music to social movements by pointing out the obvious: that merely the small number of people interested in something hardly implies its lack of importance for large numbers of other people. And, in any case, there are so many ways in which the understanding of some cultural institution or object might enlighten us about other cultural institutions and objects far more important than it, in ways we cannot foresee, that we should be very wary of rejecting, a priori, anyone's pet research project.

But these are, after all, pretty vague generalities. I have yet to suggest any reason for believing that the consideration of the possible causal connection, in one direction or the other, between absolute music and social movements should be a topic of interest to anybody. So let me see if I can come up with something to justify it.

I begin with a kind of axiom, a presupposition underlying any reasonable discussion of music with text. If one does not talk about the music as well as the text, one is not talking about the *work*. This may sound so obvious that it should go without saying. But if you dip into the vast literature on opera, for example, the most visible and extravagant of all classical musical forms, you would, I think, be surprised to find, if you are not familiar with it, how little is really said about how the music works. In so many, many cases, the critic might just as well be talking about the libretto alone and, in reality, usually is. (Perhaps that is why Joseph Kerman's *Opera as Drama* was such a revelation—here was someone who was really talking about the drama of *music*, whether one agrees with what he was saying or not.)

Let me go a little further with this thought. There is a temptation to think of vocal music, in the West, as a mixed-media art form. It is, after all, a combination of music and text. But it is both historically and, if I may say so, philosophically misleading to talk this way. For it makes it sound as if there was music, and there was language, and then people got the idea of putting them together for a combined effect. But historically it is inaccurate because as far back as one would like to go, people sang; and instrumental music, at least in its modern form, thrust itself out of vocal forms and did not predate them.

So we cannot look at a Renaissance motet, for example, and say: 'this is what the music does, and this is what the words do, and, by consequence, this is what the words and music do together'. That cannot be how the composers thought. Taking the text from the music and looking at them separately is like looking at a kidney in formaldehyde and expecting to see it perform its function.

But perhaps we can learn something here from experimental science that can help us. I heard a lecture on embryology recently in which the biologist told us about her research project, aimed at isolating the chemical agents in the frog's egg that cause some cells to become one thing, say, epidermal tissue, and other cells another, say endodermal; for in the earliest stages of development the cells are completely undifferentiated. She managed to isolate two chemical agents that seemed to be causally operative in directing cells one way or the other. Which was doing what? That was her question.

Her technique for answering the question was to alter the eggs so that they contained only *one* of the suspected chemical agents, and then see how these eggs developed: easier said than done. But when she succeeded in doing this, she found that if one of the chemical agents alone was present, all the cells became epidermal tissue, and when the other alone was present, all the cells became endodermal tissue. So she had the answer to her question.

Why couldn't we, then, take a leaf from the biologist's book and study the words without the music (chemical agent number one) and the music without the words (chemical agent number two)? We cannot do this because, I think, we would not have, then, the functioning embryo without one or the other chemical, but something more like the kidney in formaldehyde. The embryologist has preserved the functioning egg, minus one or the other chemical agent the function of which she wishes to study in isolation. However, even if the music minus the text or the text minus the music remained a functioning organism, they would be so different from the organism from which they were prised, that one would, essentially, have changed the subject. It is not like the biologist's experiment at all.

Let me suggest, however, that music history has, in a sense, performed the very experiment we want, if we look at it in the proper light.

Begin with the premiss that singing is so natural to the race that as far back as we have been human, we have been singers, and as far back as we have had language (which may also be as far back as we have been human) our singing has had words. Whether making musical sounds with physical objects—that is to say, 'instrumental music'—is also that old I do not pretend to know, the answer perhaps irretrievably lost in the mists of time. But that does not matter much to my argument.

If we now turn to the history of Western art music, it is clear that until fairly recently vocal music has been dominant, and dominant in a big way. Furthermore—and here I make a historical conjecture on precious little knowledge of the subject—modern instrumental music as we know it developed, evolved out of vocal music. That is to say, the great traditions of instrumental music that came into being in the Renaissance, Baroque, and Classical periods, and continue to flourish, did not come into being through what the evolutionists would call parallel development, like apes and humans, but one out of the other, like humans from their humanlike African ancestors (if that story is the correct one).

Suppose, now, to stick with the biology metaphor, I should be asked: 'How would a legless reptile ambulate?' I reply: 'Well, I don't know. Let's see,' and I then proceed to cut off a lizard's legs. Of course, *such* a legless reptile is not a complete, functioning organism at all, will not be able to ambulate, and will quickly die. What I ought to have done, of course, was to procure a snake and observe *it*; for a snake is a legless reptile that has evolved by natural selection to function as an autonomous organism. So if you observe a snake you will find out how legless reptiles can ambulate. Nature has, so to say, performed the experiment for us.

Returning to my subject, if I want to find out and understand fully what function music might perform in those musical forms with texts, such as song, or opera, which we think have had some effect on social movements, one strategy could be first to look at absolute music, rather than the music *in* song or opera. Why? Well, because, in a sense, if we separate the music from the text, we are cutting the legs off a lizard, whereas if we concentrate on pure instrumental music, we are looking at a snake. The point is that if we look at absolute music first, we can find out things about music's function alone that will explain why it must function as it does, when joined to a text for the purpose of *influencing a social movement*. Let me pursue this point further.

Pure instrumental music has evolved as an autonomous artistic organism. If we study what effect it can or cannot have on social movements, we will not only have discovered something of intrinsic interest to all of us, but we will also, I suggest, then be able to look at music with text with a deeper understanding of how *it* can contribute to the fomenting or facilitating of social movements—in particular, how the musical part helps it function to those ends. To return one last time to the biological analogy, we learn little about the locomotion of lizards by cutting off their legs; but we may learn something interesting about it by studying the locomotion of snakes. As nature has performed for us the 'experiment' of reptiles without legs, music history has performed for us the 'experiment' of music without texts. Let us see what this latter experiment can teach us about the influence of music with texts on social movements.

Now as I stated earlier, there are two directions that the relation of social movements to absolute music might take: from movement to music or from music to movement. The question of how social movements have influenced the pure musical parameters is, I take it, a special case of the question of how any set of non-musical ideas can, or have affected the way composers structure their music in terms of harmony, counterpoint, rhythm, dynamics, overall form, expression, and so on. The reason this is such a *hard* question to answer is that absolute music *seems*, at least, to be a kind of self-contained system, walled off from reality, something like chess, say, or pure mathematics, or mathematical logic, all of which can be pursued in almost complete isolation from the outside world of movements and ideas. One thing about them all, music included, is that they can be practised at the very highest level at a very early age, as we know from the likes of Mozart, Gauss, and Bobby Fisher. Does this tell us something about them? As for music, Goethe thought it did. 'The musical talent,' he told Eckermann, '. . . may well show itself earliest of any; for music is something innate and internal, which needs little nourishment from without, and no experience drawn from life.'[1] Hegel shared this belief.

Of course there are those who would say that the pure harmonic and structural parameters of absolute music are immune to extra-musical influence, on more or less formalist grounds; and, contrariwise, those who, on more or less anti-formalist grounds, would claim that they are influenced by the general intellectual background against which absolute music is composed. That is not a debate I want to enter into here, on one side or the other.

Music's influence on social movements rather than social movements' influence on music is my principal theme, although I strongly suspect that people who write about absolute music frequently fudge the distinction.

How, in general, might an artwork help to advance a social movement? Of course there must be many ways. I will confine myself to one. But I am sure it is a very important way, and, perhaps, the way that would most readily come to anyone's mind if the question were raised.

I think it not beyond the realm of possibility that Dickens's novels had a role in improving the way children were treated in the nineteenth century. If they did, it was, I hypothesize, because the great novelist's moving portrayals of how children were mistreated in his day changed people's beliefs about how children should be treated— changed them for the better. One important way, then, that works of art may help motivate social movements is by altering people's beliefs in ways appropriate to these movements: that is to say, instilling in

---

[1] *Conversations of Goethe with Eckermann*, trans. John Oxenford (London: J. M. Dent, 1930), 362.

people beliefs that will motivate them to help forward such movements. And they alter these beliefs by embodying, either explicitly or
(more frequently) by implication, reasons or arguments capable of
changing them.

The question that now confronts us is this. Can absolute music
change our belief systems in such a way as to motivate social movements, in the way, I am assuming, literature, movies, theatre, and
(perhaps) painting can? And that question reduces to a more basic
one. Does absolute music have either the representational potential,
or the potential for propositional content that seems to be necessary
in order to promote social movements? And that question is, clearly,
once again, a special case of the general question of musical 'content'
over which musical formalists and their adversaries have been squab-
bling, lo these many years. Are we, then, to be completely prevented
by this seemingly intractable question from making any further
progress in our attempt to understand the possible effects of absolute
music on social movements? I don't think so; and you will see why
after I have pushed our enquiry ahead a bit further.

As most of my readers will know, there has been a steadily increasing willingness, indeed eagerness on the part of music analysts, theorists, and musicologists to place elaborate content-interpretations on
all the sacred cows of the absolute music canon. None of the great
masters in the repertory, from Bach to Mahler, has escaped
unscathed. And if the label of absolute music is supposed to name a
music without propositional or representational content, there is a
large and growing number of well-known and admired musical analysts who seem prepared to say that it is a label without a reference:
that, in a word, there is no such animal. If these contemporary interpreters of the absolute music canon are correct in their interpretations then absolute music can convey as much propositional and
representational content as the nineteenth-century novel, the narrative film, or the religious paintings of the Renaissance.

To illustrate this last claim let me give a small idea of this 'new
musical criticism'—there is no room for more than that—by
adducing an example. In an essay called 'Sexual Politics in Classical
Music,' widely known to musicologists, Susan McClary writes of the
first movement of Tchaikovsky's Fourth Symphony, 'What we
have is a narrative in which the protagonist seems victimized both by
patriarchical expectations and by sensual feminine entrapment:
both forces actively block the possibility of his self development.'

This interpretation is supported both by detailed musical analysis and by appeal to the composer's own life. Of the latter, she writes: 'Such a narrative resonates strongly with Tchaikovsky's biography. As a homosexual in a world of patriarchically enforced heterosexuality, his behavior was always being judged against cultural models of "real men." '[2]

Now if we can read a number of the novels of Dickens as, in part, narratives of cruelty towards children, I suppose we can read the first movement of Tchaikovsky's Fourth, if McClary's interpretation is correct, as, in part, a narrative of cruelty to and oppression of homosexual men. And if we can conclude, as well, that Dickens was attempting either to foment a social movement against cruelty to children, or to influence favorably one already in place, by depicting in his novels the deplorable plight of children, we can at least contemplate the possibility that Tchaikovsky was, in the narrative of the Fourth Symphony that McClary finds there, trying to do the same for a social movement against cruelty towards homosexual men, by depicting their oppression in his music. Finally, we can now ask: What hope of success might each of these great artists have had, in their respective endeavors to foment or forward the respective social movements?

The formulation of this latest question should, straightaway, reveal a glaring difference between the content of Dickens' novels, *vis-à-vis* the issue of child abuse, and the content (as McClary sees it) of Tchaikovsky's Fourth, *vis-à-vis* the issue of psychological cruelty towards homosexual men. It is this, that no intelligent reader of *Bleak House*, or *Oliver Twist* can possibly come away from these works without having recognized cruelty to children represented therein, *and* that Dickens is presenting a brief against it; whereas it seems fairly clear that until very recently, *no* intelligent listener has heard the first movement of Tchaikovsky's Fourth Symphony as representing hostility towards male homosexuality and presenting a brief against *it*. It took Susan McClary to hear that and reveal it to us, *if*, that is to say, you think that is really what she has done (and I will not argue that point here). In other words, the child abuse issue is part of what might be called the 'manifest content' of the Dickens novels, whereas the homosexuality issue is part of some kind of hermeneutic, hidden, encoded content of Tchaikovsky's Fourth that

[2] Susan McClary, *Feminine Endings: Music, Gender and Sexuality* (Minneapolis: University of Minnesota Press, 1991), 76–7.

requires a very elaborate, not to say far from universally accepted interpretative strategy to reveal.

But now it ought to be clear why there is little hope that a piece of absolute music, as opposed to a novel, could possibly have any palpable effect on a social movement. For only the manifest content of an art work will be apparent to enough people, and be able to work its way with their belief systems, to either foment or facilitate a social movement. A novel might do so; perhaps *Uncle Tom's Cabin* did. Better still, a movie or television show. Absolute music, however, if it has the appropriate content at all, has it encoded, like a novel *à clef*, and so is ill-suited to influence the beliefs of large numbers of people, or, hence, to motivate their behavior. Dickens may have contributed, through his novels, to the movement to ameliorate the condition of orphaned children in nineteenth-century England. But Tchaikovsky could have had little chance of helping to eradicate gay-bashing through his symphonies, because in the case of Tchaikovsky the 'message' is in code, if it is there at all; and too few of us have the key.

Does this negative conclusion about the power of absolute music to influence social movements imply that music, when joined to a text, is powerless as well? By no means. But what it does mean is that whatever is *in* music that might possess the power must be *manifest* content. It must, that is to say, be something we can rely on all, or at least most intelligent listeners being able to recognize without the aid of complicated and frequently suspect analytical procedures. It must be manifest, not encoded content.

Well, as most contemporary philosophers of music believe, there is such a manifest, widely accessible content in absolute music, if we take the word 'content' in something other than its strictly propositional sense. Absolute music possesses *expressive* content. Which is to say that, at least within fairly general boundaries, most intelligent listeners will agree on what expressive characterization is appropriate to a piece of absolute music in the traditional repertory, at any given place.

Philosophers of music disagree about how absolute music comes to exhibit such expressive properties. And they disagree about the extent to which absolute music can *say* anything *about* the expressive properties it exhibits. But neither disagreement need concern us here. How music comes to be expressive is irrelevant to our concerns just so long as we agree that it is expressive, in the way stipulated just now, and manifestly so. And whether it can say anything about the emotions it is manifestly expressive of is just a special case of the problem we have already canvassed of whether absolute music can express the kind of propositional and representational content that literature and some of the other arts can do. Having concluded that if it can, such content is encoded, not manifest, and that only manifest content can appreciably affect social movements, the second disagreement over the expressive content of music is seen to be irrelevant to our concerns as well.

Now just because absolute music cannot say anything much, if anything at all about its expressive content, except in an encoded message, absolute music's expressive content cannot, for reasons already adduced, have any palpable effect on social movements. But it can, I wish to point out, when expressive music is joined to a text. To see how, I want to turn very briefly to the question of the role music plays in what is without a doubt the most powerful artistic influence on mass culture in our century, namely, the movies. I follow, here, the lead of the most distinguished living philosopher of film, Noel Carroll.

Carroll, developing some earlier ideas of my own in regard to music with text, calls movie music the 'modifier,' the movie the 'indicator,' as, for example: 'the music says ". . . is jaunty" and the movie specifies the blank with "the battle." '[3] In other words, the movie shot of the battle, in conjunction with music expressive of 'jauntiness,' can convey the idea that the battle is jaunty. Generalizing from this, Carroll writes:

in reaching out for music, the movie is seeking to incorporate an added, particularly powerful, augmented means of expression along with the visual, narrative, and dramatic means already at its disposal. The addition of music gives the filmmaker an especially direct and immediate means of assuring that the audience is matching the correct expressive quality with the expression at hand.[4]

Amplifying this thought, Carroll continues,

Movies are a means of popular expression. They aspire for means of communication that can be grasped almost immediately by untutored audiences. Another way of putting this is to say that moviemakers seek devices that virtually guarantee that the audience will follow the action in the way that the

---

[3] Noel Carroll, *Mystifying Movies: Fads and Fallacies in Contemporary Film Theory* (New York: Columbia University Press, 1988), 221.
[4] Ibid. 222.

filmmaker deems appropriate. . . . [G]iven the almost direct expressive impact of music, [it] assures that the untutored spectators of the mass movie audience will have access to the desired expressive quality and, in turn, will see the given scene under its aegis.[5]

The role that Carroll specifies for the expressiveness of music in the movies, to italicize, as it were, the relevant emotive tone of the shot or scene, is, of course, the same role that music has traditionally played in opera, art song, mass, oratorio, and other forms of classical music with text. Nor is expressiveness the only aspect of music, needless to say, that can serve, in such classical forms, to emphasize various aspects of the text or dramatic situation. What makes musical expressiveness special, in this regard, and the reason why it can function in the movies, which is, as Carroll says, a means of popular expression, is its unusual accessibility to the untutored audience. Musical expressiveness, in the tonal system, is immediately recognizable to anyone, with or without special musical training, as anyone knows who has tried the experiment in undergraduate classes. The price of admission is merely the natural acculturation to major-minor functional harmony and melody that anyone in the West acquires as a matter of course just by being alive.

And it is just because of the universality and easy accessibility of musical expressiveness in Western music (which is the only music I am concerned with here) that it seems the obvious candidate for that parameter of absolute music most capable of influencing mass social movements. But it cannot do so alone, in the absence of a text, or other 'indicator' (as Noel Carroll calls them). For the expressive property alone, in the context of absolute music, cannot tell us *what* the expressive property is saying to us, except in the generally inaccessible, encoded way we have identified previously.

It is, therefore, to the various popular, or at least widely accessible forms of music with text that we can look for the influence of music on social movements. And, furthermore, if my argument concerning the expressive properties of music is correct, it is to *those* expressive properties that we must principally look for the most palpable *musical* contribution to the enterprise.

Now you may have come up, by this time, with one very glaring counterexample to what I have been saying. For if what I have been

---

[5] Carroll, *Mystifying Movies:* 222.

saying is right, then we should find songs of social protest, to take but one genre of music that is supposed to influence social movements, prominently displaying a close fit between textual meaning and musical expressiveness, as, say, Schubert's songs or Bach's cantatas so clearly do. But this is not the case. Many of them, indeed, show no expressive congruence at all between text and music.

In my radicalized days, in high school, when I was as likely at a labor rally as in class, we had as our main battle strategy, to appropriate the immortal words of Tom Lehrer: 'Ready, Aim, Sing.' And the songs we sang, to the accompaniment of the ubiquitous guitar, were epitomized by one that perhaps some of you know, words by Woody Guthrie, sung to the tune of 'Pretty Redwing,' and called 'Union Maid.' Here is the first verse and chorus:[6]

There once was a union maid,
She never was afraid
Of goons and ginks and company finks,
And the deputy sheriffs that made the raids;
She went to the union hall
When a meeting it was called,
And when the comp'ny boys came 'round
She always stood her ground.

Oh, you can't scare me, I'm sticking to the union,
I'm sticking to the union, I'm sticking to the union,
Oh, you can't scare me, I'm sticking to the union
I'm sticking to the union,
'Til the day I die.

Now the tune of 'Pretty Redwing,' as regards its expressive character, has absolutely nothing to do with Woody Guthrie's words. (Imagine what Bach or Schubert would have done with 'afraid' and 'die,' although they would, I suppose, have had considerable trouble with 'deputy sheriffs' and 'company finks.') Why, then, did Woody put his words to that tune? Clearly, because this is not 'spectator music,' if I may so call it, but 'participation music.' The audience was meant to sing along, not to sit in rapt attention, as if to *Die Winterreise*. And he could rightfully assume that his audience knew this tune, or could pick it up easily because it is so simple and singable.

---

[6] The full text and musical setting of 'Union Maid' can be found in *The People's Song Book*, foreword by Alan Lomax, preface by B. A. Botkin (New York: Boni & Gaer, 1948), 70–1.

I have been talking, all along, about how spectator music might be thought to influence social movements, because that is the music I know about and know how to deal with. And if one looks to *that* music, say, to Brecht and Weill's *Dreigroschenoper* or Marc Blitzstein's *The Cradle Will Rock*, one will, I am sure, see my hypothesis borne out. But participation music is quite another thing entirely. Like spectator music, it must be readily accessible if it is to be socially motivating. But whereas spectator music must be readily accessible to perception and mind, participation music must be accessible in another way: it must, of course, be easily learnt and easily sung in groups or crowds.

Obviously, the goal of both spectator music and participation music, if it is to be socially motivating, is much the same: to impart to people the beliefs that will motivate them to action. And why *singing* Woody Guthrie's words in chorus should be more conducive to that end than just communally reciting them, like the catechism, I do not know. I do know that, as I said early on, singing must be deeply embedded in our very being, coeval with our emergence as the *human* animal. But I am sure there are others who know far more about this than I; and I will leave it to them to explain, if they can.

What I have tried to do, simply, is to show why absolute music— quintessentially a spectator art—cannot be expected to influence social movements, and why a certain aspect of it, its expressive aspect, might be a social influence, not in absolute music alone, but if joined to a text or dramatic representation, in various other forms of spectator music. For it is spectator music that I have always talked about in my other writings, and what I am talking about here.

Perhaps I have merely spent a long time telling readers something they already knew. If so, I hope I have said it, at least, in a new way— a way that will help us to understand what we already know a little bit more fully. If I have just done that, then perhaps I have performed a useful function after all, even though I convey in this chapter no new knowledge. Some things, after all, bear repeating. That is why in symphonies the exposition is frequently played twice.

Music in Memory and Music in the Moment

On occasion one reads a philosophical work that strikes what appears a mortal blow to a long-cherished, foundational belief. Less frequently, the belief so endangered is such that its falsity—if false it is—must change one's life and how one has viewed it in some radical, deeply disturbing way. I have now experienced this double shock to my belief system in reading Jerrold Levinson's book, *Music in the Moment*. For Levinson's book has presented arguments that can by no means be dismissed out of hand, against what he sometimes calls a 'dogma' of music appreciation, which has been the underlying support of my musical world since I was 12 years old. So deeply has music penetrated my life since that time that if Levinson's arguments are good, I will indeed be forced to reevaluate my whole teenage and adult life in music and, furthermore, to change fundamentally.

It is, thus, not merely an intellectual interest, but a practical one of the most compelling kind that urges me on to examine Levinson's arguments against my musical 'dogma' and its implications. For I deeply desire to preserve my musical life, and my view of how it was almost, it seems to me, miraculously transformed between the ages of 12 and 17, and I cannot do so unless Levinson is seriously mistaken in his views. Seriously mistaken I think he is, as I shall try to show in what follows. But before I try to do that, I must first present my general understanding of what Levinson's position on musical listening is. That will occupy me in the first sections of this chapter. Afterwards, in succeeding sections, I shall present my own, contrary views, and, in the process, spell out in more detail, some of the implications of Levinson's position, which he calls 'concatenationism.'

Concatenationism

Levinson is, I should say, the staunchest supporter of the great nineteenth-century philosopher of music, Edmund Gurney, and certainly the most deeply read, among my acquaintances, in that author's compendious volume, *The Power of Sound*.[1] His 'concatenationism,' he claims, is a development of Gurney's theory. But I shall not, in my exposition and criticism of Levinson, try to differentiate between what part is 'Socrates' and what 'Plato.' It shall be assumed to be Levinson throughout.

What, then, is concatenationism? 'I chose the name', Levinson says, 'because it expresses the idea that music essentially expresses itself for understanding as a chain of overlapping and mutually involving parts of small extent, rather than either a seamless totality or an architectural arrangement.'[2] This idea of musical understanding or appreciation, concatenationism, can be subdivided into four separate but related theses:

1. *Musical understanding* centrally involves neither aural grasp of a large span of music as a whole, nor intellectual grasp of large-scale connections between parts; understanding music is centrally a matter of apprehending individual bits of music and immediate progressions from bit to bit.

2. *Musical enjoyment* is had only in the successive parts of a piece of music, and not in the whole as such, or in relationships of parts widely separated in time.

3. *Musical form* is centrally a matter of succession, moment to moment and part to part.

4. *Musical value* rests wholly on the impressions of individual parts and the cogency of the successions between them, and not on features of large-scale form *per se*; the worthwhileness of experience of music relates directly only to the former.[3]

The implications of concatenationism for listening, and the reasons for believing it, will emerge slowly as this critique unwinds.

---

[1] Edmund Gurney, *The Power of Sound* (London: Smith, Elder, 1880).
[2] Jerrold Levinson, *Music in the Moment* (Ithaca: Cornell University Press, 1997), 13.
[3] Ibid. 13–14.

But what must be immediately added to the view, as sketched above, is a concept I take to be the central motivating principle that makes the whole thing work (if it does): what Levinson calls 'quasi-hearing.'

Now I take it as fairly uncontroversial that an account of musical understanding and appreciation will be, although perhaps not entirely, a matter of what can be *heard*.[4] That being the case, it must be crucial to answer the question, What *can* be heard? What *can* we hear in music? Levinson's answer is 'not very much'. That is to say, what, at any given time, we can be said to be hearing while listening to a musical work is only a very brief segment.

What do I hear? That which is presently impinging upon my auditory faculty. But such an answer immediately leads to an age-old metaphysical puzzle, certainly known at least as far back as Saint Augustine, of what might be called the paradox of the vanishing present. Everything, in other words, is either past or future, except present instants of apparently no duration whatever (or else they would be past at one end, future at the other). Without getting into such murky waters, Levinson simply has it that 'although one literally *hears* only an instant of music at a time, one generally *quasi-hears*, or vividly apprehends, a somewhat greater extent of musical material.'[5]

How far from the instant of hearing does quasi-hearing stretch? Not very far, on Levinson's view, but at least a few measures backward, in memory, and a few measures forward, in expectation. Thus, 'The experience of quasi-hearing can usefully be thought of as having three components or aspects. The first would be the *actual hearing* of an instant of music, the second would be the *vivid remembering* of a stretch of music just heard, and the third would be the *vivid anticipation* of a stretch to come.'[6] Yet, in spite of stretching both backwards and forwards in time, 'an important point is that the scope of quasi-hearing, of grasping a musical motion in one go—of seeming to hear a span of music while strictly hearing, or aurally registering, just one element of it—is generally fairly small.'[7]

With quasi-hearing now defined, there remain but two further points to cover and the reader will have at least a general idea of what Levinson calls concatenationism. The first point is that, by and large,

---

[4] For some of my views on the non-aural aspects of the work of music, see my *Authenticities: Philosophical Reflections on Musical Performance* (Ithaca: Cornell University Press, 1995), chs. 4 and 8.

[5] Levinson, *Music in the Moment*, 15.   [6] Ibid. 16.   [7] Ibid. 15.

Levinson does not think musical listening, which is to say quasi-hearing, is, vaguely speaking, a 'self-conscious' mental activity.

Quasi-hearing can be conceived as a process in which conscious attention is carried to a small stretch of music surrounding the present moment, and which involves synthesizing the events of such a stretch into a coherent flow, insofar as possible. None of that however, entails that one is consciously *aware* of quasi-hearing—that is, of attending and synthesizing—while one is doing so, or conscious *that* one is consciously aware of only a small extent of music surrounding the presently sounding event.[8]

The second point is that quasi-hearing, so defined, as 'conscious attention . . . carried to a small stretch of music surrounding the present moment . . . synthesizing the events of such a stretch into a coherent flow,' constitutes what Levinson calls 'basic musical understanding.'

We shall have occasion, further on, to look more closely at the word 'basic', in Levinson's musical lexicon, and in mine, and what it might imply. For now what is required is a general idea of what basic musical understanding is, for Levinson, beyond what we already know. 'Most abstractly put,' Levinson says, basic musical understanding is 'that way of hearing . . . that involves aurally connecting together tones currently sounding, ones just sounded, and ones about to come, synthesizing them into a flow as far as possible at every point. And this in essence means quasi-hearing some stretch of variable length surrounding the notes one is currently hearing.'[9]

The most significant implication of this view of basic musical understanding, as Levinson sees it, is that it requires no musical awareness beyond the *local*, as defined by quasi-hearing. Knowledge and conscious awareness of the larger musical forms and structures are (more or less) irrelevant for basic musical understanding. As Levinson puts the position, in one place:

If basic musical understanding can be identified with a locally synthetic rather than globally synoptic manner of hearing, then it is conceivable that with musical compositions, even complicated and lengthy ones, we miss nothing crucial by staying, as it were, in the moment, following the development of events in real time, engaging in no conscious mental activity of wider scope that has the whole or some extended portion of it as object. Of course it is rare that activity of that sort is entirely absent, but the point is that its contribution to basic understanding may be nil.[10]

---

[8] Levinson, *Music in the Moment*, 18.   [9] Ibid. 29.   [10] Ibid.

Furthermore, the strength of 'basic' seems to be (more or less) *necessary and sufficient.* In other words, one (more or less) has the whole musical kit and caboodle, as far as understanding and enjoying music goes, when one has basic musical understanding, so defined, and one cannot have either understanding or enjoyment of music without it. Levinson writes,

The adjective 'basic' in the phrase 'basic musical understanding' carries some suggestions that I endorse and others that I would prefer to exorcise. I mean to convey that such understanding is essential (to any apprehension of music), fundamental (to any further musical understanding), and central (to worthwhile musical experience of any kind)—but not that it is simple, or elementary, or rudimentary. While characterizing basic musical understanding as constituting ideal understanding of music would be going too far, such understanding does represent, I claim, a level of understanding substantially adequate to most instrumental music in the Western tradition.[11]

This, then, in brief, is concatenationism. Why should we believe it is true?

Levinson adduces three prima-facie reasons, or rather, pre-systematic intuitions about music that, he thinks, support concatenationism. First of all, we have an intuition, Levinson thinks, about 'what we ordinarily count as *knowing* a piece of music, as *grasping* it, or, in a more vernacular vein, as *getting* it.' Not surprisingly, this intuition coincides, according to Levinson, rather exactly, with concatenationism.

The kind of knowing or grasp at issue is fundamentally a matter of attentive absorption in the musical present. . . . It is plausible to identify, as the chief ground of this involvement, the capacity to quasi-hear, or aurally synthesize, a small extent of music, surrounding any present instant, which synthesizing moves progressively along the length of a piece, binding it part by part, so far as the music allows, into an organic chain.[12]

Thus, Levinson thinks, 'When someone claims that some composition, say, a string quartet by Schoenberg, does not "make sense" to him, this is *invariably* a matter of being unable to follow the musical logic from point to point.'[13]

Second, we have an intuition, 'favoring concatenationism,' that, 'One of the clearest indications that one has understood a piece of music at the basic level is one's ability to reproduce parts of it in some

---

[11] Ibid. 33.   [12] Ibid. 23.   [13] Ibid. 25. My italics.

manner—by playing, singing, humming, or whistling it—or relatedly, one's knowing how a given bit is to be continued, or what bit succeeds the bit that has just occurred.' This is so, Levinson thinks, because 'One listens with understanding when one actively registers and projects musical movement at each instant, with this understanding being reflected, as a rule, in the capacity to later give back, in some fashion, that musical movement.'[14] In short, it is a common intuition, according to Levinson, that a sure sign of understanding music, at the basic level, is being able to reproduce in some way or other just those lengths of musical line that are quasi-hearable, which is just, presumably, what concatenationism would predict.

The third intuition that Levinson thinks is supportive of concatenationism concerns the emotive properties of music. It is, Levinson believes, that just the kind of hearing embraced by concatenationism, which is to say, 'present-focused hearing,' is adequate to the perception of such emotive properties. Emotive properties are local properties not global ones. 'The emotional content of music, in other words, is not primarily communicated to a listener by large-scale formal relations, consciously apprehended, but instead by suitable arranged parts small enough to fall within the scope of quasi-hearing.'[15]

We now have before us what are pretty well the bare bones of Levinson's concatenationism, and of its 'intuitive' appeal, as Levinson sees it. But more is needed to grasp fully the impact of what he is claiming.

I said it was the most significant implication of Levinson's position with regard to basic musical understanding, as defined, that it comprises, for all intents and purposes, the total listening experience, and that (therefore) the perception of large-scale musical structure and form is just about irrelevant, contributing but negligibly to either comprehension or enjoyment. Well, that is an understatement, at least as far as I am concerned. It is not merely significant; it is startling; it is disturbing.

Given, then, the importance I am placing on these two related implications of concatenationism—the complete musical sufficiency of local listening, and the complete irrelevancy of global listening—it behooves us to look a little more closely at what further Levinson has to say in this regard. I shall attend to this in the next section, which will, essentially, complete my sketch of Levinson's position.

---

[14] Levinson, *Music in the Moment*, 26.   [15] Ibid. 27.

Against Architectonicism

The view, prevalent among musicians, music theorists, and musico-logists—that the perception or apprehension of large-scale musical form and structure contributes importantly, significantly to musical appreciation—Levinson calls 'architectonicism.' It is perhaps *the* major object of Levinson's criticism throughout *Music in the Moment*. And we must fully appreciate what its denial implies before we can fully comprehend what is disturbing about its opposite number, concatenationism.

I think the best way to get a handle on exactly what Levinson is denying, and why he is denying it, is to get down to specific cases. I shall examine two: a general structural feature of Western art music for a very large part of its history, and a specific formal structure that has been with us, as perhaps the most ubiquitous formal principle of instrumental music since the advent of Classical style, in the second half of the eighteenth century. These are musical 'unity' and 'sonata' form. If these cannot be sustained by the supporters of architectoni-cism, then I think it fair to say that architectonicism itself cannot be. We will look at unity first.

'A particularly important aesthetic quality,' Levinson begins, 'one for whose perception large-scale awareness might seem absolutely necessary, is *unity* or *coherence*.'[16] It is, it must initially be observed, the 'or' of equivalence that Levinson is invoking here, taking 'unity' and 'coherence' as names for the same thing. This is not left unstated, although it becomes obvious as the argument progresses, but is made explicit in a footnote, where Levinson writes that 'in the present dis-cussion I will be regarding unity mainly under its aspect of coher-ence, and so equating the respective terms.'[17]

With unity equivalent to coherence, the immediate result, favor-able to Levinson's concatenationism, is that unity becomes a local quality, because coherence seems clearly to be one. Unity is just coherence, and the experience of coherence is that

in coming where and when it does, a given passage in a strong sense con-tinues, as opposed to just succeeds, what has transpired up to this point. So construed, it is clear that the crucial experience of unity in a piece of music is one that can be had as the piece proceeds, without either intellectual grasp of widely separated parts or explicit conception of the whole.[18]

[16] Ibid. 58.   [17] Ibid. 58 n.   [18] Ibid. 59.

In other words, with unity construed as coherence all that the perception of unity requires is basic musical understanding, which is to say, quasi-hearing.

It thus seems to follow that the perception of large-scale thematic relationships in musical works is not necessary for unity, so construed, nor does perceiving them, when it occurs, contribute much, if anything, to the feeling of unity, which is to say, coherence, one gets in quasi-hearing the local parts of an ongoing musical work. 'Underlying relations, such as that between themes in Ravel's quartet, clearly ground many of the perceived qualities of the musical work. But conscious awareness of these underlying relations seems unnecessary in order for a piece of music to be perceived as unified by the listener.' Furthermore, 'the awareness as such does not obviously enhance this aural coherence to any significant degree.' In short, 'as regards this one very important aspect of aesthetic content [namely, unity or coherence], it is not at all clear that access to it requires large-scale reflection of any sort.'[19]

But, of course, as Levinson is forced to admit, 'conscious realizations of thematic or structural relationships . . . do commonly provide a certain distinct pleasure.' This pleasure, however, is relegated to an altogether minor, borderline significance. 'We take pleasure in the composer's cleverness for having constructed his or her music so ingeniously, and in our own for having detected that construction.' Levinson does not go as far as to say such pleasure is not 'specifically musical—that would be too strong.' But he does demote it to a 'secondary' status, and concludes that 'satisfactions such as these are arguably both not essential to basic musical understanding and relatively minor in comparison to the satisfactions inherent in basic musical understanding itself.'[20] And, indeed, it *is* hard to think of a pleasure taken even in a composer's 'cleverness,' let alone our own, as 'musical' pleasure, properly so called.

Levinson's strategy, then, in attempting to bring our perception of unity into the ambit of concatenationism, is first to construe unity, a global quality, as coherence, a local one. He then suggests, I take it, that most of what people want to say about musical unity can be said about musical coherence. Finally, whatever is left over that does seem unquestionably a global quality, he tries to convince us provides only the most marginal, if any musical pleasure, and 'musical' in only the

---

[19] Levinson, *Music in the Moment*, 60.   [20] Ibid. 61–2.

most distant, attenuated sense. Whether this strategy succeeds we will have occasion to consider later on. For now we will leave it where it is and move on to Levinson's treatment of sonata form.

Levinson frames the question of sonata form's relevance to the musical experience as follows: 'The principal question to be faced is whether having explicit awareness of a movement's sonata form during audition is crucial to auditing it successfully—to achieving basic musical understanding. Must one hear a sonata movement as such in order basically to hear it?'[21]

The way Levinson frames this question is, in an obvious way, question-begging. For he equates the question of whether conscious awareness of sonata form 'is crucial to auditing it successfully' with the question of whether it is crucial to 'achieving basic musical understanding.'

But so put, the question really answers itself. Basic musical understanding being local, sonata form global, apprehending sonata form *cannot* be crucial to basic musical understanding because as basic musical understanding is defined, apprehending global aesthetic features *cannot* be a part of it. For basic musical understanding is quasi-hearing, and apprehending global features exceeds its temporal limits. Furthermore, since Levinson has already claimed that basic understanding of music is all that is needed for 'auditing it successfully,' and apprehending sonata form cannot be part of basic musical understanding, it follows directly that 'having basic musical awareness of a movement's sonata form during audition is [*not*] crucial to auditing it successfully.'

My own view, as shall emerge more fully later on, is that what Levinson calls basic musical understanding *is* necessary for hearing music 'successfully,' but not *sufficient*, if successful listening is construed in any deeper or richer sense than merely 'musically successful audition'; furthermore, that the apprehension of sonata form, and other large-scale features of classical music *is* essential to successful musical listening, in the richer, non-minimal sense of 'successful.' But that argument is to come. What concerns us now is Levinson's case against the apprehension of sonata form as an essential ingredient of successful music listening.

Levinson begins by distinguishing two senses of what we might mean if we said that someone 'heard sonata form,' which he calls the *intellectual* sense and the *perceptual* sense. 'In the first [intellectual] sense,' he writes, 'hearing a movement as a sonata involves entertaining certain concepts in thought and relating them to current perceptions, or consciously organizing what one is perceiving under certain articulate categories'—essentially, I might add, the way I listen to sonata movements, and the way, I presume, others like me listen. 'In the second [perceptual] sense,' in contrast, 'hearing as a sonata involves not conscious thought or categorization but a disposition to register and respond to the musical progression one is presented with in a certain way.'[22] In other words, the second sense of hearing sonata form is a sense meant to be consistent with quasi-hearing, as the first sense clearly is not.

But how is the second sense of hearing sonata form really hearing sonata form at all? Sonata form has to *matter* in some way.

Levinson obviously is aware of this potential problem, and gives us an account of hearing sonata form that he thinks robust enough to make it matter, but does not necessitate our 'entertaining certain concepts in thought and relating them to current perceptions.' He writes, 'One who perceptually hears-as-a-sonata has internalized a certain norm for pieces of a given kind, and implicitly senses convergence with and divergence from that norm as presented by a particular composition. This sort of internalization does not presuppose prior abstract grasp of sonata structure.'[23] Thus, whatever conscious knowledge of sonata form might contribute to sonata-form listening, it is Levinson's view, I take it, that perceptual listening is quite enough for a successful musical experience of sonata form. So Levinson concludes, at one point, 'that the reactions and satisfactions characteristic of comprehending listening are had without cognizance of overall structure or contemplation of large-scale relations.'[24]

Now Levinson's argument up to this point is more or less acceptable to the defender of architectonic listening, who is not likely to think that one who lacks explicit technical knowledge of sonata form, or the other large-scale structural forms and techniques of the classical repertory is thereby barred from enjoyment of it. Experience amply demonstrates the falsity of such a conclusion. But the argument against architectonic listening becomes far more strident and damning as Levinson's book progresses. So further exploration is

---

[22] Levinson, *Music in the Moment*, 72.   [23] Ibid.   [24] Ibid. 84.

necessary for us to get the full impact of his case. First, *can* we hear architectonically, in the sense (or senses) in which the defender of architectonic listening, such as myself, says we can; and, second, if we can, for full appreciation *should* we?

It is difficult quite to know whether or not Levinson thinks architectonic listening is possible. Obviously, he thinks something that might fairly be called that is possible, because he repeats over and again that doing it adds little or nothing to musical understanding or appreciation. But, on the other hand, there are places where he at least hints that there is some difficulty in the very notion of architectonic *hearing*. Thus, he writes in one place, 'Broad-span aural apprehension may not be impossible, but it is inherently difficult, contraindicated by the temporally unfolding nature of music, and unnecessary, in any case, for basic appreciation of music. . . . If music is to be good it must be aurally synthesizable, ideally throughout its course, by those of moderate, rather than exceptional quasi-hearing abilities.'[25]

There are a number of points here worth mentioning. Obviously, the admission that broad-span aural apprehension may not be impossible is as close as one can get to saying it *is* impossible without actually saying so. As I gloss Levinson on that regard, he is saying, skeptically, that aural apprehension of the broad-span kind may or may not be impossible; and to say 'not impossible' rather than 'possible' also suggests skepticism about the real possibility of global listening.

Furthermore, he says that broad-span aural apprehension is 'inherently difficult,' and goes on to ascribe it to 'the aural faculties of the inherently gifted, such as Mozart . . .'[26] Now 'inherently gifted' covers a lot of ground; and, as I shall argue later on, I see no reason there should not be valuable ways of listening to music, or looking at paintings, that are not available to everyone. I have many friends who are able to get more out of the visual arts than I who are, perhaps, inherently gifted in that area. This does not suggest that they are out of the range of ordinary human beings. But, of course, if Mozart is your example of the gifts required to engage in broad-span listening, then, in reality, it is an impossible activity.

Finally, there is, I think, some confusion, in this passage, over the concept of quasi-hearing. Levinson talks at the end of the above

<hr />

[25] Ibid. 130–1.   [26] Ibid.

quoted passage about 'moderate' as opposed to 'exceptional quasi-hearing abilities.' Now as I understand the concept of quasi-hearing, it is pretty much an all or none ability: the ability to remember 'vividly' a few bars of music that have already transpired before the 'present moment' and to anticipate 'vividly' a few bars that are about to transpire. (It is remarkable how Humean this psychology is.) In that sense of quasi-hearing, one assumes that *all* normal people can acquire the ability. And in that sense of quasi-hearing, bound to a specifically stated temporal span—a 'few' bars past, a 'few' bars future—broad-span aural apprehension is, by definition, *not* quasi-hearing at all, thus, not, by consequence, 'exceptional quasi-hearing'.

But if, on the other hand, quasi-hearing is thought of as whatever any given individual can remember vividly before the present musical moment, and anticipate vividly after the present musical moment, then it does come in grades; and when the time-span is long enough, quasi-hearing *can* be broad-span hearing: when, for example, one has the musical memory of a Mozart. Construed in this way, broad-span hearing is, indeed, impossible for most of us. That is to say, if broad-span hearing is construed as 'super-quasi-hearing', only the Mozarts of the world can do it, and for all intents and purposes, we can forget about it as a viable ingredient in the aesthetics of classical music.

Now my own position will be, when I come to my critique of Levinson, that quasi-hearing be construed in the former manner. It then turns out that broad-span listening is not quasi-hearing at all, but a different kind of hearing altogether that *is* possible for many, but perhaps not all listeners. For now, however, I pass on to the question of what value broad-span listening might have on Levinson's view. As things turn out, he thinks it has little or none.

The claim that comprehending the large-scale architectonic of classical music contributes little or nothing to musical pleasure or appreciation is reiterated with great frequency in Levinson's book, sometimes with no real argument. Or, perhaps, a more accurate way of putting it is that the argument is implicit. For it follows directly from Levinson's claim that quasi-hearing provides most of the pleasure and appreciation, that anything else—notably architectonic listening—can contribute little or nothing.

Beyond that general implication of concatenationism, there are some related claims about architectonic listening that do not augur well for its importance in the musical experience. Perhaps the most frequent put-down of broad-span musical apprehension, if I may so call it, is that it is an intellectual apprehension, and, therefore, can deliver little 'musical' satisfaction.

The spontaneous, unforced, almost palpable relating, within a span of quasi-hearing, of proximate musical events into a flow virtually present at one time offers a satisfaction that all who truly love music must admit is vastly more vivid and intense than that which can be afforded by deliberate and concerted relating of widely separated musical events under the aegis of some form concept in an act of *intellectual cognition*.[27]

Another claim of Levinson's that seems meant to imply the relative unimportance of architectonic listening is that quasi-listening is a prerequisite for it. You can have quasi-hearing without architectonic apprehension, but certainly not the other way round. So, of the two, quasi-hearing is far and away the bearer of more musical satisfaction. 'The pleasure we take in *intellectual apprehension* of the large-scale form or structuring of a musical composition seems largely to presuppose the greater and more fundamental pleasure we take in its perceptually apprehendable sequential substance.'[28] (Note again the insistence on apprehension of large-scale structure being 'intellectual apprehension.')

Yet another claim of Levinson's, that seems to suggest the barely minimal contribution of architectonic listening to musical pleasure, is that musical form is spatial whereas *music* is temporal. Levinson writes, 'First, a piece's form, in the analyst's sense, is more abstract and less particularized than the piece itself. Second, a piece's form, in the sense analysis provides, is essentially spatial and static, while the piece itself is inherently temporal and directional.'[29]

It follows from the belief that music is temporal, musical form spatial, Levinson seems to think, that the grasping of musical form must be intellectual, the grasping of *music* perceptual. 'Thus, to grasp the one [music itself] perceptually is not surprisingly distinct from, and not necessarily continuous with, grasping the other [form] *intellectually*.'[30] (And again note the reiteration of the claim that grasping musical form, as opposed to grasping music, in quasi-hearing, is 'intellectual.')

From the distinction between the (supposed) spatial character of musical form and the temporal character of music there seems to

---

[27] Levinson, *Music in the Moment*, 156. My italics.
[28] Ibid. My italics.   [29] Ibid. 155.   [30] Ibid. My italics.

follow the startling conclusion that the form of a musical work is not part of the work: or at least, if that does not come down to the same thing, is not part of the *music* of the work.

What the present-absorbed, attentive, and backgrounded listener understands and consequently enjoys—the music in its developing immediacy and full sonic particularity—is not quite the same entity as the totality of abstracted structural relationships and patterns that the *intellectual apprehension* beholds, wholly or in part, and in the grasp of which is afforded an enjoyment of a different kind.

Note once again the emphasis on the 'intellectual' nature of the satisfaction musical form provides, which is supposed to imply that 'there is at least some justification, based on a distinction of objects, for denying that such satisfactions are taken in the music—the piece of music *per se*'.[31]

From all the above points we can, then, derive, in sum, a more or less blanket condemnation of broad-based, structural, or formal listening. If possible at all, and that seems in grave doubt for any listener short of a Mozart in mental gifts, the pleasures it yields up are vanishingly small, and, into the bargain, not even 'musical' pleasures at all.

Such pleasure is not only different in kind, not only directed on an object distinct from that on which basic musical understanding is focused, and not only clearly unnecessary for such basic understanding to occur. In addition, such pleasure is, first, manifestly *weaker* than the enjoyment consequent on basic musical understanding, and second, strongly *parasitic* on the achievements of basic musical understanding and the degree of enjoyment derived from it.[32]

Levinson has much more of a critical nature to say about structural and formal listening than I have yet presented, or have space to present. But at this point the reader has, I think, a reasonably good grasp of concatenationism, of the supposed reasons for believing it, and of the consequent critique of architectonicism, for me to get on with my own critical remarks. My resistance to Levinson's view has, indeed, already begun to peak out of my exposition of it, as fair as I have tried to be in my presentation. And my objections can no longer be silenced.

---

[31] Levinson, *Music in the Moment*, 155.   [32] Ibid.

A Personal Interlude

This chapter began in something of a passionate mode. I have, over the years, read a lot of books on philosophy, and on music, with which I have been in substantial disagreement. Few have penetrated me as deeply, where I live, as Levinson's. And although it may be a violation of philosophical etiquette to do so, I cannot help sharing with the reader from whence this passionate reaction to Levinson's claims derives its passionate side. In short, I am going to regale the reader, briefly, with the story of my life.

From the ages of 5 to 12, I achieved, like most people, what Levinson calls basic musical understanding. In other words, I came to quasi-hear tonal Western music.

What was somewhat unusual, perhaps, but hardly unique, and certainly not something of which I want to boast, was that, along with the pop music, and the folk music that was then in circulation among the children of parents of liberal or radical tendencies, I was, during these years, an avid listener to the classical repertory—at least that part of it that my mother possessed in a small collection of 78 rpm records, and, for the times, not so small for people of our station in life. Thus, along with the Andrew Sisters and the big bands, Woody Guthrie and Pete Seager, I also listened with great pleasure and concentration to Beethoven's Fifth Symphony and Emperor Concerto, Haydn's Surprise Symphony, Mozart's G-minor Symphony and Brahms's First, Frank's D-minor Symphony, and even some of the Brandenburg Concerti, in addition, later, to Wanda Landowska's recording of the Goldberg Variations.

During this period I also received some lessons, now and then, on the piano and clarinet, from boring and ineffectual teachers who made ignorance in matters musical seem infinitely more desirable than whatever musical knowledge they possessed and were attempting, unsuccessfully, to impart to me. But between the ages of 12 and 17, something happened in my life that was closer, I guess, than anything I have experienced since, or expect to experience in the future, to a mystical experience: a religious conversion. I fell off the horse, and my relation to music changed forever.

From age 12, in quick succession, three spectacular comets entered my orbit. I was blessed with the tutelage of three charismatic musicians and teachers of music who left me forever a new and different human being. Before that time I perceived as through a glass darkly. Afterwards, music opened up to me like a flower in bloom. In short, I learned, from the inside and the outside, through performance and through analysis, and even through some of the rudiments of composition, the inner secrets of music, at least so far as my talent and ability allowed.

Now when I say that I learned music, I of course mean that I learned a lot about it. That this changed my musical life does not, of itself, contradict anything that Levinson claims in his book. But I have compared what happened to me with the kind of ecstatic, mystical experience that does not merely change or add to your *beliefs*, but radically alters your *experience* as ell. And such was the case with my musical conversion. I not only knew more things about music, but experienced it thenceforth in a radically different way. My *listening* changed.

My listening became *both* more architectonic and more locally detailed. Furthermore, my appreciation and enjoyment of classical music increased exponentially. Looking back on my listening before my enlightenment, it seemed as if I had been doing it while anesthetized.

But if Levinson is right, if concatenationism is right, then that cannot have happened as I perceive it to have done. I must be in thrall to an illusion: a myth of how my musical enjoyment and appreciation spiked after my musical conversion. For it is Levinson's view that the kind of additions to my listening habits that I acquired from my charismatic teachers could have produced only a very small increase, if any, in my musical enjoyment and appreciation, or else a very large increase in my basic musical understanding. That, however, does not match my recollection. I do not see how my basic musical understanding, already acquired, could have increased enough to account for my radical change of musical life. And, as I have said, that change was so dramatic in the increase of my enjoyment of the classical repertory from what came before, that the prior experience pales in comparison. The new was different not merely in quantity but in kind.

This biographical excursion which, brief though it has been, has perhaps already gone on too long, may, I hope, give the reader some idea of why my reaction to Levinson's book has been not merely disbelief, but *passionate* disbelief. However, our discipline teaches us (or some of us, anyway) that passion is no substitute for rational argument. So having now, perhaps unwisely, worn my heart on my sleeve,

I had better put passion aside (to the extent I can) and get down to some philosophical nuts and bolts.

Counter-Intuitions

Levinson, as we have seen, begins his defense of concatenationism with three 'intuitions' about music that he believes we share, and that he believes concatenationism supports. I am not sure 'intuition' is the right word here because these beliefs about music hardly seem to me to have the kind of widespread acceptance that, for example, such ethical intuitions have, as 'Killing is worse than letting die,' and the like. Indeed, I do not share Levinson's first intuition, I do not wholly share his second, and although I do share his third, I do not think it supports concatenationism.

The first intuition, the reader will recall, is that when we say someone 'knows', or 'grasps', or 'gets' a piece of music, we mean merely that that person can make sense of its local happenings. He or she can follow the piece from moment to moment, present event to next present event, without feeling any sense of disorientation. The local process from event to event seems familiar and right. But when someone says he does not grasp a piece of music, does not get it, that it 'does not make sense to him, this is *invariably* a matter of being unable to follow the musical logic from point to point.' The example that Levinson cites, to illustrate and back up this claim, is an excellent one for his cause: a string quartet by Schoenberg. For I think he is right on the money in his claim that when a musically untutored but experienced concertgoer says that he doesn't get it, he is indeed admitting that, as Levinson says, 'it is a matter of being unable to follow the musical logic from point to point.' In other words, he has not internalized the musical grammar. In Levinson's terms, he does not have basic musical understanding.

The problem is that the Schoenberg example is far from ordinary. Indeed, it is unusual and highly biased in Levinson's favor. Note what Levinson claims. When we say we don't get the Schoenberg, we are admitting that we cannot follow the local musical logic from point to adjacent point. And this is a stand-in for all examples, apparently, because we are supposed to infer from it that invariably, all the time, cases of not getting it are like the case of the Schoenberg. But this is far from the truth. Because most of the music in the modern concert repertory is music written in the same basic musical 'logic,' which is to say, the major/minor harmonic system, and since we *all* possess basic musical understanding of that system, as a natural birthright, it is *seldom* that we ever don't get it the way we don't get the Schoenberg. That happens only when we meet with music not written within the system of major/minor tonality: for example, twelve-tone serialism, or non-Western musics, or music from the Middle Ages and early Renaissance, where the music is modal, the third still a dissonant interval, and the writing horizontal rather than vertical.

What, then, does my companion mean when, after listening to the fourth movement of Mahler's Ninth Symphony, she says to me: 'I don't get it'? She surely does *not* mean that she cannot make sense of the local happenings, that she is 'unable to follow the musical logic from point to point.' It is written in the same harmonic language as 'Melancholy Baby.' It is that she is lost, all at sea; she doesn't have the big picture; she doesn't know where anything belongs, or why. The movement lasts 28 minutes. The reason she 'gets' 'Melancholy Baby' but not the first movement of Mahler's Ninth is not because she can't follow the local musical logic of the latter. It is because its dimensions and complexity of structure require, in addition to basic musical understanding, a map of the territory and attention to it: in short, architectonic listening.

Classical music, because of its temporal dimensions alone, if for nothing else, makes demands on a listener that the two 8-bar phrases of a popular ballad do not. The demands go far beyond basic musical understanding. But people frequently say of classical music, 'I don't get it.' And they cannot mean they don't, in Levinson's sense, basically understand it. Seldom do they mean *that* because seldom do they meet with music outside the major/minor system, the system which they have had basic musical understanding of since childhood. Levinson's intuition, then, that when someone says of music, 'I don't get it,' 'this is *invariably* a matter of being unable to follow the musical logic from point to point,' is a false intuition, or, perhaps more accurately, no intuition at all. Concatenationism finds no support from that quarter.

Levinson's second intuition is also flawed, it seems to me, although there is an element of truth in it as well. Certainly, it is never an indication that someone *does not* basically understand a piece of music when she can whistle or hum a few bars. But it is very far from being an infallible sign of understanding. For example, it is far from clear that a listener completely uninstructed in the ways one must attend to the modal and contrapuntal music of the Middle Ages and early Renaissance even has a basic musical understanding of it though she can hum or whistle fragments of it with ease. And the same would be true, I think, for much non-Western music that is hummable. A person can give a recognizable rendition of a fragment of classical Chinese music and still honestly say, 'I don't get it,' where it is, clearly, the 'I don't get it' of the Schoenberg quartet, not the Mahler symphony.

Actually I do not think the 'reproducability' intuition has much to tell us either way: it supports neither concatenationism nor architectonicism.

Levinson's third intuition, that musical expressiveness is a local phenomenon, not (usually) a global one, is far more significant. It also happens, I think, to be true. But the relevance of this truth is not as clear as Levinson would have us believe.

There have been many writers on music, and still are some, who think that music is basically an emotive art form in some special, uniquely important way, even a 'language of the emotions.' For such writers, to be able to perceive the expressive properties of music constitutes, for all intents and purposes, total comprehension and full appreciation. But if the expressive properties of music are local properties, and, therefore, perceivable through basic musical understanding, then, for such writers, basic musical understanding would provide total comprehension and full appreciation.

Now I do not suggest Levinson *is* one of those who attributes such heavy significance to music's expressive properties; nevertheless, I believe he places heavier significance on them than I do. Thus, for Levinson the third intuition pulls more strongly in the direction of concatenationism than it does for me. For although I do think expressive properties are very important to some kinds of music, I think they are of little importance to others; and, all in all, I place them lower rather than higher on my scale of musical importance.[33]

In any case, it is not surprising to me that expressive properties, for the most part, require only basic musical understanding for their apprehension. For we know that they are the musical properties that lay listeners are most likely to take hold of first, which is why, of

---

[33] I am speaking here, let it be remembered, of pure instrumental music. Vocal music is quite another matter. There the emotive relationship between music and text is of vital importance.

course, they are the stock-in-trade of program annotators and others who write for a lay musical audience.

Thus, though I share the third intuition with Levinson, I find it perfectly compatible with *my* architectonicism. I am perfectly content to place *both* basic musical understanding *and* the perception of music's expressive properties at a lower level of musical attainment than does Levinson, global features at a far higher level. But fully to spell out where the level of importance lies, for me, of what Levinson calls basic musical understanding, it is to global features that we must now turn.

A Defense of Architectonicism

Architectonicism I take to be the position that global listening is not everything but that it is not nothing either: rather, that it contributes a very substantial part of the satisfaction to be had from classical music. Concatenationism denies this. And our critical examination of concatenationism so far reveals that at least the prima-facie reasons Levinson offers for accepting it—the three 'intuitions'—do not support the view. None the less, for all of that, concatenationism may yet be true. And, for all of that, Levinson may well be right that architectonic listening is impossible, or not musical listening at all, but intellectual, or productive of negligible pleasure beyond that produced by quasi-hearing. All of these charges must be met before I can convince the reader, as I hope I can, that although what Levinson calls basic musical understanding does play a crucial, important, indeed necessary, part in our enjoyment and appreciation of classical music, so too does global, architectonic listening, as well as listening to musical 'detail.'

Let us first take a critical look at Levinson's attempt to gather musical unity under the concatenationist umbrella. Recall that Levinson distinguishes between musical unity and musical coherence, but, in the end, concentrates on coherence, in an effort—quite successful in my opinion—to show that musical coherence is purely a matter of local listening, quasi-hearing: in other words, basic musical understanding.

But that leaves musical unity to be accounted for; and although Levinson does argue that it may have an aesthetic pay-off as a contribution to musical coherence—hence a local pay-off that can manifest itself in quasi-hearing—that is far from enough to write it off as a global feature requiring architectonic listening.

I present, in what immediately follows, my own view of musical coherence, musical unity, and their relation (or rather lack thereof) as not so much a refutation of any argument Levinson has given in this regard, but as a defense of the proposal that unity is an impor- tant feature of some classical music; that it requires something beyond quasi-hearing—namely, architectonic hearing—for its apprehension. The question of how large a contribution to musical satisfaction and appreciation apprehension of unity makes I will postpone for the time being; it will be relevant further on.

In an early work of mine I presented the view, 'unconvincingly', Levinson thinks,[34] that unity in music is basically a matter of 'monothematic structure'.[35] I still remain convinced of this view, although I would certainly find a less obscure way of expressing it than I managed then. I am not sure just why Levinson finds it uncon vincing except for the suspicion that he is confounding unity with *coherence*, which is certainly not a matter of monothematic structure.

So let me say, simply, that so far as I can see, writers about music consistently point to the monothematic structure of music, whether it be the recurrence of themes, theme fragments, motives, or chords, harmonic progressions, even sonorities (for example, the persistent pizzicato in the cello, in the second movement of the third Rasumovsky Quartet), when they are talking about how a composi tion or movement is 'unified'; in virtue of what it is unified, in what its unity consists. This structure is put in place by composers, when it is put in place, with, one must assume, a great deal of care and trouble. I take it as axiomatic that they intend it to be perceived— and, I shall argue, consciously perceived—by the astute listener.

But monothematic structure—henceforth 'unity'—is independent of coherence, in the obvious sense that music can be coherent with out being unified, and unified without being coherent. Many, I think most, of Mozart's instrumental movements, for example, are not unified yet are supremely coherent. That is to say, they have no uni fying, monothematic structure; yet each segment seems to the listener to follow logically from the previous one: the sequence seems just right. Haydn's instrumental movements, on the other hand, charac teristically display overarching monothematic structure and coher ence as well.

---

[34] Ibid. 60 n.
[35] Peter Kivy, *Speaking of Art* (The Hague: Martinus Nijhoff, 1973), 5–9 *et passim*.

However, it is perfectly possible, and not infrequent, for music to be unified and not coherent. Music written by composers who are good craftsmen but not of the first rank frequently has the one feature but not the other. Aristotle, the *fons et origo* of our concepts of both artistic unity and artistic coherence, well knew this distinction. When he said, in the *Poetics*, that a tragedy must have a beginning, a middle, and an end, connected as following logically the one from the other, he was talking about *coherence*; and when he said that a tragedy should comprise one complete action he was talking about *unity*, and one of the 'unities' it became.

When music is unified, whether or *not* it is coherent, that unity can only be perceived by architectonic listening. And I take it that that is done by being consciously aware, whether during the first listening if you are good at this sort of thing, or after many if you are not, that you are locally hearing something you perceive to be thematically connected with something you remember hearing previously. When this conscious awareness occurs in your local listening, it provides deep *musical* satisfaction, as I shall argue more fully later on. But this sort of listening requires not only practice and effort, but explicit musical knowledge as well. And, of course, it requires, as a prerequisite, basic musical understanding, in Levinson's sense.

Thus, to sum up, coherence, the logical connection of local parts, is quasi-heard, and is a function of basic musical understanding. Unity, which is to say monothematic structure of some kind, is heard by being consciously aware, during quasi-hearing, that what you are hearing is thematically connected with what you have heard, perhaps many measures previously or even in a previous movement entirely. Each experience provides musical satisfaction, and each is indispensable to full, rich appreciation and enjoyment of classical music.

Moving on, now, to sonata form, which is a stand-in for musical form in general, we will recall that Levinson wants to distinguish between what he calls *intellectual* listening, and *perceptual* listening. The latter kind, which Levinson endorses, is a listening in which one can be sensibly said to 'hear' sonata form without any explicit knowledge of it, or conscious awareness, while listening to it, that one is hearing it. Such hearing of sonata form, which Levinson is at pains to insist requires merely basic musical understanding, is cultivated by continual listening alone, and does not require explicit musical instruction.

Such *perceptual* listening to sonata form as Levinson describes, I confess I have some difficulty in accepting. I tend to doubt that one hears sonata form, in any robust sense, if one does not possess the concept, and does not hear the music as answering to it in whatever particular way it does. Nevertheless, I am prepared to give Levinson the point. But what Levinson characterizes as *intellectual* listening to sonata form, and which he rather thoroughly bashes, I think it imperative to rehabilitate. For on my view and in my own experience it makes a major contribution to the listening experience of a certain kind of listener, and his or her musical pleasure. I count myself one such listener. And if what Levinson says is true, I am certainly a deluded listener.

I do not intend to present in detail an account of musical appreciation and understanding. I have done that elsewhere.[36] What I do intend is to try to answer Levinson's critique of architectonic and other cerebral varieties of musical perception. But as I do so, I will certainly be defending my own views and expatiating upon them at the same time. I begin with the claim that such perception is at best difficult and at worst impossible. I then move on to the further claim that, where possible, it is productive of little or no true musical satisfaction.

Why should we think it impossible to perceive music architectonically? It seems to have a lot to do, Levinson thinks, with the obvious, uncontested fact that music is 'temporal,' usefully contrasted with painting in this regard. 'Now, one can "perceive the whole" of a piece of music if one wishes to call it that, by successively perceiving all of its parts, as one might do with a painting of some size, but one cannot do what in the case of a painting is fairly easily done, namely, have a single perceptual experience of it in its entirety.' Architectonic hearing, then, the full perception of a movement's sonata form, for example, would be tantamount to having 'a single perceptual experience of it in its entirety', 'a synoptic perception, or beholding, of the whole . . .' which is possible in painting, a non-temporal art, but not in music, a temporal one.[37]

It is of more than passing interest that what Levinson says is an impossible way to hear music—that is, in a single synoptic perception—was, for a long time, thought to be just the way Mozart *did*

[36] Peter Kivy, *Music Alone: Philosophical Reflections on the Purely Musical Experience* (Ithaca: Cornell University Press, 1990).
[37] Levinson, *Music in the Moment*, 20.

perceive it, at least in his imagination; and this notion, I find, still lingers on among unwary readers of a letter supposedly by Mozart himself, which has been decisively proved spurious on more than one occasion.[38] In that letter, pseudo-Mozart tells us how he can hear in his head one of his finished compositions: '. . . I can survey it, like a fine picture or a beautiful statue, at a glance. Nor do I hear in my imagination the parts *successively*, but I hear them, as it were, all at once.'[39]

This spurious letter has had a damaging effect on the psychology of musical perception ever since it was noticed, and quoted by William James in *The Principles of Psychology*. The apparent endorsement by Mozart of a way of perceiving music that seems to fit perfectly the description, 'synoptic listening', or 'architectonic listening' to a T has made it seem as if this is all that can reasonably be meant by such descriptions. It certainly fits Levinson's description; and Levinson is absolutely right in flatly rejecting it as impossible. If *this* is what architectonic or synoptic listening amounts to, then there is truly no such thing short of the mind of God, if the reports about *Him* are true.

But, surely, there is a perfectly possible mode of listening, properly called architectonic or synoptic, that does not require the absurd notion of hearing a temporal sequence atemporally. It is the mode I have already alluded to, of perceiving the present musical moment, so to say, through the lens of one's conscious memory of what has transpired, and expectation of what is to come. It does require having the 'plan in your head.' It does *not* require either the intellect of God, or of Mozart, to do it. It *does* require deep and concentrated attention; and, yes, it requires explicit musical knowledge of musical form, structure, syntax, style, and history. And that it does should be no embarrassment to the one who claims it, or require excuses. Why shouldn't there be music that yields up its greatest satisfactions only to those willing and able to do the work?

But why, it may be asked, should architectonic listening require anything *beyond* deep, concentrated attention? Why, in particular,

---

[38] See Peter Kivy, 'Mozart and Monotheism: An Essay in Spurious Aesthetics,' *Journal of Musicology*, 2 (1983), 322–8; repr. in Kivy, *The Fine Art of Repetition: Essays in the Philosophy of Music* (Cambridge: Cambridge University Press, 1993), ch. 10.

[39] From the English trans. of the letter, repr. in Edward Holmes, *The Life of Mozart* (New York: Harper, 1868), 329. The fabricator of this letter was the editor of the *Algemeine Musikalische Zeitung*, J. F. Rochlitz. It was first published in that periodical in 1815.

should it require the kind of knowledge suggested above? A long answer to these questions cannot be essayed here, although more bits and pieces will emerge as I go on.[40] Briefly, however, architectonic listening, and other forms of local and non-local listening that go beyond basic musical understanding, require a frame of reference. There will be no pay-off in musical satisfaction, from the kind of deep and concentrated attention I am talking about, unless one is trying, in the act, consciously to place what one is hearing within some schemata at one's disposal. And these schemata, whether structural or syntactic, stylistic or historical, are the stuff of a good musical education, whether taught or self-taught. When listening, in other words, one is trying to find one's way on a map in one's possession, not trying to make up a map from scratch. That does not mean the map will not be changed by what one hears, if it does not fit into the map you bring to your listening. (The recapitulation turns out to be a 'false' recapitulation, the rondo turns out to be a sonata movement after all, etc.) But some map or other you must have, or the kind of listening I am talking about will be as unfruitful for you as deep and concentrated observation of natural phenomena without a hypothesis to test. It would be the musical version of Baconian science: blind without concepts.

Such architectonic listening as I am talking about, then, I have insisted is hard-won but eminently possible. I indulge in it myself and I am neither a genius nor a professional musician—nor am I a freak; I have plenty of company in my listening habits. However, if the charge of impossibility is answered, the charge that such listening is empty of true musical satisfaction beyond that provided by basic musical understanding remains. The best Levinson can say of the fruits of architectonic listening, if achieved, is that: 'Even then, of course, it behooves us to remember that it is essentially icing—though sometimes of the most impressive sort—on the musical cake, and not the cake itself. The basic point is that if the cake is not in place, there's nowhere for the icing to go.'[41] Well, not as I hear it. As I hear it, music is a seven-layer cake. Basic musical understanding certainly constitutes the bottom layer, and perhaps more layers above. Architectonic and other forms of non-basic musical listening certainly comprise the top layer, and other layers below—not, by any

---

[40] For my previous thinking see my *Music Alone*.
[41] Levinson, *Music in the Moment*, 157.

means, icing on the cake, but the cake itself. Of course it goes without saying that you can't have the last layer without the first. Of course it goes without saying that you can't have the superstructure of a house without its foundation although you *can* have the foundation without the house. That obvious fact does not make the foundation more important than the rest of the house except in that one respect. (You can't *live* in the foundation.)

So we must now go through, one by one, those reasons adduced by Levinson for the claim that architectonic listening, when (or if) possible, is not productive of any substantial musical satisfactions.

1. *The satisfaction taken in architectonic listening is 'intellectual' (therefore) not musical satisfaction.* There runs through Levinson's book a decided anti-intellectual strain that is nowhere more apparent than in the insistence that hearing architectonically can produce only, *merely* intellectual satisfaction. Sometimes the claim seems to be that because the satisfaction is intellectual, it cannot therefore be *musical*. This seems to be without foundation. The satisfaction taken in architectonic listening is, of course, intellectual in some pretty obvious senses. It requires thinking—conscious, self-reflective thinking—while one is listening. It requires possessing explicit musical concepts such as sonata form, canon, inversion, stretto, counter-subject, answer, episode, and so on. All of that is, of course, a function of intellect.

Call architectonic listening 'intellectual listening' if you like; call the satisfaction it produces 'intellectual satisfaction' if you like. But do not take the illicit step from 'intellectual listening' to 'not listening to music,' or from 'intellectual satisfaction' to 'non-musical satisfaction.' Knowing the major events of Beethoven's life or the minutiae of a Bach autograph produce what anyone would call 'intellectual satisfaction.' If, after listening to a very complicated fugue for the first time I go to the score afterwards to see if at one spot where the texture was so thick I could not hear it, the subject and its inversion really were combined, I get what can fairly be called 'intellectual satisfaction' in the process. But let us not confuse this with hearing consciously the subject and its inversion combined, in concentrated hearing, under just those concepts. That produces *musical* satisfaction, satisfaction in the sounds of music, perceived under consciously entertained descriptions.

If you think, furthermore, that musical satisfaction is sensual satisfaction, satisfaction to the sense of hearing, so do I. But intellectual musical satisfaction *is* sensual satisfaction, satisfaction to an external sense, as satisfaction, for example, in the understanding of mathematical equations is not. There is, after all, mindless sex and thoughtful sex. Both, I should say, are sensual pleasures *par excellence.* (Most people I know prefer the latter.)

But that is not all there is to Levinson's devaluation of intellectual satisfaction in musical listening. There is the further claim that, to remind you of a previously quoted passage, the satisfaction produced by basic musical understanding 'all who truly love music must admit is vastly more vivid and intense than that which can be afforded by deliberate and concerted relating of widely separated musical events under the aegis of some form concept in an act of *intellectual cognition.*'

That sounds present to the hearing are more vivid than those remembered is, I guess, a harmless enough truism if one does not, like Hume, try to make too much philosophical mileage out of it. When one's memories equal or exceed one's present perceptions, I suppose 'delusion' or 'hallucination' would be the correct diagnosis. But when 'intense' is added to 'vivid,' shouldn't we begin to demur?

Surely a memory can be experienced as intensely as any perception. (Isn't that what Proust is all about?) One can, in reverie, be experiencing a memory far *more* intensely than what is present to the senses, and not be crazy.

When one claims, as I do, that architectonic listening is as important as quasi-hearing, one surely is not committed to the notion that in musical listening, memory of what you have heard many measures before is as vivid in your present experience as your present perception of present sounds. What one may well be committed to is that quite sensible notion that your memories (and expectations) are experienced intensely, and that they contribute that intensity to the experience of musical listening to a very substantial degree.

Architectonic listening scarcely requires the premiss that memory and expectation are as vivid as present perception. It does require that they can be intense, nor have I any trouble with the premiss that they are, at times, as intense as any other musical experience. Of course they must be a part of present experience, which is another way of saying, if it needs really to be said, that you cannot listen to music unless you listen to music. And that brings us to the second claim of Levinson's against the importance of architectonic listening that I want to consider.

2. *The pleasure we take in intellectual apprehension of form and structure is parasitic on the (therefore?) greater pleasure of basic musical understanding.* Levinson insists, on numerous occasions, that basic musical understanding, as he describes it, is a necessary condition for any other form of musical understanding. In this I heartily agree, and am also in substantial agreement with the way in which Levinson characterizes basic musical understanding. It seems to me to be right on target.

But where Levinson seems at least to infer from the fact that basic musical understanding is a necessary condition for any musical appreciation at all—which I think is right—the conclusion that it therefore must constitute virtually *all* music appreciation, I think he has made a serious mistake, as I have already suggested. It simply does not follow that because basic musical understanding is a necessary condition for architectonic and other forms of musical understanding, it must make the dominant or larger contribution to our musical satisfaction. It is, on my view, basic musical literacy. It is the foundation, and the foundation is not the whole house, only a part, although, it is to be granted, the part *sine qua non*.

It is, I think, a point of no importance if one wants to say that the *sine qua non* is, *ipso facto*, the most important element. If one does want to make that claim about basic musical understanding, I have no quarrel with it, just so long as one dos not take it to mean, *ipso facto*, that it makes the greatest or dominant contribution to musical satisfaction, except in the obvious sense that without it there would be no musical satisfaction at all.

That being said, we can now move on to consider a series of further claims which, taken together, comprise a blanket condemnation of architectonic listening as a substantial (or even, perhaps, minimal) contribution to musical satisfaction. It will be essential to examine them together.

3. *Musical form is spatial; music is temporal.*

4. *From (3) it follows that the grasping of musical form is intellectual whereas the grasping of music is perceptual.*

5. *From (3) it also follows that the musical form of a musical work is not part of the musical work.*

6. *From all the above, and particularly (3), (4), and (5) together, it follows that satisfaction taken in the grasping of musical form is not musical satisfaction.*

That musical form is spatial I can only take to be a claim based on the conflation of musical form with its mode of representation. It is an unfortunate choice of words to have started calling sonata, variation, rondo, and so forth 'forms' at all, for the obvious reason that 'form' is a word more closely connected in our common usage with two-dimensional or spatial images ('the human form divine'). But musical forms are not, except metaphorically (although the metaphor is ubiquitous) musical 'shapes'. They are *temporal patterns*.

Of course, as Henri Bergson made much of, we represent time spatially. But that is, after all, beside the point. When we think of form, when we are conscious of it in music, we are not thinking spatially (whatever that means) nor are we thinking of a spatial feature. We are thinking about the temporal pattern of a temporal art.

Now if it is supposed to follow that because musical form is spatial, grasping it is intellectual rather then perceptual, then, to begin with, since musical form is *not* spatial, there is no need, on those grounds, for calling it intellectual. In any case, we have already dealt with the charge that architectonic listening is intellectual listening, and concluded that nothing very troublesome follows from that concerning the musical satisfaction such listening might provide. So we can put any further consideration of it aside.

But if it is supposed to follow from the spatial character of musical form that it cannot be a proper part of the musical work, which is, we all agree, a temporal entity, that implication fails for the simple reason that, as I have just argued, musical form is *not* spatial, although its representation (in textbooks and other places) is. Nevertheless, there may be some other reason to believe that musical form is not part of the musical work, although I am not clear what exactly that reason might be.

Levinson says, in one of the quotations already cited, that musical form, 'in the analyst's sense, is more abstract and less particularized than the piece itself'. I am not sure what that means. I suppose it is true that when the analyst talks in her textbook about sonata form, that is an abstraction. But the sonata form I hear *in* the first movement of Beethoven's Fifth Symphony is a particular: it is the particular instantiation of sonata form in that particular symphonic movement. It is, to take a leaf from the schoolmen, *in re*, not *ante rem*. I do not see why the particular form of a particular work is any more an abstraction than a particular local quality of that work: a particular modulation, voice leading, or harmonic progression.

All that being said, I think we can make fairly quick work of the argument that musical form being spatial, or an 'abstraction', cannot be a proper part of the musical work, which is temporal and a particular. Since, as I have argued, musical form *is* temporal and particular, when instantiated in a particular work, there seems no argument from that direction, anyhow, that musical form is not a proper part of music.

Furthermore, if one wishes to argue that musical form not being temporal but spatial and thus not a part of the (temporal) musical work, satisfaction in it cannot, obviously, be *musical*, that is an argument that cannot possibly be maintained since its premises are false. Musical form is temporal, not spatial, part therefore of the musical work that instantiates it; satisfaction in it, therefore, *musical* satisfaction, satisfaction taken in a *musical* part, is a part *of* the musical work.

I have argued now at some length that those reasons of Levinson's that I have had time to examine, purporting to show musical satisfaction taken in architectonic listening to be minimal or non-existent, do not do the job. There are, indeed, other arguments I have not had time to examine. But it would place an undue burden on the reader—if I have not done that already—to vet them all. And it seems time, at this point, to press on to some appropriate conclusion.

I began this essay by stating that my objections to Levinson's concatenationism were not merely 'intellectual' but 'passionate' as well. But I think it fair to say that Levinson's own views are expressed with some considerable degree of passion too, which makes itself particularly evident in his concluding remarks. I will make my own conclusion by suggesting what the source of his passion is, for I think in doing that I will be able to paint, in brighter colors, just what it is that separates us.

Music and Democracy

The idea of the country club, closed to all but the high born, racially pure, and religiously correct, is an idea anathema to the democratic American spirit. Classical music, I believe, is seen by many, especially in the United States, in the same light: one of culture's country clubs—membership restricted.

What further reinforces this perception of classical music as a preserve of the aristocracy is its apparent hermetic character. Popular music, which America has excelled in and exported to the world, is open to all: it is wholly transparent; what you hear, first time through, is what you get. But classical music requires a key, a code book. It requires an *education*, referred to, venomously, by Nicholas Cook, as the 'appreciation racket'.[42] Levinson quotes the remark with at least apparent approval.[43]

Levinson's own final plea for concatenationism, against the 'appreciation racket,' I cannot help but see infused with a democratic ideal of classical music freed from the clutches of the country-club crowd, open to all. And who can quarrel with that? Certainly not I.

Levinson's peroration, I think it fair to say, is suffused with 'democratic passion,' and framed in combative terms: no less than a defense of the common man against the forces of musical aristocracy and privilege.

Qualified concatenationism stands plain as a defense of the intuitive listener, assuming he or she is dedicated to acquire the appropriate listening background, and takes to heart the gentle commandment of adequate rehearings. Concatenationism is intended, in particular, as a defense of such a listener against purveyors of intellectual appreciation of music primarily in terms of theoretical concepts, formal schemes, and spatial diagrams, and as a prophylactic or restorative against the fear or guilt occasioned by such approaches to appreciation.[44]

It is hard to miss the emotive tone with which this passage is imbued. The 'intuitive listener' is in need of protection. But from whom? From the charismatic teachers who brought me gifts, and for precious little monetary reward? No: you don't need protection from a teacher. So these folks are now styled 'purveyors.' (The king's 'purveyors' were essentially the king's robbers—hence the unsavory connotation of the word.)

The indictment continues:

It is dispiriting to think of the many persons fully capable of appreciating the glories of classical music . . . who have turned away without even venturing to cross the threshold, disheartened by the mistaken belief, which music theorists and commentators often do little to dispel, when they are not actively promoting it, that elaborate apprehensions of the form and technique of music are necessary to understanding it, and thus to reaping its proper rewards. But the plain truth is that to appreciate any music of substance, the thing to do is listen to it, over and over again.[45]

---

[42] Nicholas Cook, *Music, Imagination, and Culture* (New York: Oxford University Press, 1990), 164. For some further opinions of mine concerning Nicholas Cook, see my review of his book in the *Journal of Aesthetics and Art Criticism*, 50 (1992).
[43] Levinson, *Music in the Moment*, 174 n.   [44] Ibid. 173–4.   [45] Ibid. 174.

Again, one cannot miss the highly charged emotional tone of the expression: classical music closed to deserving people by a kind of conspiracy of the intellectual élite (self-styled, should one add?). These conspirators are the 'music theorists and commentators' who 'do nothing to dispel,' and even actively promote the notion that musical knowledge is necessary for appreciating the classical music repertory. There is surely more than a hint of duplicity here on the part of the 'purveyors.' The theorists and commentators are excoriated for doing nothing to dispel the élitist ideology, and for even promoting it. But why *should* they dispel it if they believe it? So if one excoriates them for acquiescing in it, one must believe that they do not believe it. It's a conspiracy against the common man: it's the 'appreciation racket'.

One can only sympathize with the spirit of Levinson's appeal: the wish to open the glories of classical music to all is a wish one must share, at least if one shares the American dream. No less than Levinson, I despise the suggestion that classical music should not be open to all. The question is what that really might mean. I also think the glories of general relativity should be open to 'all.' What might *that* mean? They are not open to *me*. And I do not suspect an élitist, anti-democratic conspiracy to deprive me of my rights in that regard.

The 'democratizing' of classical music, like so much democratizing that goes on nowadays, carries with it the danger of leveling. The democratic ideal of being 'open to all' is, after all, a *political* ideal. That is to say, it concerns the lifting of artificial political constraints, barring people, for various unsavory reasons, from having free access to all those institutions and means necessary for the pursuit of life's goods. It is not to be confused with the ideal, if that is what it is, of bringing everything down to the level at which everyone can *seem* to have every one of life's goods, no matter what their natural endowments, inclinations, or training might be; without, in other words, doing the work.

Indeed, I think the glories of classical music should be open to all, in the political sense. All should have access to the means by which the glories of classical music can be made available to them. But that does not mean telling them the big lie that all they need to do is listen, over and over again, and that musical training is a kind of conspiracy, a 'racket' to deprive them of their birthright. They should be told the awful truth that classical music is difficult to penetrate; that work is required; that it will only open up its glories to those who are willing to do the *real* work.

Levinson suggests that people turn away from classical music because they have been bamboozled by the purveyors of theory. There is a much simpler explanation. They turn away because they try to listen to it as they listen to popular music, which requires no explicit, consciously entertained musical knowledge at all, and, quite predictably, do not enjoy the experience. The reason popular music is *popular* is that it is 'easy listening.' The reason classical music is not is that it requires, at least for its full, rich effect, knowing stuff.

In rather a significant slip, so it seems to me, Levinson writes, in defense of knowledgeless listening, 'One need only position oneself, through familiarity, *in the right musicological space*, and then be willing to listen closely and repeatedly, until the unique shape of a given musical entity engraves itself on the mind's ear.'[46]

Now I take it that Levinson must mean, by 'the right musicological space,' the right historical space, since it is music history people usually mean, nowadays, when they refer to 'musicology,' even though it originally had wider implications. In saying this, Levinson, of course, gives evidence of the musical times in which we live, which are distinctly historicist times. I share with Levinson the notion, if indeed that is the notion he is promulgating here, that classical music must be appreciated, at least to some substantial degree, in its historical context. Indeed, it is fair to say that this is one crucial respect in which it differs from most popular genres. But it seems to me that Levinson must also think we can place music historically just by listening, just 'through familiarity,' which is to say, through basic musical understanding. And that seems to me absolutely untrue.

I am reminded, here, of a story I was told, years ago, by a musician who at the time was the principal oboe of the Metropolitan Opera orchestra. He himself was known by the players for his 'musical learning.' And on the strength of that, a trombone player, who had been with the orchestra upwards of twenty years, asked the oboist one day, 'Say, who came first, Verdi or Mozart?'

Now the reason I find this story utterly believable is that I do not think it is possible, for all the pure listening in the world, to figure out whether Mozart came before Verdi or Classical style before Romantic. If Levinson thinks, as I do, that listening to classical

---

[46] Levinson, *Music in the Moment*, 174, My italics.

music successfully requires having some idea of its periodization, then I cannot see how he can avoid thinking, as I do, that it requires historical knowledge of music, acquired in the usual way history is: by reading and instruction. It requires, in short, the 'musicology racket,' or at least its popular retailers, the program annotators and writers of record sleeves.

But has not Levinson, thereby, let the fox into the henhouse? Like other rackets, the musicology racket doesn't work alone. How can you put music in its historical place without stylistic analysis, structural analysis, theory—the lot? All these 'rackets' work together, comprising the 'musical mob.'

Of course I am far from suggesting that one needs a doctoral degree in music to enjoy Bach and Beethoven. But one does, after all, have to know which one came first; and one then has to know a lot of other things too. Maybe one also needs some natural gifts. I do not think anyone is certain about that. So in the absence of such certainty, I will go on thinking that anyone who can appreciate music at all can acquire the knowledge and skills requisite for deeply enjoying classical music, if he or she has the will to do it. I see no reason at all, however, certainly none Levinson has given, for believing that all one needs is basic musical understanding of the kind one acquires through the pores, just by listening.

Levinson thinks that the purveyors of musical knowledge have produced, as he puts it, 'fear and guilt' in those seeking entrance into the temple of classical music. The high priests are seen as saying: *Zurück*! I think, rather, that the guilt tripping goes in the other direction. Knowledge is taking a beating these days; and it is the ones who venture to suggest that some real intellectual work is required for classical music to open its temple doors who are made to feel the guilt: the guilt of élitism, of snobbery, of all those other undemocratic vices so much feared in the academy.

Well, why shouldn't there be some music that is difficult? And why shouldn't we admit to it? Spinoza said that everything is as difficult as it is excellent. Perhaps that is going too far. But, anyway, as we give two cheers for musical democracy, can't we at least give one cheer for the appreciation racket? After all, as any bootlegger or drug dealer will tell you, you can't have a racket without a clientele *and* a good product. As well, every successful racket needs, of course, *protection* from the police—in the case of the appreciation racket, the idea police, otherwise known as philosophers. I am of that number,

you will say; and so I am. However, every police force has its reneg-
ades, its rogue cops. I, my friends, am working for the rackets.⁴⁷

---

[47] Subsequent to my writing of the essay that became this chapter I returned from
my summer break to find waiting for me in my office mail box the April 1999 issue of
British Journal of Aesthetics, with an article by Roy W. Perrett, 'Musical Unity and
Sentential Unity.' Perrett, like me, is critical of Levinson's concatenationism, and
offers an alternative to it and to architectonicism which he calls 'relationalism.' There
are some points in his paper with which I am in sympathy, although I think the architectonicism he rejects is a stronger version than the one I defend. He also notes the relevance of the spurious Mozart letter to the discussion. However, his essay in no way
influenced mine, which was written before his came into my ken; and it is now too late
for me to comment on it any further here.

How to Forge a Musical Work

It is difficult for the younger philosophers of art to quite realize what state the discipline was in when the students of my generation entered graduate school in the late 1950s and early 1960s. It was, frankly speaking, a desert with one great oasis: Monroe Beardsley's *Aesthetics: Problems in the Philosophy of Criticism* (1958). Furthermore, the British analytic philosophers of those years, whom we wished so to emulate, had declared Aesthetics a non-subject. Taste, criticism, art, and beauty were, they argued, not susceptible of a philosophical critique. For a graduate student in philosophy to declare an interest in Aesthetics, the 'dreary science,' was an embarrassment.

Fortunately for me and those of my contemporaries who wished to pursue Aesthetics, a small group of distinguished American and British philosophers refused to believe the exaggerated reports of its demise. I will not name them, for fear of leaving someone important out. But on anyone's list there would be the name of the late Nelson Goodman. It is impossible to overemphasize the invigorating effect that the publication, in 1968, of *Languages of Art* had upon us; for Goodman was already a towering figure in contemporary Anglo-American philosophy. *The Structure of Appearance* loomed over us like a mountain peak that only the bravest and most skilled could hope to scale. And *Fact, Fiction and Forecast* was the subject of close scrutiny and vigorous debate. Anyone who could not discourse at length on grue and bleen was simply not yet a qualified practitioner of the art, no matter what else he or she was capable of. On top of all that, the *style* of *Fact, Fiction and Forecast* was a wonder to us all. That such philosophical depth and rigor could be expressed in such lucid and, yes, jaunty American prose seemed utterly miraculous.

Thus the very fact that the great Goodman should have turned his hand to the philosophy of art instantly made it not just respectable but a vital center. For me, it meant that I no longer needed to blush when I said to someone, 'I do aesthetics.'

Certainly one of the most intriguing chapters in *Language of Art*, and one of the most controversial, was the one called 'Art and Authenticity.' It was there that Goodman made the distinction, now an integral part of our philosophical vocabulary, between what he called 'allographic' and 'autographic' arts. Part of that distinction, or an implication of it, however you want to look at it, was the result that musical works, as opposed, say, to paintings or statutes, could not be forged. You could, of course, forge a musical manuscript; but all you got when you did that was just another score of the same work. And if you 'forged' Brahms's Fifth Symphony all you got was a symphony by you. Forging musical works, on Goodman's analysis, was simply an ontological impossibility.[1]

This chapter is what might be described as an oblique response to Goodman's position on musical forgery. I present below an example, so I believe, of what it might mean to forge a work of music: not a bizarre or outré example, but what I take to be a perfectly straightforward one—no ontological gimmicks or logical tricks. I propose, simply, a commonsense narrative of what I think any ordinary person would describe as 'forgery' in a robust, ordinary, language sense. It is not, in other words, philosophical science fiction, but just the sort of thing that might land you in the slammer.

It is not, either, an answer to Goodman's challenge, as I have said, in any but a tangential way. But it seems fair to say that it was Goodman who put the question of forgery into the position of a central concern for philosophers of art. It seems altogether appropriate, therefore, that I should offer, in his memory, an essay on musical forgery, as un-Goodmanian as it may be.

A musical work is best and most easily forged as a collaborative enterprise, involving a trained historical musicologist, a composer-theorist with a gift for mimicking other composers' styles, and an experienced embezzler with a good hand.

First one must choose the work to be forged. A good candidate is a work the original autograph of which is lost, for example, J. S. Bach's Partita in A minor for Unaccompanied Flute. 'The composition survives in a single manuscript that was written out by two copyists, one

---

[1] Nelson Goodman, *Languages of Art: An Approach to a Theory of Symbolism* (Indianapolis: Hackett, 1968), 112–22.

of whom, known in the literature as Anonymous 5, was associated with Bach in both Köthen and Leipzig.'[2]

In preparation for their collaboration, the composer and musicologist should make themselves as familiar as they can with Bach's style in general, his style in writing for the flute, and, especially, the style of the Partita. (A computer may be of help to them here.) Meanwhile, the forger of signatures should have obtained microfilms of a good selection of authenticated Bach manuscripts, and applied himself assiduously to the mastering of Bach's very elegant musical script.

When these preparations have been well and properly made, the composer and musicologist must then combine their skills to produce a version of Bach's work that, in various well thought-out ways, differs in musical details from the extant surviving manuscript, and from the published editions that have been made from it.

The composer and musicologist are now ready to present the results of their labors, in the form of a fair copy of the Partita, to the forger who, in the meantime, has mastered Bach's musical hand. He then produces a forgery of a Bach manuscript of the Partita, based on the fair copy he has been given, properly distressed, dirtied, and aged, which purports to be the authentic, long-lost original manuscript of the Partita, in the composer's own hand, and which the musicologist claims to have found in the attic of a hovel on the outskirts of Leipzig. He publishes his 'research,' in the form on an article, in the prestigious *Journal of the American Musicological Society*: Bärenreiter-Verlag publishes, in facsimile and performing edition, the 'newly discovered,' 'authentic' version of the work—the now accepted authoritative version—and on the strength of this research, the musicologist is tendered a full professorship in the Harvard music department. (The composer and forger get a flat fee for their trouble.)

I suggest the proper description of what has taken place here is that the composer, musicologist, and handwriting specialist have, together, forged a musical work, namely, Bach's Partita for Unaccompanied Flute. Notice, they have also forged a Bach manuscript, as a means to their nefarious end of work forgery; but actually, a work can perfectly well be forged without the added difficulty of manuscript forgery if a proper narrative is concocted for the source of the work forgery. (For example, the musicologist claims to have copied the work from a manuscript in the composer's hand subsequently destroyed in a bombing

² Robert L. Marshall, *The Music of Johann Sebastian Bach: The Sources, the Style, the Significance* (New York: Schirmer Books, 1989), 211.

raid during the Second World War.) The manuscript forgery is just icing on the cake.

Now it may be replied at this point that what these three scoundrels have done is not forge a musical work, that being, for well-known Goodmanian reasons, a metaphysical impossibility. All they have done, for all their considerable trouble, has been to produce, through rather unconventional means, another version of the work, to add to the extant contemporary manuscript and the various versions made out of it by a long line of editors.

But that response is only partly correct. The collaborators have, indeed, produced another version of the Partita. They have also, however, produced a forgery of *the work*. For to produce a version of the work *is* to produce the work: a version of the work *is* the work, *in one of its versions*. And in the circumstances in which they have produced their version of the work they have, *ipso facto*, produced a forgery of the work: a forgery that pretends to be the authoritative version. In other words they have forged the authoritative version of the work.

But consider now the following case. In one of those wildly improbable coincidences, dear to the hearts of philosophers, the lost original manuscript of the Partita for Unaccompanied Flute turns up. Lo and behold, our forgers' fake manuscript is, note for note, exactly the same as the authentic one. Is the forgery, then, really a forgery? After all, there is no difference between it, the work, that is, and the work that the authentic manuscript notates. They are the same version of the same work.

Compare this to the case of the long-awaited super xerox that can make a copy of an oil painting, molecule for molecule, identical with the original. The molecule-for-molecule copy of the Mona Lisa is, on most everyone's ontology (except for those who think painting is an allographic art) a forgery, assuming it is done with the appropriate motives, etc. If it is the case that the molecule-for-molecule copy of the Mona Lisa is a forgery, and the note-for-note copy of the manuscript of the Flute Partita is not, does this cast any doubt on the claim that there is a clear case, as outlined above, in which musical works can be forged?

I would answer as follows. The difference between forgery of musical works and forgery of paintings is, ontologically, that when versions of a musical work are note for note identical, they are the same version of the same work, hence cannot bear the relation of forgery to original, whereas, when copies of a painting are molecule for molecule identical with the original they are, obviously, still distinct paintings and, hence, can be forgeries.[3]

Of course, as the above story shows, the ontology of musical forgery differs in some important ways from that of painting forgery. But what of that? It is hardly surprising, since the ontology of musical works differs from the ontology of paintings in some important ways, at least according to most theorists. However, the point is that the ontology of musical works does not exclude the forgery of musical works, as has customarily been thought, witness the example of the Bach Flute Partita adduced above. There is only one way to describe that example that captures our intuitions of what has taken place, nor is this case of forgery 'forgery' in some weird, attenuated sense. The description is perfectly straightforward: a work of music, Bach's Partita in A-minor for Unaccompanied Flute has been *forged*.

In conclusion, musical forgery, properly so called, seems to be ontologically possible, practically possible, and probably not worth the trouble.[4]

---

[3] Jerrold Levinson, in a private communication, suggests an alternative interpretation of this example. He writes, 'If you believe you are concocting something, and represent the result as other than what you believe it to be (that is, your concoction), then I don't see why that isn't forgery, even when the result, by "improbable coincidence," is a "happy" one. And I think this point is independent of your (apparently still robust) preference for a musical ontology where works with the same sound/tonal structures are necessarily the same works.'

[4] I am grateful to Noel Carroll and Jerrold Levinson for reading an earlier version of this paper, and for helpful criticism of it. I am, of course, entirely responsible for the remaining errors.

BIBLIOGRAPHY

ADDIS, LAIRD, *Natural Signs: A Theory of Intentionality* (Philadelphia: Temple University Press, 1989).

—— *Of Mind and Music* (Ithaca: Cornell University Press, 1999).

ALPERSON, PHILIP, *What is Music? An Introduction to the Philosophy of Music* (New York: Haven, 1987).

ARISTOTLE, *Nicomachean Ethics*, trans. Martin Ostwald (Indianapolis: Bobbs-Merrill, 1962).

BOTKIN, B. A., and LOMAX, ALAN, *The People's Song Book* (New York: Boni & Gaer, 1948).

BOUWSMA, O. K. *Philosophical Essays* (Lincoln, Nebr.: University of Nebraska Press, 1969).

CARROLL, LEWIS, *Alice's Adventures in Wonderland, Through the Looking Glass and the Hunting of the Snark* (New York: The Modern Library, n.d.).

CARROLL, NOEL, *Mystifying Movies: Fads and Fallacies in Contemporary Film Theory* (New York: Columbia University Press, 1988).

CHAMPLIN, T. S. 'Tendencies,' *Proceedings of the Aristotelian Society*, New Series 91 (1991).

COOK, NICHOLAS, *Music, Imagination, and Culture* (New York: Oxford University Press, 1990).

DAVIES, STEPHEN, *Musical Meaning and Expression* (Ithaca: Cornell University Press, 1994).

—— 'Transcription, Authenticity and Performance,' *British Journal of Aesthetics*, 28 (1988).

DICKIE, GEORGE, 'The Myth of the Aesthetic Attitude,' *American Philosophical Quarterly*, 1 (1964).

EGGEBRECHT, HANS HEINRICH, *J. S. Bach's 'The Art of Fugue': The Work and its Interpretation*, trans. Jeffrey L. Prater (Ames, Ia.: Iowa State University Press, 1993).

EINSTEIN, ALFRED, *Mozart: His Character, His Work*, trans. Arthur Mendel and Nathan Broder (London: Oxford University Press, 1945).

FISH, STANLEY, *Is There a Text in this Class?: The Authority of Interpretive Communities* (Cambridge, Mass.: Harvard University Press, 1980).

GOETHE, JOHANN WOLFGANG VON, *Conversation of Goethe with Eckermann*, trans. John Oxenford (London: J. M. Dent, 1930).

GOODMAN, NELSON, *Languages of Art: An Approach to a Theory of Symbolism* (Indianapolis: Hackett, 1968).

GURNEY, EDMUND, *The Power of Sound* (London: Smith, Elder, 1880).

HANSLICK, EDUARD, *Music Criticism, 1846–99*, ed. Henry Pleasants (Baltimore: Penguin, 1963).

—— *On the Musically Beautiful: A Contribution Towards the Revision of the Aesthetics of Music*, trans. Geoffrey Payzant (Indianapolis: Hackett, 1986).

HARTSHORNE, CHARLES, *The Philosophy and Psychology of Sensation* (Chicago: The University of Chicago Press, 1934).

HOLMES, EDWARD, *The Life of Mozart* (New York: Harper, 1868).

KANT, IMMANUEL, *Anthropology from a Pragmatic Point of View*, trans. Mary J. Gregory (The Hague: Martinus Nijhoff, 1974).

—— *Critique of Aesthetic Judgement*, trans. James Creed Meredith (Oxford: Clarendon Press, 1911).

—— *Critique of Judgement*, trans. J. H. Bernard (New York: Hafner, 1961).

KERMAN, JOSEPH, *Contemplating Music: Challenges to Musicology* (Cambridge, Mass.: Harvard University Press, 1985).

KIVY, PETER, 'Auditor's Emotions: Contention, Concession, Compromise,' *Journal of Aesthetics and Art Criticism*, 101 (1993).

—— *Authenticities: Philosophical Reflections on Musical Performance* (Ithaca: Cornell University Press, 1995).

—— *The Corded Shell: Reflections on Musical Expression* (Princeton: Princeton University Press, 1980).

—— *The Fine Art of Repetition: Essays in the Philosophy of Music* (Cambridge: Cambridge University Press, 1997).

—— 'Mattheson as Philosopher of Art,' *The Musical Quarterly*, 70 (1984).

—— *Music Alone: Philosophical Reflections on the Purely Musical Experience* (Ithaca: Cornell University Press, 1990).

—— 'A New Music Criticism?' *The Monist*, 63 (1990).

—— *Osmin's Rage: Philosophical Reflections on Opera, Drama and Text* (Princeton: Princeton University Press, 1988).

—— *Philosophies of Arts: A Study in Differences* (Cambridge: Cambridge University Press, 1997).

—— 'Review of Nicholas Cook, *Music, Imagination, and Culture*', *Journal of Aesthetics and Art Criticism*, 50 (1992).

—— 'Something I've Always Wanted to Know About Hanslick,' *Journal of Aesthetics and Art Criticism*, 46 (1998).

—— *Sound Sentiment: An Essay on the Musical Emotions* (Philadelphia: Temple University Press, 1989).

—— 'Thomas Reid and the Expression Theory of Art,' *The Monist*, 61 (1978).

—— (ed.), *Essays in the History of Aesthetics* (Rochester: University of Rochester Press, 1992).

KRISTELLER, PAUL O., 'The Modern System of the Arts (I),' *Journal of the History of Ideas*, 12 (1951).

—— 'The Modern System of the Arts (II),' *Journal of the History of Ideas*, 13 (1952).

LANGER, SUSANNE K., *Philosophy in a New Key: A Study in the Symbolism of Reason, Rite and Art*, 2nd edn. (New York: Mentor Books, 1959); 3rd edn. (Cambridge, Mass.: Harvard University Press, 1978).

LERDHAL, FRED, AND JACKENDUFF, RAY, *A Generative Theory of Tonal Music* (Cambridge Mass.: MIT Press, 1985).

LEVINSON, JERROLD, *Music, Art, and Metaphysics: Essays in Philosophical Aesthetics* (Ithaca: Cornell University Press, 1990).

—— *Music in the Moment* (Ithaca: Cornell University Press, 1997).

—— *The Pleasures of Aesthetics: Philosophical Essays* (Ithaca: Cornell University Press, 1996).

MCCLARY, SUSAN, *Feminine Endings: Music, Gender, and Sexuality* (Minneapolis: University of Minnesota Press, 1991).

MARSHALL, ROBERT L., *The Music of Johann Sebastian Bach: The Sources, the Style, the Significance* (New York: Schirmer Books, 1989), 211.

MATRAVERS, DEREK, *Art and Emotion* (Oxford: Oxford University Press, 1998).

MATTHESON, JOHANN, *Der vollkommene Capellmeister*, trans. Ernest C. Harriss (Ann Arbor: UMI Research Press, 1981).

MEYER, LEONARD B., *Emotion and Meaning in Music* (Chicago: University of Chicago Press, 1956).

—— *Music, the Arts and Ideas: Patterns and Predictions in Twentieth-Century Culture* (Chicago: University of Chicago Press, 1967).

—— 'A Universe of Universals,' *Journal of Musicology*, 16 (1998).

PERRETT, ROY W., 'Musical Unity and Sentential Unity,' *British Journal of Aesthetics*, 39 (1999).

PLATO, *Phaedo*, trans. by G. E. M. Grube (Indianapolis: Hackett, 1977).

RADFORD, COLIN, 'Emotions and Music: A Reply to the Cognitivists,' *Journal of Aesthetics and Art Criticism*, 47 (1989).

—— 'How Can We Be Moved by the Fate of Anna Karenina?' *Proceedings of the Aristotelian Society, Supplementary Volume*, 49 (1975).

—— 'Muddy Waters', *Journal of Aesthetics and Art Criticism*, 49 (1991).

REESE, GUSTAVE, *Music in the Renaissance* (New York: Norton, 1954).

SCHOPENHAUER, ARTHUR, *Die Welt als Wille und Vorstellung* (2 vols.; Stuttgart: Suhrkamp Taschenbuch Wissenschaft, 1993).

—— *The World as Will and Idea*, trans. R. B. Haldane and J. Kemp (Garden City, NY: Dolphin Books, 1961).

—— *The World as Will and Representation*, trans. E. F. J. Payne (2 vols.; Indian Hills, Colo.: Falcon's Wing Press, 1958).

SCHROEDER, DAVID P., *Haydn and the Enlightenment: The Late Symphonies and their Audience* (Oxford: Clarendon Press, 1990).

STEVENSON, ROBERT LOUIS, *Dr. Jekyll and Mr. Hyde, and Other Stories*, ed. Jenni Calder (Harmondsworth: Penguin Books, 1979).

STRUNK, OLIVER (ed.), *Source Readings in Music History* (New York: Norton, 1950).

TREITLER, LEO, 'The Early History of Music Writing in the West,' *Journal of the American Musicological Society*, 35 (1992).

——, 'The "Unwritten" and "Written Transmission" of Medieval Chant and the Start-up of Musical Notation,' *Journal of Musicology*, 10 (1992).

UEHLING, THEODORE E., Jr. *The Notion of Form in Kant's Critique of Aesthetic Judgment* (The Hague: Mouton, 1971).

WEGMAN, ROB C., 'From Maker to Composer: Improvisation and Musical Authorship in the Low Countries, 1450–1500,' *Journal of the American Musicological Society*, 99 (1996).

WOLLHEIM, RICHARD, *The Mind and its Depths* (Cambridge, Mass.: Harvard University Press, 1993).

INDEX